THE UNIVERSITY OF MICHIGAN
CENTER FOR CHINESE STUDIES

MICHIGAN PAPERS IN CHINESE STUDIES
NO. 23

"PROLETARIAN HEGEMONY"
IN THE CHINESE REVOLUTION
AND THE CANTON COMMUNE OF 1927

by
S. Bernard Thomas

Ann Arbor

Center for Chinese Studies
The University of Michigan

1975

*Open access edition funded by the National Endowment for the Humanities/
Andrew W. Mellon Foundation Humanities Open Book Program.*

Printed and bound by CPI Group (UK) Ltd, Croydon, CR0 4YY

ISBN 978-0-89264-023-2 (hardcover)
ISBN 978-0-472-03827-5 (paper)
ISBN 978-0-472-12792-4 (ebook)
ISBN 978-0-472-90188-3 (open access)

To

Evelyn

CONTENTS

ACKNOWLEDGMENTS

Research for this study was much facilitated by a Fulbright-Hays Research Fellowship for 1969-1970 and by two small research grants from Oakland University in 1969 and 1973. I am indebted for their many kindnesses and expert assistance to the directors and staffs of the Universities Service Centre in Hong Kong, the Hoover Institution at Stanford University, the Asia Library of The University of Michigan, and the Kresge Library of Oakland University. I wish to thank Professor Daniel Bays of the University of Kansas, Professor Renate Gerulaitis of Oakland University, and Tanya Marcotty for their generous help. I am grateful to Professor Robert C. Howes of Oakland University for expert translations from the Russian sources used. I want also to express my great appreciation to Mr. Shih-chen Peng of Oakland University's Chinese language faculty for his unstinting and invaluable assistance with difficult and sometimes barely legible Chinese microfilm materials. The hours we have spent together on this and other projects over recent years have further cemented our good friendship.

As is true of so many of my colleagues at Oakland, I owe very special thanks to Marian Wilson, our extraordinarily talented editorial secretary, who, with her customary skill and devotion, took the manuscript through successive drafts to the final copy. Any errors in fact or interpretation are of course solely my responsibility. My greatest debt and gratitude is expressed in the dedication.

S. Bernard Thomas

LIST OF ABBREVIATIONS

ACFL	All-China Federation of Labor
CCP	Chinese Communist Party
CC, CCP	Central Committee, Chinese Communist Party
CI	Communist International or Comintern
ECCI	Executive Committee, Communist International
CPSU	Communist Party of the Soviet Union
KMT	Kuomintang

INTRODUCTION

The Communist-organized Canton uprising of December 11, 1927, which proclaimed the Canton Commune or Soviet, proved to be a short-lived and disastrous affair lasting less than seventy-two hours. However, it immediately thereafter took on and long retained a meaningful symbolic role in the intricate fabric of ideological formulations, policies and strategies which marked the Chinese Communist movement and its relations with the Comintern during most of the decade following the collapse of the Commune. It was the Canton revolt, the Comintern proclaimed on the first anniversary of the Commune, which constituted "the banner of the new Soviet phase in the Chinese revolution."[1] A careful review of the political and rhetorical uses of the Canton Commune in both Comintern and Chinese Communist sources may throw some additional light on the complex and often ambiguous policy lines of the post-1927 soviet stage of Chinese Communism, particularly on the key issue of "proletarian hegemony" and its link to the urban-rural strategic relationship. Indeed, as I shall note, continuing references to and assessments (or the absence thereof) of the Canton uprising in Chinese Communist and Soviet Russian commentaries since 1949 appear to have a certain relevance to similar issues in postliberation China as well.

The Canton Commune was in fact an unmitigated disaster for the Communist revolutionary movement in China. Though it was marked by great heroism and was at least in part the expression of a still powerful radical labor movement in that city, the revolt was nevertheless speedily and ruthlessly crushed with severe losses to the Communist cadre nucleus in Canton, thus largely destroying the strong organizational base the party had been able to build in that original stronghold of the nationalist revolution.[2] The Commune failed to mobilize or involve the workers of Canton in very substantial numbers, either in the preparation for or the unleashing of the uprising or in the formation of the soviet itself;[3] at the same time, it exposed the strongly anti-Communist sentiments of many of the organized skilled workers in that city (such as the powerful Mechanics' Union) and the deep antagonisms that rent the Canton labor movement.[4] It failed also to develop a coordinated strategy with existing rural revolutionary movements in eastern Kwangtung (particularly the Hai-lu-feng soviet), nor did it initiate or lead important new rural uprisings in the immediate vicinity of Canton in support of the Commune.[5] Much

1

less could the Canton Commune be pointed to as a "spark" which subsequently ignited broader and more successful revolutionary actions. Though some individual stragglers fleeing the collapse of the Commune may ultimately have found their way to the base established by Mao and Chu Te on Chingkangshan, a much greater and more direct spin-off in this regard could clearly be claimed for the earlier Nanchang and Autumn Harvest uprisings.[6] And above all, the Canton revolt proved highly counterproductive on the very score for which its significance was particularly acclaimed: though the Comintern declared in February 1928 that as a result of the Commune the Chinese workers "have now the right to claim their historical role as leaders of the great Chinese revolution,"[7] in fact the bloody defeat of the Commune, coming in the wake of the ruthless suppression of the Communist-led labor organizations in Shanghai, Hankow, and other major urban centers, only served further to "turn off" the urban workers for a full generation as a committed nucleus and driving force of Communist political and military action. "After the Canton Commune," Liu Shao-ch'i told Nym Wales in 1937, "the power of the workers' unions was completely destroyed." Only in Shanghai, he added, did the workers retain some "hidden power" for a time.[8] Despite its tragically heroic aspects, the Canton Commune can thus in reality best be viewed, in contemporary Maoist parlance, as a "negative example" of revolutionary policy and strategy, rather than as the harbinger for the soviet stage of the Chinese revolution it was continuously asserted to be. A 1934 Comintern account of the soviet movement in China declared, for example, that it was the Canton workers in December 1927 "who raised the flag of the Soviets and unfurled this banner so broadly that it became a beacon for the forces of the Chinese revolution who were split and scattered as a result of the temporary Kuomintang victory."[9]

Whether or not the uprising was initiated, as is often asserted, on "direct orders" from Stalin or the Stalin-directed Comintern,[10] the decision to seize Canton accorded generally with the much more "leftist" insurrectionary policy guidelines adopted by the Chinese Communist leadership, under the close scrutiny and guidance of Comintern representatives, during the second half of 1927. And one of these representatives, Heinz Neumann, played a major role in planning and implementing the rising, working closely with the local Communist leadership in Canton.[11] When the Commune proved a disaster, subsequent Comintern analyses sharply criticized what were considered to have been the many tactical and strategic errors of the on-the-spot leadership (including the Comintern representative), but at no time was the larger significance, the overall goals, or the ideological framework and political program of the Commune denigrated or disavowed in any way. If it had been considered politically desirable, the entire venture could readily have been dismissed as merely an ill-advised "putsch" engineered by local leaders and Comintern operatives misinterpreting directives from on high, and thus as an adventurist example to be disowned rather than a heroic model to be revered, [12] particularly since the February 1928 ECCI Ninth Plenum had also complained that the CCP Party Center had been kept in "complete ignorance . . . of the Canton events. "[13]

Yet basically the Canton Soviet, which declared itself to be "the organ of the revolutionary democratic dictatorship of the workers and peasants," can be viewed as at least the symbolic culmination of a policy line which the Comintern had been evolving under Stalin's direction during the previous eighteen months in response to sharply shifting developments in China and in the process of countering the criticisms and challenges of the Trotsky-led Left Opposition. And while the uprising was finally acknowledged to have been, strategically, a "rear-guard action" of a receding revolutionary wave, it played a significant ideological role for the revolutionary period ahead by setting the appropriate proletarian political parameters for the "democratic dictatorship of workers and peasants" of the ensuing, primarily rural soviet period. The Commune served also, in a figurative sense, to place the post-1927 CCP-led revolution more firmly within the internationalist orbit of the Comintern-led proletarian world revolution, and it carried as well certain longer-term political and strategic implications for the ultimate course of the Chinese revolution. And, as I have already suggested, post-1949 Chinese and Russian assessments of the Canton Commune have apparently continued to speak to some of these same issues.

The Communist aim of proletarian hegemony in the Chinese revolution was given concrete expression through the Canton Commune--reflected in the policies and strategies that led to the uprising, in the makeup and program of the Soviet setup in Canton, and in the subsequent assessment of the revolt by the Comintern and the CCP. This study will describe these developments and, with the further ideological treatment given the Commune serving as a backdrop, will then examine the continuing evolution and ultimate transformation of the proletarian line and the concept of proletarian leadership in the post-1927 history of Chinese Communism.

FOOTNOTES

1. "The First Anniversary of the Canton Revolt" (Theses of the Agitprop of the ECCI), International Press Correspondence (Inprecorr), VIII: 89 (December 13, 1928), 1696.

2. Harold Isaacs, The Tragedy of the Chinese Revolution, 2nd ed. rev. (Stanford, 1961), pp. 290-291. J. C. Huston, American consul in Canton, estimated that in the week of December 13-20 alone, some 3,000-4,000 radicals and suspected radicals were summarily executed. "Peasants, Workers and Soldiers Revolt of December 11-13, 1927, at Canton, China" (December 30, 1927), p. 28, Hoover Library microfilm. Hereafter cited as Huston Report.

   The CCP itself stated that 5,700 persons had been killed in the December 14-19 aftermath of the uprising. "In Memory of Fallen Heroes--5700 Workers, Peasants and Soldiers of Canton," Bolshevik (Pu-erh-se-wei-k'o), no. 12 (January 1928), p. 354, included as a document in L. P. Deliusin, ed., Kantonskaia Kommuna [The Canton Commune] (Moscow, 1967), p. 207. Hereafter cited as Kantonskaia Kommuna. This important Russian-language collection of essays and documentary materials on the Commune was issued under the auspices of the Institute of the Peoples of Asia of the USSR Academy of Sciences for the fortieth anniversary of the Canton uprising. I will give only the English translation of titles cited from this collection.

3. Yeh T'ing's (Communist military commander in the Canton uprising) report on the Canton insurrection, cited in A. Neuberg, Armed Insurrection, trans. Quentin Hoare (London, 1970), pp. 127-128; and "Resolution on the Chinese Question," Ninth Plenum of the ECCI (February 25, 1928), Inprecorr, VIII: 16 (March 15, 1928), 322.

   Armed Insurrection is a well-known Comintern revolutionary manual which includes a major chapter on the Canton insurrection. It was originally published in 1928 in Germany, and in a French edition (with slight editorial changes) in 1931. The translation cited above is based on both editions and contains also an important new introduction ("How We Wrote Armed Insurrection") by a former German Comintern functionary, Erich Wollenberg, who was apparently involved in the Moscow discussions which led to the original preparation and publication of this book. Wollenberg, among other things, dispels the former widely accepted view that "A. Neuberg" was in reality Heinz Neumann, the Comintern representative in Canton during the uprising. Wollenberg states that the book was in fact prepared by members of the Red Army staff in Moscow and then turned over to Ercoli (Togliatti), head of the Comintern "Agitprop" division for editing and publication. Armed Insurrection, pp. 9-11. Neumann's widow, Margarete Buber-Neumann, gives an essentially similar attribution in a 1967 book in which she denies "the rumor stubbornly surviving until today" that Neuberg and Neumann were identical. Kriegsschauplätze der Weltrevolution. Ein Bericht aus der Praxis der Komintern, 1919-1943 [War theaters of the world revolution. An account of the practices of the Comintern, 1919-1943] (Stuttgart, 1967), p. 101.

4. An article in the Comintern journal stated that "The yellow union of the engineering workers was active as a counterrevolutionary force, both during and after the Canton rising, and even before, and competed with the generals in the slaughter of the workers." John Pepper, "Position and Tasks of the Chinese C. P. After the Canton Rising," Communist International, V: 6 (March 15, 1928), 159.

The anti-Communist, pro-KMT unions included also the provincial federation of Kwangtung unions (Kwangtung General Union), of about thirty unions, most of them craft workers, with a membership of some 30,000. Jean Chesneaux, The Chinese Labor Movement, 1919-1927, trans. H. M. Wright (Stanford, 1968), pp. 304-305.

Consul Huston reported that "armed squads of the anti-Communist Mechanics Union joined the police and soldiers in searching out and executing on the spot their foes and political enemies among labor." Huston Report, pp. 25-26. See also the account by a Kuomintang labor leader of the 1920s and 1930s, Ma Chao-chun, History of the Labor Movement in China, trans. Peter Liang (Taipei, 1955), p. 159.

5. The ECCI, in a first-anniversary statement on the Commune, listed among "the fundamental causes" of defeat "the isolation of Soviet

Canton from the districts of the peasant insurrection." "The First Anniversary of the Canton Revolt," p. 1697. Comintern representative Heinz Neumann subsequently acknowledged to the Comintern that "At the moment of the insurrection, there was no important revolutionary movement among the peasants adjacent to Canton. The peasants were completely isolated; no aid could be expected from them." M. N. Roy, Revolution and Counter-Revolution in China (Calcutta, 1946), p. 559.

6. The greater part of the elite cadet training regiment (Chün-kuan Chiao-tao T'uan) which had spearheaded the Canton revolt were able to flee to the Hai-lu-feng area, where virtually all soon lost their lives in the suppression of the soviet there in the early months of 1928. Only 60 of the original 1,200 survived. Nym Wales, Red Dust (Stanford, 1952), pp. 150-152; and Shinkichi Eto, "Hai-lu-feng--the First Chinese Soviet Government," China Quarterly, no. 9 (January-March 1962), part 2, p. 179. For personal reminiscences by survivors, see Hui-i Kuang-chou ch'i-i [Reminiscences of the Canton uprising] (Shanghai: Wen-i ch'u-pan she, 1959); and Nym Wales and Kim San, Song of Ariran, 2nd ed. rev. (San Francisco, 1972), pp. 161-211.

7. "Resolution on the Chinese Question," p. 322.

8. Nym Wales, The Chinese Labor Movement (New York, 1945), p. 56. Liu of course was referring to the Comunnist-led or influenced unions. By 1930 the CCP reported that industrial workers made up less than 2 percent (some 2,000) of the total party membership. Chou En-lai, "Report to the Third Plenum" (September 24, 1930), in Conrad Brandt et al., A Documentary History of Chinese Communism (Cambridge, Mass., 1952), p. 206. Hereafter cited as Documentary History.

9. J. Johanson and O. Taube, "The Soviet Movement in China," in Räte China [Soviets in China] (Moscow-Leningrad, 1934), p. 41. Hereafter cited as Soviets in China. Titles from this important German-language collection of reports and documents will be cited in English.

10. See, for example, Leon Trotsky, "Stalin and the Chinese Revolution" (August 26, 1930), in Problems of the Chinese Revolution

(New York, 1966), p. 291; Benjamin I. Schwartz, Chinese Communism and the Rise of Mao (Cambridge, Mass., 1951), pp. 105-106; Isaacs, Tragedy of the Chinese Revolution, p. 282n; Buber-Neumann, War Theaters of the World Revolution, pp. 212, 218; and her earlier book, Von Potsdam nach Moskau (Stuttgart, 1957), pp. 181-183. On the other hand, Hsiao Tso-liang, in line with his thesis that Moscow's policy line for the Chinese revolution had shifted in the latter part of 1927 to a strategy of primary focus on the countryside as the revolutionary center, questions much of the available evidence directly linking Stalin and the Comintern in Moscow either to the specific planning of the Canton revolt or to actual orders initiating this clearly urban-centered revolutionary event. "Chinese Communism and the Canton Soviet of 1927," China Quarterly, no. 30 (April-June 1967), 71-74; and Chinese Communism in 1927. City vs. Countryside (Hong Kong, 1970), pp. 145-147.

Mrs. Buber-Neumann, in citing what she asserts was Stalin's telegraphic instructions to Neumann on the eve of the uprising ("act in a way that you can take responsibility for"), states that by this rather ambiguous message Stalin gave the starting signal for the revolt. She adds that by this formula, Stalin "also saddled the Canton leadership with full responsibility" should the uprising fail. War Theaters of the World Revolution, p. 218.

For official Nationalist Chinese allegations of direct Russian involvement in the uprising, see enclosure No. 6, Huston Report: December 22, 1927, a dispatch from the Commissioner of Foreign Affairs for Canton to Consul Huston on "Participation of Russians in the Recent Communist Trouble in Canton." Five Russian staff members and six Chinese employees of the Soviet Consulate in Canton were seized and shot after the revolt collapsed. Report of former Soviet consul, addenda to Huston Report.

11.   Mrs. Buber-Neumann states that Besso Lominadze, a young Stalin confidant, was sent to China after the July 1927 CCP break with the Wang Ching-wei-led Wuhan government, bringing with him the new leftist policy line. In the fall of 1927, she continues, Stalin dispatched Heinz Neumann to China with instructions to meet Lominadze and go with him to Canton to take over the leadership of the projected uprising there. War Theaters of the World Rev-

olution, pp. 209-212. Lominadze attended the CCP's key
August 7 Emergency Conference as Comintern representative,
and apparently also the important November Political Bureau
enlarged session, returning to Moscow prior to the Canton revolt to attend the Fifteenth Congress of the CPSU in December.
Hsiao Tso-liang, Chinese Communism in 1927, p. 145. Neumann,
who also attended the November Political Bureau session, served
as on-the-spot representative of the Comintern in Canton and as
a leading force in the insurrection there. Roy, Revolution and
Counter-Revolution, pp. 558-559.

12. The ECCI Ninth Plenum's criticisms of the Canton rising could
easily have been used to condemn the revolt as a putsch lacking
necessary mass support. The line was indeed a finely drawn
one in Comintern discussions at the time, a subject I shall
deal with later in this study.

13. "Resolution on the Chinese Question," p. 322. Nevertheless,
the CCP Central Committee in early January 1928 endorsed and
praised the Commune as "having an extraordinarily great effect
on the overall development of the Chinese revolution at the present stage." "The Meaning [Significance] and the Lessons of the
Canton Commune" (January 3, 1928), in Warren Kuo, Analytical
History of the Chinese Communist Party (Taipei, 1968), I, 417.

The Soviet Russian government itself, in strongly protesting the
execution of several of its consular officials in Canton by the
anti-Communist forces suppressing the Commune, denied that
the revolutionary movement in China or elsewhere was the work
of "Soviet agents." Statement by People's Commissar of Foreign
Affairs Chicherin, December 22, 1927, in Xenia J. Eudin and
R. C. North, Soviet Russia and the East, 1920-1927 (Stanford,
1957), pp. 384-385. A December 14 Comintern appeal for
worldwide revolutionary support for the Canton Commune declared the revolt to be "an event of really worldwide historical
significance." See text of the Appeal in ibid., p. 384.

IDEOLOGICAL AND POLITICAL BACKGROUND
TO THE UPRISING

The political concept of the "democratic dictatorship of the proletariat and the peasantry," originally devised by Lenin in 1905 to meet the Russian revolutionary situation at that time, [1] was revived in Communist policy pronouncements on China during the period of KMT-CCP collaboration in the 1920's. It came to be a general political formula to define or describe the structure that revolutionary political power would hopefully and ultimately take during the course of the pre-socialist stage of the Chinese revolution. During this stage, "bourgeois" tasks (primarily the agrarian revolution and anti-imperialist nationalist objectives) remained to be accomplished through a multiclass coalition led by the CCP-supported Kuomintang. However, "proletarian hegemony" would increasingly emerge within this coalition, transforming it into a "democratic dictatorship," and thus lay the basis for a subsequent transition to a fully socialist stage of proletarian dictatorship. In November 1926, for example, Stalin declared that the form of the "future revolutionary power" which was expected to emerge from the Kuomintang-led coalition would be "something in the nature of a democratic dictatorship of the proletariat and the peasantry" which, he added, would be "a power marking a transition to China's non-capitalist or, more exactly, Socialist development."[2] At the same time, Stalin rebutted those calling for immediate formation of peasants' soviets in China, arguing that "it is not possible to organize soviets in the countryside bypassing the industrial centres of China," and "the question of organizing soviets in the Chinese industrial centres is not on the agenda at the moment."[3] Thus a "democratic dictatorship" poised for the transition to socialism was projected as the aim of the CCP-KMT alliance, to be achieved through a Kuomintang which had been further revolutionized and transformed by Communist mobilization of the masses. And when the time for soviets arrived, they would be organized in both urban and rural areas with leadership stemming from the urban industrial centers.[4]

After Chiang Kai-shek's April 1927 anti-Communist coup (looked upon in ideological terms as the betrayal of the revolution by the national bourgeoisie), but during the period of continuing CCP collaboration with the "Left" KMT at Wuhan, Stalin, arguing against the position of the Left Opposition at the ECCI Eighth Plenum, rejected the idea of

9

an immediate Communist move to organize soviet power in China.[5] The Plenum itself called for "transforming" the Wuhan government "into the political centre of the workers' and peasants' revolution and into an organ of the revolutionary democratic dictatorship of the proletariat and the peasantry." And since the (Left) KMT was the organization in which "the proletariat works together with the petty bourgeoisie and the peasantry . . . the proletariat cannot claim hegemony in the country without the Communist party--the party of the working class--claiming hegemony within the Kuomintang."[6]

But despite this notion of CCP "hegemony" within the KMT, when the time for transition to the proletarian revolution and the organization of soviets had arrived, the CCP would emerge independently as a "bloc without," exercising direct and exclusive revolutionary leadership. Thus, as Stalin stated it at that time, since "the formation of soviets of workers' and peasants' deputies is the preparation for the transition from a bourgeois-democratic revolution (primarily equated by Stalin with the agrarian revolution) to a proletarian revolution, to a Socialist revolution," then "not only during the dictatorship of the proletariat but also before such a dictatorship, during the formation of the soviets . . ., the Communist Party has to leave the KMT in order to conduct the preparation for the Chinese October under its own exclusive leadership."[7] The move to soviet power was therefore specifically linked to a direct and presumably short-term transition to proletarian-Communist power--a transition for which the emergence of a "democratic dictatorship" would be the "take-off" point. Stalin underscored the urban, anti-bourgeois focus of this projected soviet stage, declaring that the "Communists will be empty phrasemongers if they do not conform to the policy of expropriation of the bourgeoisie, as soon as they have Soviets of workers' and peasants' deputies."[8]

In July, after the Communist break with Wuhan, Stalin stated that "now . . . the slogan of the formation of soviets can become a really revolutionary slogan if (if!) in the near future a new and powerful revolutionary upsurge is set ablaze." The CCP was still instructed to work under the KMT banner, in a struggle to replace the "discredited KMT leadership by "a revolutionary leadership." Meanwhile, propaganda for the idea of soviets should be carried out, but "without running ahead and without forming soviets right now."[9] The thesis now propounded by Stalin was that the completion of the unconsummated tasks of the bourgeois-democratic phases of the Chinese revolution were now devolving upon the "next stage of the Chinese revolution, to the Soviet stage."[10]

Thus the uncompleted, basically agrarian tasks of the bourgeois revolution[11] were now meshed with those of the soviet stage of direct transition to socialism, with the two soon to converge in the concept of a CCP-led democratic dictatorship of workers and peasants, to be created through Communist-organized soviet power. A kind of "great leap forward" revolutionary strategy emerged, as CI-CCP policy veered to the left in the post-Wuhan period, in an effort simultaneously to carry through both the above stages so that on the crest of this new "upsurge" the revolution could be brought to the threshold of socialism and proletarian dictatorship. In the context of this compressed strategy, the crucial agrarian revolution was viewed in convulsively violent jacquerie terms, for which radical rural revolutionary power based on the poorer peasantry and the rural "semi-proletariat" could be directly coordinated with and harnessed to urban-focused, increasingly anti-bourgeois struggles to build the proletarian hegemony considered so crucial to the strategy of transition.[12] In these latter months of 1927, CCP formulas and policies for the projected transitional stage turned towards the "Trotskyist"-tinged concept of a "permanent revolution." Trotsky himself, however, linked this idea to his assertion that the Chinese revolution, although in a period of recession, had already entered a new post-bourgeois phase of proletarian-led socialist revolution, for which the theory of the democratic dictatorship of workers and peasants was both anachronistic and unworkable.[13]

Thus the CCP's famous August 7 Emergency Conference called on the party to work "to obtain a hegemony of the working class in order to realize a workers' and peasants' dictatorship,"[14] and an August 23 Central Committee circular declared that the current tasks of the revolution could be carried out only under such a "revolutionary democratic dictatorship of workers and peasants," adding that "this democratic revolution against the bourgeoisie undertaken by the proletariat and peasants [is] a revolution that opposes both Chinese and foreign bourgeoisie and which can and should grow and become a socialist revolution."[15] While not yet calling for organization of soviets (only "propaganda"), it stated that "the Soviet of workers, peasants and soldiers is a revolutionary form of political regime which provides assurance that the democratic dictatorship of the workers and peasants will advance directly to the socialist dictatorship of the proletariat."[16]

In late September, in the wake of the Nanchang and Autumn
Harvest uprisings, Stalin moved directly to endorse soviets, though
on the assumption that these new developments marked "a new upsurge of the revolution in China," in which case "Soviets can and
actually will become the main force that will rally around itself
the workers and peasants of China directly under Communist leadership."[17] A subsequent Pravda article of September 30, "The Tasks
of the Chinese Revolution," also took note of the "new revolutionary
élan in China" resulting from the presumed (and short-lived) successes of the "Southern Revolutionary Army" under Ho Lung and Yeh
T'ing moving through eastern Kwangtung in the aftermath of the Nanchang uprising.[18] The article acknowledged that the new upsurge
did not originate in the urban industrial centers ("where counter-
revolution has for the time being gained the upper hand") but in the
peasant guerrilla movement and through revolutionary military forces
operating in coordination with peasant risings. But in projecting the
future course of these revolutionary developments, Pravda outlined
a scenario reminiscent of Stalin's November 1926 stipulations on the
circumstances under which a move to peasant soviets would be
acceptable: "As revolution spreads to industrial centres it will be
possible to create there soviets of workers', soldiers' and artisans'
deputies on which the new revolutionary government or governments
will rest in the beginning." Thus "the soviet slogan, from being a
propaganda slogan, must develop into an action slogan." In the
countryside, the article continued, power should go to the revolutionary peasant unions and committees which "must be converted
into Soviets of peasant deputies."[19]

Thus while the revolutionary thrust had shifted to the countryside, the new upsurge was postulated on the assumption of the revolution's rapid spread to "industrial centres" where the political
center of gravity of a new soviet power would be located.[20] Indeed,
it was clearly assumed that this "spread" to urban centers was the
direct and immediate objective of the revolutionary forces under Ho
Lung and Yeh T'ing, which had already occupied Swatow and were
expected to move on Canton, thus making the entire province of
Kwangtung the "revolutionary centre."[21] The politically supportive
though crucial revolutionary role of the peasant movement in creating
the new soviet power was evident in the tasks set: for the peasant
soviets, "their business must be to rouse as large sections as possible of the Chinese peasantry for revolution," while it is on the
projected urban soviets that "the new revolutionary government" was
to rest.[22] This consistent urban political orientation was clearly

expressed in a Comintern article written in March 1928, well after the defeat of the Ho Lung-Yeh T'ing forces in the Ch'ao-chou-Swatow area in early October[23] and of the Canton Commune in December. It declared that "the great gains which the Communist Party of China has to show for the period just elapsed are the August conference (the August 7 Emergency Conference), which put an end to opportunism, the southern expedition to Swatow and the Canton revolution."[24]

Despite the Nanchang and Autumn Harvest setbacks, and in line with the post-August 7 Ch'ü Ch'iu-pai party leadership's view that the Chinese revolution had entered a new upsurge, policy veered further to the left at the enlarged session of the CCP Central Committee's Provisional Political Bureau, held in Shanghai November 9-10, 1927, and attended by Comintern representatives Neumann and Lominadze. It further delineated the strategy of linking the rural and urban revolutionary movement under urban political leadership in the move to soviet power. The session thus called for organizing "the spontaneous revolutionary struggles of the masses," combining the sporadic and scattered peasant uprisings into large-scale actions and, under appropriate conditions, coordinating worker uprisings with those of the peasantry in a combined insurrection. "The responsibility of the Party is to lead workers in their daily struggle, to build up the revolutionary tide of the broad masses, to organize uprisings to provide leaderships [sic] in armed struggle, and to make cities the guiding centers of spontaneous peasant insurrections."[25]

The November Plenum saw in the "new upsurge of peasant risings" a key indicator of the "prolonged but permanent nature" of the Chinese revolution. It declared that the "wave of the peasant risings calls forth a workers' movement which, while still weak, is coming to meet the peasant wave." It summed up the rural-urban revolutionary relationship: "To maintain contact between the revolts of the workers and the risings of the peasants--this is the most important task of the party. Without leadership and assistance from the working class, the purely peasant risings cannot lead to complete victory."[26]

Though the Plenum spoke of the prolonged character of the Chinese revolution, it viewed the stages of revolution in highly compressed political terms, focusing primarily on the tasks and strategies of socialist transition.[27] As a Comintern source subsequently observed, despite the severe defeats the Communists had suffered in the six months following Chiang Kai-shek's April Shanghai coup, the Chinese

Party Center in late 1927 reaffirmed the view that "the situation in China remained immediately revolutionary, and that the slogan of insurrection was still appropriate."[28] Urban insurrection was seen as the key link in carrying the new peasant upsurge directly onto the path of socialist transition. The view of Kwangtung as a major center of this upsurge was highlighted by the establishment on November 7 of soviet administrations under Communist leader P'eng P'ai in Haifeng and Lufeng (Hai-lu-feng) counties of eastern Kwangtung, some 150 miles east of Canton.[29] The Canton uprising of December 1927 clearly found a place in this overall strategy.

But as the Chinese revolution in fact moved into a protracted rural phase after 1927, the ill-fated Canton Commune came to play a vestigial political role in the CI-CCP effort to maintain, under these new revolutionary conditions and over a longer-term basis, the "urban vantage point" and the policy implications inherent in the worker-peasant relationship which characterized the strategic perspectives of the November Plenum.

FOOTNOTES

1. Hélène Carrère d'Encausse and Stuart Schram, <u>Marxism and Asia</u> (London, 1969), p. 19; Schwartz, <u>Chinese Communism</u>, pp. 88-89. The Leninist concept strongly implied proletarian dominance or "hegemony" in this dual class dictatorship, though it also envisaged a dual party structure as well.

2. November 30, 1926, speech delivered in the Chinese Commission of the ECCI, in <u>Stalin on China</u> (Bombay, 1951), p. 8.

3. <u>Ibid.</u>, p. 10.

4. Stalin had added that peasant soviets could only be established during a "maximum upsurge of the peasant movement" and "in the hope that the industrial centres of China had already broken down the barrier and entered on the phase of forming a soviet power" (<u>ibid.</u>).

5. "The Revolution in China and the Tasks of the Comintern," speech to Eighth Plenum of the ECCI, May 24, 1927, <u>Communist International</u>, IV: 10 (June 30, 1927), 200-207.

6. "Extracts from the Resolution of the Eighth ECCI Plenum on the Chinese Question" (May 30, 1927). In Jane Degras, ed., <u>Communist International, 1919-1943</u>, 3 vols. (London, 1956-1965), II, 388.

7. "Talk with Students of the Sun Yat-sen University" (May 13, 1927), in <u>Stalin on China</u>, pp. 35-36.

8. "The Revolution in China and the Tasks of the Comintern," p. 206.

9. "Comments on Current Affairs on China," <u>Pravda</u>, July 28, 1927, in <u>Stalin on China</u>, p. 77. These views were further amplified by Moscow on August 9, to the effect that if Communist efforts to "revolutionize the KMT" fail, and should "the revolution make a fresh advance, then it will be necessary to change the propagandist slogan of Soviets into a slogan of immediate fight and to proceed at once to the organization of workers', peasants', and artisans' Soviets." "Resolution on the International Situation" (passed by the "Joint Plenum of C.C. and C.C.C. after hearing

Comrade Bukharin's report of 9 August 1927"), Inprecorr, VII: 48 (August 18, 1927), 1072.

10. "The International Situation and the Defense of the U.S.S.R." (August 1, 1927), in J. Stalin on Chinese Revolution (Calcutta, 1970), p. 196.

11. "The agrarian revolution constitutes the foundation and content of the bourgeois democratic revolution in China," Stalin stated in May 1927. "The Revolution in China and the Tasks of the Comintern," p. 206.

12. The famous Hai-lu-feng Soviet, established in eastern Kwangtung under P'eng P'ai's leadership in November 1927, closely reflected these strategic concepts in its extreme confiscatory land policies (including "landed farmers" as targets), its extermination of landlords and their families, and its antimerchant policies. Shinkichi Eto, "Hai-lu-feng--The First Chinese Soviet Government, II, 175-176.

On the other hand, in the aftermath of the failures of the August 1 Nanchang uprising and the subsequent "Southern Expedition" to Swatow, and of the Autumn Harvest uprising in September, CCP policy documents criticized their failure adequately to "arouse" the peasant masses (in revolutionary support of the military forces for whom the occupation of urban centers had been essentially the main objective), and thus castigated them for failing to pursue more radical land policies and for not ruthlessly carrying out or permitting the extermination of "local bullies and evil gentry." See "Central's [the party's Central Standing Committee] Announcement (No. 13): On the Matter of the Defeat of Yeh and Ho" (October 14, 1927), in C. Martin Wilbur, "The Ashes of Defeat," China Quarterly, no. 18 (April-June 1964), pp. 38-44; and "Excerpts from the C.C.P. Politburo Resolution on Political Discipline" (November 14, 1927), in Karl A. Wittfogel, "The Legend of 'Maoism,'" part 2, China Quarterly, no. 2 (April-June 1960), pp. 32-33.

The October 14 party statement outlined a labor-oriented, strongly anticapitalist strategy as well as an antigentry position in projecting a move to Communist-organized soviet power and a workers' and peasants' dictatorship. Wilbur, "Ashes of Defeat," pp. 43-44.

13. Trotsky, "The Canton Insurrection," in Problems of the Chinese Revolution, pp. 133-146.

14. Schwartz, Chinese Communism, p. 95. It was not until September 19, however, that the CCP finally abandoned the KMT banner as the instrument of this dictatorship (ibid.).

15. "Resolution on the Political Task and Policy of the Chinese Communist Party" (August 23, 1927), in Kuo, Analytical History, I, 441.

16. Ibid., p. 447.

17. "The Political Complexion of the Russian Opposition" (September 27, 1927), J. Stalin on Chinese Revolution, p. 214.

18. Inprecorr, VII: 56 (October 6, 1927), 1238.

19. Ibid., p. 1239.

20. Rue states in this regard that "throughout October and November he [Stalin] was urging the Chinese Politburo to organize at least one Soviet in a large city." John E. Rue, Mao Tse-tung in Opposition (Stanford, 1966), p. 77.

21. Tang Shin-she, "The Victorious Advance of the Revolutionary Troops on Canton," Inprecorr, VII: 56 (October 6, 1927), 1237. A 1967 Soviet source reaffirms that the objective of the southern campaign of the Nanchang forces was "to liberate Canton" and reestablish the revolutionary base in the south. T. N. Akatova, "The Working Class and the Canton Commune," Kantonskaia Kommuna, p. 50.

22. "The Tasks of the Chinese Revolution," p. 1239.

23. Chang Kuo-t'ao, The Rise of the Chinese Communist Party, 1928-1938, vol. II of the autobiography of Chang Kuo-t'ao (Lawrence, Kas., 1972), 30-31. Chang states that the Ch'ü Ch'iu-pai central party leadership had earlier conveyed instructions (through Kwangtung party leader Chang T'ai-lei) to abandon Ch'ao-chou and Swatow and concentrate the Nanchang forces in the Hai-lu-feng area and build there a Workers' and Peasants' Red Army in combination

with the local peasants (ibid., p. 28). Chang, who was critical of and hostile to Ch'ü, presents this incident as a factor in undermining the morale of the Swatow forces, and which contributed to their defeat and virtual destruction shortly after. If authentic, such an order was presumably in accord with the subsequent strategy of concentrating forces in a strategically more secure area of Communist-led peasant risings much closer to Canton. In fact, as I shall note, after some apparent initial misgivings following the defeat of the Nanchang forces (see Kuo, Analytical History, I, 386), the Party Center moved during November to map out a coordinated revolutionary strategy for Kwangtung in which a Canton uprising was to play a central role. One suspects, however, that the instructions to proceed to the Haifeng-Lufeng area may have come only after the defeat of the Swatow forces; and in fact no such move occurred until then. Akatova, "The Working Class and the Canton Commune," p. 5. Mrs. Buber-Neumann writes that "Since the overrunning of Swatow the Comintern had sent one or two telegrams nearly daily with the urgent summons to trigger off uprisings in Canton and other cities." War Theaters of the World Revolution, p. 212. See also nn. 20 and 21, above.

24. Pepper, "Position and Tasks of the Chinese C. P.," p. 159.

25. From the November Plenum's political resolution on the party's current tasks, cited in Kuo, Analytical History, I, 389; also summarized in Hsiao, "Chinese Communism and the Canton Soviet of 1927," p. 63. (A lengthy portion of the Plenum's political resolution was published in Inprecorr, VIII: 5 [January 26, 1928], 121-123). The Plenum affirmed also the insurrection slogan of soviets as the instrument of a proletarian-led dictatorship of workers and peasants. Kuo, Analytical History, I, 390.

26. Cited in Eudin and North, Soviet Russia, pp. 307-308.

27. The Plenum's political resolution thus declared that "the Chinese revolution must solve its democratic tasks as thoroughly as possible and, in its rapid progress, must enter upon the Socialist path." Inprecorr, January 26, 1928, p. 123.

28. Neuberg, Armed Insurrection, p. 108.

29. V. P. Iliushechkin, "The Peasant Movement in Kwangtung, 1924-1927," Kantonskaia Kommuna, p. 80.

THE RISE AND FALL OF THE CANTON SOVIET

Preparations for the Uprising

As the CCP leadership in November 1927 focused on Kwangtung as a continuing center of revolutionary upsurge,[1] it saw the revolutionary potential there not only in the comparatively high incidence of peasant risings in that province,[2] but also in the still remaining core of the powerful Communist organizational base which had been built up in the Canton labor movement, primarily in the course of the massive 1925-1926 Hong Kong-Canton strike and boycott struggle.[3] Communist influence had centered in the left-wing Canton Workers' Delegates Conference (or Council) which reportedly represented some 150,000 unionists in the spring of 1926, and perhaps 200,000 by early 1927.[4] As an additional result of the general strike and boycott against British-ruled Hong Kong and the foreign concession area (Shameen) in Canton, a unique situation had developed. Tens of thousands of strikers had left Hong Kong for nearby Canton, where a Strike Committee and a Strikers' Delegates Conference had been established which functioned virtually as a "second government" in that city.[5] The thirteen-member Strike Committee was firmly under Communist leadership, with Su Chao-cheng and Teng Chung-hsia playing prominent roles. The committee had its own armed forces of almost three thousand strike pickets; it took charge of the boycott; and it handled the housing and feeding of the Hong Kong strikers, ran educational programs, and published a weekly newspaper.[6] On the other side of the coin, however, Canton throughout this period also remained the base of the powerful Mechanics' Union and the 30,000-strong Kwangtung provincial federation of unions--both of them conservative organizations, mostly of skilled and craft workers, which adopted an increasingly antagonistic anti-Communist stance as the influence and power of the Communist-led labor organizations expanded.[7]

Though the sixteen-month strike struggle was settled in October 1926 after prolonged negotiations, the arrangements and organizational structure created during the strike persisted, and some 20,000 Hong Kong strikers remained in their communal living quarters on the outskirts of Canton, including among them the several thousand military-trained strike pickets under the Workers' Delegates Conference.[8]

Kwangtung at this time was under the control of Li Chi-shen, a leading KMT military figure who commanded the garrison forces in the Canton area and served as governor of the province. Through him pressure built up against the left labor forces during the early months of 1927, abetted by the mounting hostility of the anti-Communist unions. In the wake of Chiang Kai-shek's April coup, Li Chi-shen moved openly against the left, arresting some two thousand Communists and union militants. A number of Communist labor leaders were executed and the strike pickets were disarmed. Over forty of the unions affiliated with the Workers' Delegates Conference were "reorganized" and placed under a newly formed Revolutionary Labor Federation in which the anti-Communist unions played key roles. [9]

Chang Fa-k'uei, a former subordinate of Li Chi-shen, had earlier become a key commander in the KMT's Northern Expedition armies, for which the Canton region had been the staging area. Chang played a key role in the takeover of the Wuhan area in August 1926, and as leader of the famous "Ironsides" Fourth Army he was closely associated with the Wang Ching-wei left KMT leadership at Wuhan. His army at that time also included the pro-Communist forces which later staged the Nanchang uprising of August 1, 1927. In October 1927 Chang moved his troops back to the Canton area, where a struggle for power developed with Li Chi-shen. Included among Chang's forces that marched south was the Communist-oriented cadet training regiment (chün-kuan chao-tao t'uan) from the Wuhan Military-Political Academy under the command of Yeh Chien-ying. [10] Chang Fa-k'uei had disarmed this regiment in the aftermath of the Nanchang revolt. According to Yeh Chien-ying, the regiment anxiously weighed the possibility of revolt during the march to Canton, but were persuaded by their Communist party committee to bide their time and follow Chang to Canton where a more propitious revolutionary opportunity would present itself. [11]

Chang Fa-k'uei (joined in Canton in November by left KMT leaders Wang Ching-wei and Ch'en Kung-po) made some initial advances to the left forces in Canton. However, in the face of a resulting rising tide of labor strikes and demands, left-wing demonstrations and attacks on the headquarters and leaders of the various "reorganized" unions during October, [12] Chang and Wang Ching-wei moved against the reactivated left. The Workers' Delegates Conference (or Council) once again went underground and, abandoning earlier plans for a general strike, dispersed its forces in small groups throughout the city. The Strike Committee was closed down, and virtually all of the more than 20,000 Hong Kong strikers remaining in the city were forced by the authorities to leave the Canton area --a serious blow to the Communists who had looked to the well-organized strikers and their armed underground contingents as the key proletarian revolutionary core in planning for an uprising. [13]

There now remained underground in Canton only some 2,000 of the Hong Kong strikers and 500 former pickets of the Strike Commit-tee. The latter became the nucleus of the worker Red Guard which the Communists began hurriedly to organize in late November. The pickets were joined by secret detachments from left-wing unions, with altogether some 2,000 workers assembled in the Red Guard, which was given an elaborate organizational structure under the supreme command of a committee of five. It suffered, however, from a severe shortage of arms and little military training. [14]

On November 17 the Chang Fa-k'uei group launched a coup which drove Li Chi-shen from Canton, triggering an open armed struggle between the two factions and their various military allies in the Kwangtung-Kwangsi area. Chang was now compelled to move virtually all of his troops towards the Kwangsi border, leaving only the cadet regiment (which Chang had now found it necessary to rearm), a guard regiment, and police forces in Canton. The Communists, who already largely controlled the 1,200-man cadet regiment, appar-ently succeeded also in infiltrating many of their cadres and former strike pickets into the guard regiment as well. [15] However, various headquarters guard detachments in the city, as well as some 3,000 troops under a local anti-Communist military chieftain (Li Fu-lin) controlling the Honam island section of Canton across the Pearl River, remained untouched by Communist influence. [16]

It was in this heightened revolutionary atmosphere and new military opportunity that the CCP Central Committee in Shanghai formulated on November 18 its directive to the Kwangtung provincial committee to prepare a province-wide worker-peasant uprising cen-tering on Canton. [17] These instructions in turn formed the basis of the Kwangtung party committee's November 26 decision to proceed with an insurrection in Canton. [18] The November 18 directive outlined an eleven-point program for an armed uprising in city and country-side to set up Communist political power in Kwangtung. It included instructions for revitalizing the revolutionary unions and workers'

councils in Canton (the beginnings of a soviet system) to launch
struggles leading to a general strike and the seizure of power. It
also called for the mobilization of the peasants for jacquerie-style
uprisings (killing the landlords and local bullies and dividing the land),
particularly in eastern Kwangtung, in order further to strengthen and
expand the soviet areas there. In the immediate rural environs of
Canton, the peasant movement was to be coordinated with a Canton
uprising by acting to destroy or cut off land and water communications to the city. The scattered peasant risings throughout the province were to be broadened and merged; those to the north and west
of Canton were to focus on harassing, subverting and destroying the
armies of the rival militarist factions engaged in internecine struggle. [19]

On receipt of the Central Committee's instructions, the Kwangtung provincial committee on November 26 set about preparing for
an armed uprising in Canton. [20] It set as its main tasks the formulation of a political program, military preparations, preliminary
formation of a Canton Soviet, mobilizing the workers through the
red unions, intensifying work among the soldiers, and establishing
contact and coordination with the peasant movement. [21] On this last
point, the Kwangtung and Canton party committees maintained liaison
with the Hai-lu-feng soviet and transmitted directives and orders to
the latter's party organs. The party had also organized a secret
peasant training school in Canton and worked to develop the peasant
movement in the general vicinity of the city. [22]

In this province-wide coordinated strategy, the creation and
maintenance of a proletarian revolutionary center in Canton was
clearly pivotal. [23] As a recent Soviet account of the uprising has
described the overall plan, "the workers, having seized power in
Canton, were to unite with the rebelling peasants and set up a revolutionary base in the south of China." [24] And the immediate strategic aim of the peasant movement (as was noted in subsequent Communist postmortems on the Canton failure) was expected to be to help
guarantee the successful establishment and consolidation of Soviet
Canton as the guiding political center of a resurgent revolutionary
Kwangtung.

Apparently in response to feelers from Chang Fa-k'uei for
Communist support in defending Canton against Li Chi-shen, the
Kwangtung party committee on November 28 issued an appeal to the
people [25] which in effect rejected these overtures by demanding as a

prerequisite the reestablishment of the freedom and full authority of the Communist-led labor organizations and the arming of the workers under the latter's auspices as the core of a revolutionary new political power in Canton. The party committee called instead for a broad worker-peasant-soldier struggle to transform the militarists' war into a revolutionary war for soviet power. "The eyes of all of China are directed at us, the decisive hour of battle is approaching soon," the manifesto declared.[26]

A five-man revolutionary military commitee was set up at this point to take overall leadership of the impending insurrection. It was headed by the Kwangtung party leader, Chang T'ai-lei, with Yeh T'ing named commander-in-chief of the military forces.[27] Yeh, however, arrived in Canton only a few hours before the uprising was launched, a fact which seriously weakened his leadership effectiveness, with particularly detrimental consequences on the course of the struggle after Chang T'ai-lei was killed on December 12.[28]

On December 7 the Kwangtung Committee secretly convened a "worker-peasant-soldier congress" in Canton under the protection of worker Red Guards, which took the final decision on the uprising, now set for December 13.[29] It also established a sixteen-member executive committee of a Canton Soviet as the political organ of the insurrection, with ten members representing the underground Council of Workers' Delegates, three the revolutionary soldiers, and three the peasants' unions of the environs of Canton--though only one of this last group actually took part in the work of the soviet.[30] The plan (never consummated) was to elect a full 300- to 400-member soviet after the takeover of power.[31] During the final days of intensified secret meetings and preparations, the question of whether to call a general strike in advance of an armed revolt was thrashed out, and though sentiment at first strongly favored such a strategy, tactical considerations and the prevailing circumstances ultimately led to the decision to move ahead directly to armed action.[32] The failure (or inability) to mount a general strike was later to be pinpointed in Communist postmortems as one of the key factors in the speedy defeat of the Commune. Comintern functionary Lozovsky commented, for example, that because of the absence of a general strike, "not until they heard the thunder of the guns and the fighting in the streets did the masses realize that the revolt had begun."[33]

On December 10 Chang Fa-k'uei (apparently alerted by Wang Ching-wei from Shanghai of the impending revolt) sent forces under his front-line commander, Huang Hsi-hsiang, back to Canton to disarm the cadet regiment and to take repressive measures against the Red Guards and red labor organizations there. Under these circumstances, the revolutionary military committee hastily advanced the date of the uprising to the early morning hours of December 11.[34] Subsequently, in early January 1928 the Party Center affirmed the correctness of this decision. To have delayed the move even for a few days, it declared, would have resulted in the disarming of the revolutionary troops, the return of the main anti-Communist military forces to Canton, and the imposition of a severe "white terror."[35] Chang Kuo-t'ao reports in his memoirs that when news of the uprising (which he calls "the most important action taken by the CCP's central authorities under Ch'ü Ch'iu-pai's leadership") reached Shanghai, "Ch'ü was very happy, imagining the uprising would succeed." Chang adds (perhaps self-servingly) that his own suggestion that the Canton revolutionary forces should be promptly transferred to the Hai-lu-feng soviet area "was regarded as one of 'escapism,' designed to discourage the mutineers."[36]

The balance of military forces in the immediate Canton area on the eve of the insurrection, according to a later report by Communist commander Yeh T'ing, pitted revolutionary forces of about 4,200 men against a total of some 7,000 government troops (including police).[37] While the anti-Communist forces had a particularly marked superiority in weaponry and training,[38] these factors were somewhat balanced by the "softening" effects of Communist subversion on many of these troops, in contrast to the revolutionary dedication and courage among the poorly armed and trained Red Guards. On the other hand, armed detachments of the anti-Communist Mechanics' Union, totaling some 750 men, stood ready actively to oppose the Communists; foreign warships at Canton could be expected to render assistance to the government forces; and some 50,000 troops in the contending armies of Chang Fa-k'uei and Li Chi-shen were within two or three days' march of Canton.[39] Only a genuinely mass revolt in Canton linked to a rising tide of coordinated peasant revolutionary activity (particularly in the immediate vicinity of the city) could offer the prospect of sustaining the revolt beyond a few days. But this was not to occur, and the Canton insurrection, launched on a precariously narrow revolutionary base and virtually isolated from outside support, was doomed to rapid and disastrous defeat.

The Course of the Struggle

The plan reportedly drawn up by the leaders of the insurrection outlined a three-stage operation.[40] In the initial phase the spearheads of the revolt--the cadet regiment and the Red Guards--would move to disarm government troops and police, occupy the key military, police and government centers, free all political prisoners, and capture the main arms depot and arsenal. The weapons thus secured would be used to form large new worker battalions; at the same time, through a general strike mounted in conjunction with these initial operations, the worker masses would be mobilized in support of the newly proclaimed Canton Soviet, which could then move rapidly to implement its social revolutionary program. In the second stage, the revolutionaries would root out all counterrevolutionary elements in the city and move to destroy the military forces on Honam island. In the final stage (only vaguely sketched out in advance), a consolidated Red Canton, drawing the peasant masses into the struggle, would move out to confront the remaining militarist forces in the province.[41]

The uprising, launched in the predawn hours of December 11, succeeded quickly in achieving most of the strategic objectives of the first stage, though some key military headquarters, the Tungshan area where the leading KMT military chieftains resided, and the main arms depot and arsenal were not captured. And Honam remained an anti-Communist bastion and command post throughout the life of the Commune, with Li Fu-lin's troops pressing the insurgents hard, while the armed detachments of the Mechanics' Union went into the battle against the insurrectionists.

Though some five hundred peasant activists from nearby areas entered the Canton fighting,[42] the expectation that the neighboring peasantry could be mobilized to cut off rail, water and road communications in support of the Canton struggle failed of realization,[43] while aid from the more distant Hai-lu-feng soviet did not materialize.[44] And though the Communists were at first able to some degree to augment their initial military strength by incorporating some military defectors and released political prisoners into their ranks, they were unable to implement their plans for the rapid and massive expansion of their armed forces.[45] Later Communist reports declared that over 20,000 workers had joined the uprising on the first day, but the severe shortage of weapons, the poor organization and inadequate leadership, and the lack of any military training or experience among the workers largely nullified the effectiveness of their participation, whatever the actual numbers involved.[46] Teng Chung-hsia, the Communist labor leader and a participant in the revolt, in citing this 20,000 figure, noted that the Red Guard units (themselves mostly unarmed) who gathered in every part of the city, were followed about by large numbers of unarmed and unorganized workers.[47] The fact that a large part of the remaining radical leadership elements among the workers had been siphoned off into the Red Guards also greatly impeded the Communists' ability to mobilize the worker masses.[48]

The inability of the Communists to organize a general strike either prior to or in conjunction with the uprising also severely reduced the possibilities for alerting, preparing and organizing the laboring masses of Canton in support of the soviet.[49] Hundreds or even thousands of courageous fighters could not substitute for an indispensable broad mass movement encompassing tens of thousands of workers, Comintern labor head Lozovsky subsequently observed.[50] This weakness was further aggravated by the CCP's failure effectively to work with the rank and file of the powerful "yellow" union organization, and by the eroding effects on the formerly 200,000-strong radical labor movement in Canton of the repressive and "reorganizational" measures taken in the city since April 1927 and by the dispersal from Canton of the Hong Kong strikers,[51] who had been the most activist left-wing force in the Canton labor movement. Yeh T'ing subsequently reported that "the great masses did not take part in the insurrection at all; two big meetings produced a not very satisfactory result. . . . We were not able to make use of all our comrades, and consequently there is nothing astonishing if the workers were very badly organized. Most of the soldiers who had been disarmed simply dispersed around the city. . . . The armed detachments of the engineering [mechanics] union, wearing white armbands, chased their red brothers and shot them."[52] And Teng Chung-hsia acknowledged that, despite the strenuous efforts made by the Kwangtung Party Committee and the Council of Workers' Delegates, "only a minority of the workers of Canton actively participated in the uprising, and in this sense, the social base of the uprising was insufficiently broad."[53]

The death of Chang T'ai-lei, the most commanding figure of the uprising, on the second day of the fighting, proved an additionally serious blow to both the political and military leadership of the Canton Soviet. By the early hours of December 13, with the now joined forces of Chang Fa-k'uei, Li Chi-shen and Li Fu-lin, aided by Chinese and foreign naval forces, closing in on the beleaguered and depleted insurgent forces from all sides, the Canton Commune collapsed after a fifty-eight-hour existence.[54] The great majority of the Red Guards perished in courageous but hopeless last-ditch resistance, though most of the cadet regiment and some of the Red Guards (altogether about 1,500 men) managed to escape from the city and ultimately find their way to the Hai-lu-feng area, where most of them were to lose their lives in the suppression of the soviet there in the early months of 1928.[55] Military commanders Yeh T'ing and Yeh Chien-ying found refuge in Hong Kong; Heinz Neumann also escaped and returned to Moscow where he was to take an active part in the 1928 Comintern debates on the Canton debacle. The failure to prepare a contingency plan for retreat from Canton added greatly to the losses suffered by the revolutionary defenders of the city.[56]

The CCP reported that the retreat had left 4,000 revolutionary fighters dead on the streets of Canton;[57] and in the bloody week of ruthless terror that followed, perhaps as many as 5,700 suspected radicals in Canton were summarily killed or executed.[58] The American consul in Canton reported that in the house-to-house searches "the color of red on the neck of one of the inmates [from hastily discarded red insignia] meant instant death not only for the marked man, but for many others in the building. . . . About 1,000 members of the various unions which were known to be affiliated with the Communists were arrested wholesale and herded together in one of the large theaters, from which place they were taken out in groups of fifty and shot."[59] Five Russian members of the Soviet consular staff in Canton were seized and publicly executed for alleged complicity in the revolt.[60] M. N. Roy, the famous Asian Comintern figure of the 1920's, writing in 1930 as a bitter critic of Comintern policy, called the Canton uprising "the most tragic event in the entire history of the Chinese revolution. . . . It completed the defeat of the working class and placed it out of combat for a long time."[61] Yet subsequent CCP and CI pronouncements were strongly to assert that the political significance and symbolism of the Canton Commune overrode its acknowledged defects and disastrous failure. "There is a symbolic significance," a Comintern representative wrote in March 1928, "in the fact that Canton, the cradle of the bourgeois revolution, has now also become the cradle of the proletarian revolution in China."[62] The urban-proletarian vanguard revolutionary role of the Canton Commune was to be a strongly reiterated theme in

Communist commentaries and reports on the uprising, as the Chinese revolution moved into its Communist-led soviet stage.

FOOTNOTES

1. Abortive plans for insurrectionary action in Wuhan and its vicinity had earlier (late October) been formulated by the Hupeh Provincial Committee of the CCP. Hsiao Tso-liang, "The Dispute Over a Wuhan Insurrection in 1927," China Quarterly, no. 33 (January-March 1968), pp. 108-111.

2. Kwangtung reportedly had a total of twelve peasant uprisings from May to December 1927, the highest number of any province. A. G. Afanasiev, "The Heroic Uprising of the Proletariat of Canton, December 11-13, 1927," Kantonskaia Kommuna, p. 7.

3. Chesneaux, Chinese Labor Movement, pp. 290-303.

4. Ibid., p. 298; and Akatova, "The Working Class and the Canton Commune," p. 49. The Third National Labor Congress, held in Canton under Communist leadership in May 1926, represented another high point in CCP influence in the Canton area.

5. Chesneaux, Chinese Labor Movement, p. 293.

6. Ibid., pp. 292-293.

7. Ibid., pp. 303-306.

8. Huang P'ing, "The Canton Uprising and Its Background," Soviets in China, p. 142. Huang P'ing served as Commissar of Foreign Affairs in the Canton Soviet. His report is also contained in the Chinese volume, Kuang-chou Kung-she (Canton Commune) (n.p.: Proletarian Bookstore, 1930). This latter source hereafter cited as Canton Commune.

9. Chesneaux, Chinese Labor Movement, p. 371; Akatova, "The Working Class and the Canton Commune," p. 47.

10. Reminiscences of the Canton Uprising, pp. 1-4. Yeh Chien-ying himself joined the CCP in September 1927. Donald W. Klein and Anne B. Clark, Biographic Dictionary of Chinese Communism, 1921-1965 (Cambridge, Mass., 1971), II, 1005.

11. Yeh Chien-ying, "Ta Ko-ming shih-pai yü Kuang-chou ch'i-i" [The failure of the great revolution and the Canton uprising],

Jen-min jih-pao [People's daily] (Peking), July 30, 1958. Hereafter cited as Yeh, "Canton Uprising."

12. Teng Chung-hsia later reported that there were pressures from among the workers to launch an uprising in mid-October, but that the Kwangtung Party Committee had discouraged such hasty and ill-prepared moves at that time. [Teng] Chung-hsia, "Kuang-chou pao-tung yü Kung-ch'an-tang-ti ts'e-lüeh" [The Canton uprising and the tactics of the CCP], in Canton Commune, p. 46.

13. Ibid., p. 53; Akatova, "The Working Class and the Canton Commune," p. 53. Some of the expelled strikers reportedly broke through to join the partisan forces in the Hai-lu-feng soviet area. Akatova, p. 52.

14. Ibid., p. 53. The Red Guard apparently also included some 400 peasants from the Canton environs. Huang P'ing, "The Canton Uprising and Its Background," p. 143.

15. Yeh, "Canton Uprising."

16. Neuberg, Armed Insurrection, p. 114.

17. [Teng] Chung-hsia, "Canton Uprising and Tactics of the CCP," pp. 38-39, 42.

18. "The Significance and Lessons of the Canton Uprising" ("Kuang-chou pao-tung chih i-i yü chiao-hsün"), January 3, 1928, decision of the Provisional Political Bureau of the CCP Central Committee, in Ch'ü Ch'iu-pai, Chung-kuo ko-ming yü Kung-ch'an-tang [The Chinese revolution and the Communist party] (n.p., June 1928), supplement 2, p. 246. Teng Chung-hsia stated that the Party Center decided on the uprising before receipt of the news of Chang Fa-k'uei's coup, but in anticipation that it would occur very shortly (p. 38). Hsiao Tso-liang has contended that the Party Center in Shanghai neither endorsed nor knew about the Canton rising beforehand. Chinese Communism in 1927, p. 138. However, the Party Center's January 3, 1928, directive cited above maintained that the Kwangtung Party Committee acted in compliance with the November 18 directive in planning the insurrection, as did Teng Chung-hsia in his report referred to above. And Ch'ü Ch'iu-pai, in his tribute to the fallen leader

of the Canton uprising, Chang T'ai-lei, written in the immediate aftermath of the Commune's defeat, lauded Chang for having carried out the instructions of the party "to organize the uprising in Canton," "In Memory of Chang T'ai-lei," Bolshevik, no. 12 (December ?, 1927), in Kantonskaia Kommuna, p. 131. The specific timing and preparations for the revolt presumably were not made known to the Party Center. The 1928 account of the insurrection in the Comintern's Armed Insurrection noted on this latter point that "The Central Committee of the Communist Party had not learnt in time of the decision of the Kwangtung provincial committee to launch the movement in Canton on 11 December," p. 127 (emphasis added). And when the February 1928 ECCI Ninth Plenum spoke of "the complete ignorance of the national party centre of the Canton events," this must be interpreted in similar fashion, particularly since this resolution itself endorsed the revolt in the name of the Comintern. "Resolution on the Chinese Question," p. 322.

Both Chinese and Soviet Communist sources in recent years have reiterated that the Kwangtung committee's decision to launch the Canton uprising was in accord with the November instructions of the Party Center. Yeh, "Canton Uprising," and Afanasiev, "Heroic Uprising," pp. 10-11.

19. [Teng] Chung-hsia, "Canton Uprising and Tactics of the CCP," pp. 38-42.

20. Ibid., p. 42; Afanasiev, "Heroic Uprising," p. 11.

21. "Significance and Lessons of the Canton Uprising," p. 248.

22. Ibid., p. 253. Neuberg, Armed Insurrection, p. 113.

23. Ch'ü Ch'iu-pai stated at the Sixth CI Congress in August 1928 that "a whole series" of risings had occurred on December 13 and 14 in Kwangtung and in the vicinity of Canton, "uprisings in which workers and peasants took power. These uprisings were suppressed just as their centre, Canton, had already been crushed." "The Lessons of the Chinese Revolution" (Co-report of Comrade Strakhov [Ch'ü Ch'iu-pai]), August 15, 1928, Inprecorr, VIII: 68 (October 4, 1928), 1253.

24. Afanasiev, "Heroic Uprising," p. 28.

25. "Appeal of the Kwangtung Provincial Committee of the CCP to the People, with a Call to Revolt" (November 28, 1927), Bolshevik, no. 9 (probably early December 1927), pp. 250-256, included as a document in Kantonskaia Kommuna, pp. 202-206.

26. Kantonskaia Kommuna, p. 205.

27. Afanasiev, "Heroic Uprising," p. 11; Neuberg, Armed Insurrection, p. 113.

28. Neuberg, Armed Insurrection, p. 113.

29. Yeh, "Canton Uprising."

30. [Teng] Chung-hsia, "Canton Uprising and Tactics of the CCP," p. 48. Two-thirds of the members of the Soviet executive committee were workers, according to Teng (ibid.).

31. Huang P'ing, "Canton Uprising and Its Background," p. 154. A mass rally was held on the second day of the uprising (December 12) which ratified the previously chosen executive committee and called for the election, through worker, peasant and soldier organizations of a full soviet within three days (p. 161). But the Canton Commune was already beleaguered and was shortly to fall.

32. Ibid., p. 155.

33. Lozovsky, "Lessons of the Canton Revolt" ("Kuang-chou pao-tung-ti chiao-hsün"), Canton Commune, p. 6.

34. Huang P'ing, "Canton Uprising and Its Background," p. 155; Yeh, "Canton Uprising."

35. "Significance and Lessons of the Canton Uprising," pp. 247-248.

36. Rise of the CCP, II, 50.

37. [Ch'en] Shao-yü, "Report on the Canton Uprising" ("Kuang-chou pao-tung chi-shih"), November 1, 1928, Canton Commune, p. 139.

38. The Red Guards reportedly possessed fewer than fifty guns. Ibid.; Neuberg, Armed Insurrection, pp. 115-117.

39. Neuberg, Armed Insurrection, pp. 121, 126.

40. Ibid., p. 118.

41. Ibid. The consolidation process was to be facilitated by organizing peasant forces on the outskirts of Canton to help seal the city off from enemy contingents advancing on Canton. Yeh, "Canton Uprising."

42. Huang P'ing, "Canton Uprising and Its Background," p. 161.

43. [Teng] Chung-hsia, "Canton Uprising and Tactics of the CCP," p. 56; Neuberg, Armed Insurrection, p. 111; Huang P'ing, "Canton Uprising and Its Background," pp. 164-165. Though a few hundred peasants attacked a rail station and an arsenal on the outskirts of Canton, Teng Chung-hsia stated that there were no party cells among the peasantry in the Canton environs and that work among them had not been done well.

44. Wales, Song of Ariran, p. 163.

45. Neuberg, Armed Insurrection, pp. 120, 123.

46. [Teng] Chung-hsia, "Canton Uprising and Tactics of the CCP," pp. 50-52; Neuberg, Armed Insurrection, p. 120. Actually only the few hundred former Hong Kong strike pickets among the Red Guards had received training in handling firearms. Akatova, "The Working Class and the Canton Commune," p. 54. According to a 1967 Soviet account, 20,000 workers, 2,000 soldiers, 2,000 peasants, 800 freed political prisoners, and 2,000 members of the Communist Party and Communist Youth Corps took an active part in the revolt. Afanasiev, "Heroic Uprising," p. 28.

U. S. Consul Huston, basing himself on KMT police and military estimates, reported that the revolutionaries were able to "entice" only some "3000 or more workers" to join the insurrection--mostly in looting the city, he added. Of these, he stated, perhaps 1,000 were "riffraff" rather than "Communist workers." Huston Report, pp. 18-19.

34

47. [Teng] Chung-hsia, "Canton Uprising and Tactics of the CCP,"
    p. 52. Ch'ü Ch'iu-pai stated that "there were about 4-5 thou-
    sand workers constantly crowding about the general staff of the
    insurrection in the course of two days clamouring for arms."
    "The Lessons of the Chinese Revolution," p. 1253.

48. [Ch'en] Shao-yü, "Report on the Canton Uprising," pp. 188-189.

49. Lozovsky, "Lessons of the Canton Revolt." pp. 7-9.

50. Ibid., p. 6.

51. [Teng] Chung-hsia, "Canton Uprising and Tactics of the CCP,"
    p. 53. From a high point of 200 unions affiliated with the
    Council of Workers' Delegates in early 1927, the now under-
    ground council retained links with some sixty unions on the eve
    of the insurrection (ibid.). According to estimates given by
    Huston, a maximum of 8,000 of these radical unionists were
    Communists prior to the revolt. Huston Report, p. 19.

52. Yeh T'ing's report on the Canton insurrection, cited in Neuberg,
    Armed Insurrection, pp. 127-128.

53. [Teng] Chung-hsia, "Canton Uprising and Tactics of the CCP,"
    p. 52. In particular, there was little participation in the up-
    rising by Canton's handicraft workers and shop clerks. [Ch'en]
    Shao-yü, "Report on the Canton Uprising," p. 189.

54. V. Lominadze, "The Anniversary of the Canton Rising," Com-
    munist International, VI: 5 (January 30, 1929), 135.

55. Neuberg, Armed Insurrection, p. 122; Huston Report, p. 25;
    Wales, Song of Ariran, pp. 184-200. See also Introduction,
    n. 6.

56. Afanasiev, "Heroic Uprising," p. 31. Neuberg, Armed Insur-
    rection, p. 122.

57. "Second Appeal of the CCP to the People in Connection with the
    Canton Uprising" (CC, CCP, December 17, 1927), Bolshevik,
    no. 9 (December ?, 1927), in Kantonskaia Kommuna, pp. 196-
    201.

8. See Introduction, n. 2. Communist sources usually state that the revolutionary regime executed about 100 "counterrevolutionaries" during the brief duration of the soviet. See, for example, Neuberg, Armed Insurrection, p. 124.

9. Huston Report, p. 26. Huston particularly noted the role of the Mechanics' Union squads in the killings. "The .members of this group which had not the slightest legal sanction, either in law or by custom, carried out executions whenever and wherever they willed. Anybody who had shown the slightest sympathy for the Reds or their doctrines was ruthlessly exterminated, one black sheep in a house subjecting the whole family to execution" (p. 27). See also Introduction, n. 2.

0. Enclosure No. 5, Huston Report. Six Chinese servants from the consulate were also executed.

1. Roy, Revolution and Counter-Revolution in China, pp. 562-563.

2. Pepper, "Position and Tasks of the Chinese C. P. , " p. 159.

CI-CCP EVALUATIONS OF CANTON, 1928-1931

Despite its speedy and largely foredoomed collapse, the Canton Commune took on a special political meaning in that for the first time in the Chinese revolution it had proclaimed a government of the "revolutionary democratic dictatorship of workers and peasants" based on soviet power under direct Communist leadership, located in a major urban revolutionary center, and created through what was at least in part a workers' insurrection. The Commune had unfolded the approved socialist-oriented objectives of the transition period, and "proletarian hegemony" had been formally asserted in the 10-3-3 worker, peasant, soldier ratio of its sixteen-member Soviet executive, and in the selection (in absentia) of Su Chao-cheng, the prominent Kwangtung Communist labor leader and an organizer of the Hong Kong-Canton strike, as chairman of the revolutionary government proclaimed at a mass rally on December 12.[1] The rural-based Hai-lu-feng soviet area, on the other hand, which functioned on an organized and elected basis from early November 1927 to early March 1928, never formed a "central" government nor did it use the "democratic dictatorship" designation.[2] The proclaimed role of "Soviet Canton" as the guiding political center for the entire revolutionary movement in Kwangtung was reflected in the declared intention of the Canton Soviet to "ratify" (p'i-chun) the list of government members of Hai-lu-feng,[3] and in the appointment (in absentia) of P'eng P'ai, the Hai-lu-feng leader, as Commissioner (Commissar) of Land in the new Canton revolutionary government, with the Hai-lu-feng peasants asked to send delegates to Canton.[4] At the same time, the view of peasant risings as jacqueries designed to promote a general revolutionary wave linked to the urban revolutionary center was evident in the Canton Soviet's appeal to "all peasants in Kwangtung to rise up strongly forthwith and confiscate all land, exterminate landlords and rich farmers [local bullies and evil gentry?], to pay neither rent nor taxes, to repay no loans and to destroy all title deeds and promissory notes and to organize a village Soviet government. The Canton Soviet will not fail to send red troops to help you."[5]

For the workers of Canton, the Soviet decreed an eight-hour day, wage increases for all workers, and generous state aid to the unemployed. It ordered state control of banks, railways, mines, factories

and steamships, cancellation of debts and loans, confiscation of the
property of all (big) capitalists, worker control of production, and
recognition of the Communist-organized All-China Federation of Labor
(ACFL) as the sole organizational structure for the labor movement.
It saluted the Third International as "the leaders of the world revolution. "[6]

Pravda on December 12 greeted the uprising as confirmation
that, contrary to the assertions of the opposition, "the [Chinese]
revolution lives and strides resolutely forward. "[7] And as already
noted, the Comintern on December 14 saluted the then already defeated revolt as "an event of really worldwide historical significance. "[8] The CCP Center under Ch'ü Ch'iu-pai in early January
hailed the importance of Canton as the first example of an urban
soviet government in China and in the whole of colonial Asia. The
proletariat, the January party resolution stated, had now clearly
asserted its vanguard role in the Chinese revolution. [9] Trotsky, on
his part, while labeling Canton a hopeless "adventure, " at the same
time saw in it confirmation of the heroic revolutionary political ca-
pacities of the Chinese proletariat. [10] Reiterating his thesis that the
bourgeois stage of the revolution had come to a close with the KMT
victory, Trotsky saw verification of this in the proletarian character
and strongly anti-capitalist program of the Canton Commune, which
exhibited "the features of the coming [proletarian-socialist] stage of
the Chinese revolution. "[11] He thus pointedly asked, in his oft-cited
query, "If these are the methods of a bourgeois revolution, what will
the proletarian revolution in China look like?"[12]

And in keeping with the "leftist" line regarding a new revolutionary upsurge in China, with its notions of immediate, coordinated
rural-urban armed uprisings and rapid transition to the socialist revolution, the Canton revolt was also initially saluted in such terms by
the CCP leadership[13] and by the continuing proponents of this line in
the Comintern, notably Neumann and Lominadze. [14] The latter,
writing in the Comintern journal soon after the defeat of the Commune,
declared, "China is entering a period of development and intensification
of extremely ruthless civil war. Ahead lie fresh gigantic struggles and
conflicts. The Canton rising is only the beginning of a new stage. "[15]

It was quickly apparent, however, that Canton did not in fact
presage such a new upsurge, and given the actual state of affairs in
China in the wake of the uprising, a reassessment was clearly in

order. Factional infighting between "left" and "right" positions apparently marked the discussions at a Comintern-organized Chinese Conference held in Moscow in early 1928 which hammered out an evaluation of Canton as well as new political-strategic guidelines for the Chinese revolution. These decisions were then incorporated in the definitive resolution on the Chinese question adopted by the ECCI Ninth Plenum held in February, immediately following the Chinese Conference.[16] While the Canton events were a subject for further bitter exchanges between the two factions at the Sixth World Congress of the CI in the summer of 1928,[17] that Congress (and the CCP Sixth Congress also held in Moscow just prior to the CI gathering), fully endorsed and reaffirmed the position taken on Canton by the Ninth Plenum.

The rightist faction, probably supported by Bukharin,[18] focused on the errors and shortcomings in the planning and execution of the uprising, pointed to its inadequate mass base, and strongly inferred that "objective factors" in the overall situation had foredoomed the revolt to failure--a view carrying critical overtones towards the CI-CCP policy makers.[19] The left spokesmen, led by Lominadze, Neumann, Ch'ü Ch'iu-pai and other CCP representatives, countered by attacking the above views as veering towards Trotsky's "putschist" characterization of Canton,[20] asserted the genuinely proletarian social character of the uprising, acclaimed the correctness, significance, and positive achievements of the insurrection, and maintained their view of a continued revolutionary upsurge in China and the validity of the armed insurrection policy.[21] While the policy stance which emerged from the Ninth Plenum incorporated many of the criticisms of Canton raised by the right[22] and also rejected leftist contentions of a continuing upsurge in China, it nevertheless endorsed the basic leftist position on the overall merits and significance of Canton-- which was itself transmuted into a "rearguard battle" at the subsequent Sixth CCP Congress.

In its Chinese resolution the ECCI Ninth Plenum thus moved away from the notion of a new revolutionary upsurge moving rapidly and directly into the socialist stage (in an uninterrupted or "permanent" revolution), with remaining bourgeois tasks simultaneously resolved in the course of this transition.[23] In seeking to "decompress" this strategic line, the Plenum stressed instead the continued "bourgeois-democratic" character of the revolution,[24] and warned against the Trotskyist implications of permanent revolution, which ignored "the

profound national peculiarity of the Chinese revolution as a semi-
colonial revolution." The first revolutionary wave had ended in
"terrible defeats," and in the subsequent regrouping of class forces,
the workers and peasants now confronted a counterrevolutionary coalition (though rent by conflicts) of imperialists, feudal and militarist
forces, and the bourgeoisie.[25]

Acknowledging the absence of a new national revolutionary
upsurge, the resolution pointed to portents of a new advance, symp-
toms of which were "not only the heroic insurrection of the workers
of Canton," but primarily the peasant risings in progress in various
parts of China. But the revolution was developing unequally: "whereas
in some provinces the peasant movement develops further, in some industrial centres, the labour movement is bled white and subjected to
unexampled white terror and experiencing a certain degree of depression." The tactical line of the CCP under these conditions must be
to "prepare for the broad upsurge of a new revolutionary wave," for
which the central task was the winning over of the masses of workers
and peasants.

The resolution called on the CCP to increase in every possible
way its work among organized labor, while in building a network of
peasant organizations it called for special attention "to work among
the rural poor and separately organizing the rural proletarian elements." In leading the "spontaneous guerrilla actions of the peasants,"
the party was cautioned that "these actions can be transformed into a
victorious national uprising only on condition if they will be linked up
with the new upsurge of the revolutionary wave in the proletarian
centres." It called on the party to prepare and organize "simultaneous
and coordinated action in the villages and towns of several neighboring
provinces,"[26] and directed attention specifically to the "sovietized districts," where the main task was to carry out the agrarian revolution
and to organize Red Army detachments with the ultimate aim of forming
a united national Red Army.

Though the resolution warned against "putsches" and against any
tendency "to play with insurrection," and despite the specific listing
of a damaging set of "blunders" committed in the Canton uprising
which could easily have been used to underline these warnings,[27] it
instead declared the Canton insurrection to have been "a heroic attempt
of the proletariat to organize a Soviet Government in China," and as
"having played an enormous role in the development of the workers'

and peasants' revolution." Thus, despite the errors made, the Chinese workers now have "the right to claim their historical role as leaders of the great Chinese revolution."[28]

As Communist strategy in China thus moved towards a more extended revolutionary perspective, with primary emphasis on a more protracted rural revolution, the Canton Commune took on a special political connotation. In the task of preparing and organizing a new upsurge that would again put the revolution in high gear, the large urban centers were expected to play their crucial and central role in the transition to a "Chinese October." The Canton revolt and its political program had provided the revolutionary example and established the credibility of the Chinese proletariat for this eventual leading role.[29] This clearly transcended the immediate inappropriateness of the Commune's socialist-oriented program and of its ill-conceived insurrectionary strategy.[30] As the revolution moved into the hinterland, the Canton Commune served politically and symbolically to assert the "proletarian soul" of that revolution and the political leadership of "the city over the village," issues which remained basic throughout all the subsequent history of Chinese Communism.

The Sixth Congress of the CCP, held in Moscow under close Comintern guidance from June 18 to July 11, 1928, enunciated policies which Richard C. Thornton, in a recent analysis of the 1928-1931 period, describes as "merely a crystallization of the ideas first disclosed in the (ECCI) Ninth Plenum's resolution."[31] Thornton characterizes the strategy outlined by the Sixth Congress as one of protracted struggle, which called on the CCP to carry out "a broadly conceived, sophisticated strategy of guerrilla warfare" in the countryside and "political subversion" of the cities, with the rural buildup of Communist power apparently being "the main focus," while in terms of overall strategy the party's urban activities were to play "a key diversionary role."[32]

But from a longer-term perspective the party's urban strategy might more justifiably be described as a key preparatory and organizational one, for the intent was evidently for the political center of gravity to remain in a Party Center rooted (if precariously) in an urban environment and exercising direct leadership over the rural soviet movement.[33] In this context, it was vitally important for the party to rebuild its links with labor organizations and directly to support urban labor interests and struggles as the foundation for

restoring and developing the Communist urban political base.[34] There
was an equal determination to coordinate a Communist-led workers'
movement with the rural struggle and to "proletarianize" party, army
and soviet organs in the countryside,[35] to press for economic and
agrarian policies in the soviet areas geared to rural proletarian forces
and interests,[36] and to pursue a decidedly anticapitalist overall policy line. All this would prepare the ground for a new revolutionary
upsurge in one or more provinces, once again linking rural and urban
insurrection, with the political locus of power focused on the cities
under a proletarian-led dictatorship of workers and peasants poised
for the "growing over" into the proletarian socialist revolution.[37]

The 1928 Comintern treatise, Armed Insurrection, in pointing
to the importance of "the participation of the peasant masses in the
preparation and execution of armed uprisings," emphasized "The
indispensable preconditions for success in the organization and
operations of the revolutionary peasant armies are: a) the proletarian and semi-proletarian composition of these armies, b) the
presence of a nucleus of industrial workers and communists who
form their military and political cadre, c) the coordination of their
operations with the revolutionary struggle of the urban proletariat."[38]
At the Sixth CI Congress, Ch'ü Ch'iu-pai, noting the growing vitality
of the peasant revolutionary movement in contrast to the "depression
in towns and in the Labour Movement as a whole," added: "The
question arises: If a victorious insurrection of the proletariat, such
as that in Canton, does not take place and if this victory cannot be
stabilized--would in such situation a victory of the Chinese revolution,
at least in a few provinces, be thinkable? We must answer this
question in the negative."[39]

The Sixth CCP Congress specifically endorsed the Ninth Plenum's
assessment of the Canton Commune, and in a definitive formulation
declared that the Commune "began the third stage of the Chinese
revolution, the period of the Soviets."[40] But "objectively speaking,
the Canton Commune became 'a rearguard fight' in the stage of revolutionary failure."[41] The Commune had "world historical significance,"
and party headquarters on all levels were called upon "to make a
careful study of the rich experiences [accumulated] in the heroic
struggle of the Cantonese proletariat."[42]

The Sixth World Congress of the Comintern, meeting in Moscow
during August-September 1928, reiterated and endorsed the line for
China already spelled out in the Sixth CCP Congress. Rejecting "the

attempt to look upon the Canton uprising as a putsch, " it again stressed Canton's role as "the last powerful onslaught" in the ebbtide of a receding revolutionary wave, and linked the revolt specifically to the key objectives of the revolutionary period now again beginning to unfold. It was thus the insurrection of "the heroic Canton proletariat, which under the slogan of Soviets attempted to link up the agrarian revolution with the overthrow of the Kuomintang and the establishment of the dictatorship of workers and peasants."[43] Accordingly, it remained "the banner of the new, soviet stage of the revolution." Pointing to the example of Canton, the CI proclaimed: "Let the future insurrection of the broadest masses of the workers and peasants, organized on the basis of the sound and tested principles of Leninism, supported by the international proletariat, be a victorious October for China."[44]

In projecting its strategic line for the Chinese revolution during 1928, the CI-CCP leadership had stressed its "national peculiarity" as a "semi-colonial revolution."[45] Though the revolution's immediate goals remained primarily the anti-imperialist nationalist struggle for unity and independence and the social revolutionary overturn of China's massive agrarian system, the Canton events and the Canton proletariat had at the same time placed the revolution in an "internationalist" framework, and the Commune was thus portrayed as both symbol and evidence that the Chinese revolution, no matter what its immediate prospects, necessary strategies, or national "peculiarities," could be kept on course and find its proper place in the Soviet-led proletarian world revolution. The nature of the relationship and of the link between an increasingly "peculiar" peasant-nationalist content and the "proletarian-internationalist" perspectives and outlook of the revolution was also to become a basic issue in Chinese Communism. Canton thus emerged neither as a strategic and political blunder and aberrant deviation from the move to a primarily rural-centered strategy nor as merely an expedient proletarian symbol to obscure the "unorthodox" peasant-based strategy of the post-1927 Communist revolutionary movement. Instead, it found an authentic place as an urban proletarian revolutionary milestone and political yardstick as the CI and the CCP moved to fashion and implement the new strategic-political revolutionary guidelines for China.

The Sixth CI Congress' overall theoretical position on the urban-rural, industrial-agricultural, international-national relationship, projected on a world revolutionary scale, was strikingly summed up as follows:

Colonial revolutions and movements for national liberation play an extremely important part in the struggle against imperialism and in the struggle for the conquest of power by the working class. Colonies and semi-colonies are also important in the transition period because they represent the world rural district in relation to the industrial countries, which represent the world city. Consequently, the problem of organizing Socialist world economy, of properly combining industry with agriculture is, to a large extent, the problem of the relation towards the former colonies of imperialism. . . .

Thus, in rousing the workers in the home countries for the struggle for the dictatorship of the proletariat, the progress of the world revolution also rouses hundreds of millions of colonial workers and peasants for the struggle against foreign imperialism. In view of the existence of centres of Socialism represented by Soviet Republics of growing economic power, the colonies which break away from imperialism economically gravitate towards and gradually combine with the industrial centres of world Socialism, are drawn into the channel of Socialist construction, and by skipping the further stage of development of capitalism as the predominant system, obtain opportunities for rapid economic and cultural progress. The Peasants' Soviets in the more developed ex-colonies [China's category] group themselves politically around the centres of proletarian dictatorship, join the growing Federation of Soviet Republics, and thus enter the general system of the world proletarian dictatorship. [46]

Thus, while supporting a strategy of "rural" colonial revolution, the Comintern linked this politically to the leadership of the "urban" proletarian socialist center--a macrocosmic version of the Chinese revolutionary strategy and program formulated during 1928.[47] Since by Marxist definition the proletariat was the most socialist-minded and internationalist-inclined class, the proletarian city would presumably serve a national function analogous to that of the "world socialist city" internationally and also be the best guarantee that the national revolutionary movements would enter the socialist system of "world proletarian dictatorship."[48]

CI-CCP reports and commentaries on Canton during the years up to the establishment of the soviet republic in Kiangsi, consistently underlined its relevance to the direction and goals of the Chinese revolution outlined above. While Trotsky in 1928 pointed to Canton as final confirmation of the defeat of the proletarian forces, declaring that it was "absurd to believe that one can march towards a peasant insurrection when the proletarian masses are departing,"[49] CI-CCP pronouncements cited Canton in affirming that the post-1927 "peasant war" could and would develop along the class lines of the worker-peasant dictatorship first proclaimed in China by the Canton Soviet, as the road to the declared goal of a Chinese October.

In the immediate wake of the uprising, the Chinese Party Center had declared that Canton had forged a closely knit revolutionary alliance between the proletariat and the peasantry. The uprisings of the peasant masses, it stated, had become a "powerful echo" (or response) to the workers' uprising, and Canton had proclaimed to every peasant in Kwangtung that only under the leadership of the proletarian soviet government could they acquire land.[50] Heinz Neumann reiterated this point at the Sixth CI Congress, asserting that "since the Canton uprising the Chinese peasant knows that he can receive land, peace and freedom only from the hands of the workers, from the Soviet power."[51] A Comintern tribute to Chang T'ai-lei, fallen Kwangtung party leader, voiced this concept as follows: "It was clear to Chang that if the town did not take the lead of the civil war in the village, and if the C.P. did not develop the struggle to the highest pitch, that of revolution, then the Wuhan [sic, Kwangtung] workers and peasants would not have sufficient support."[52]

The role of the Canton Commune in emphasizing the "proletarian internationalist" facet of the Chinese revolution was illustrated in major commentaries on the Commune in the wake of the 1928 CCP-CI Congresses. An official ECCI analysis on the first anniversary of the Commune declared: "In the Canton revolt the Chinese proletariat came out as a mighty revolutionary force, as the hegemoneous leader of the oppressed classes of China. The proletariat of Canton pointed out to the hundreds of millions of the exploited people of China, India, and other Eastern countries, the real, the only correct road to freedom."[53] The event was hailed as "a conquest for the whole world proletariat . . . inasmuch as the struggle of the Chinese proletariat is part and parcel of the struggle of the international proletariat against world imperialism."[54]

A collection of reports on the Commune by Russian and Chinese Communists dating from this same period and published in a Chinese edition in 1930 under the title, The Canton Commune (Kuang-chou

Kung-she), [55] also stressed its role in the internationalization of the revolution. For example, Ch'en Shao-yü (Wang Ming), soon to emerge under Comintern auspices as a dominant figure in the CCP, wrote in a lengthy November 1928 report on the uprising that the Commune had openly proclaimed to the people of the world that the "spectre of communism" not only "haunted" Europe (in the phrase of the Communist Manifesto), but had also enveloped the "backward Far Eastern continent as well." The coolies of China, despite their backwardness, were as heroic and progressive as the proletariat of Paris (of the Paris Commune) and Russia. The Soviet flag thus no longer flies only over the Russian one-sixth of the land surface, "it has also become the red symbol of liberation for millions of China's toiling masses."[56] By establishing a Soviet regime in a backward colonial country, the uprising "advanced the world revolution still another step."[57] Ch'en declared the uprising to have been an inevitable culmination of the class struggle in China, and particularly in Kwangtung. He lauded the political program of the Commune and called for continued struggle for its realization.[58] The Canton defeat, he concluded, had served as a "rehearsal" for the future nationwide victory, and had proclaimed to the world that the latter would be "a victory of the Chinese October!"[59]

Comintern functionary Lozovsky similarly pointed to Canton's beacon role for the Eastern revolutionary movement and cited the short-lived soviet's historical significance in having given concrete political form to the worker-peasant democratic dictatorship through which the tasks of the bourgeois-democratic revolution could be completed in preparation for the transition to the socialist revolution.[60] Huang P'ing (Foreign and Internal Affairs Commissioner in the Canton Soviet) concluded his report on the uprising by declaring it to have been the "turning point which showed the working class and the poor peasantry of China the new road to power, the only power capable of freeing them from the landowners, the bourgeoisie, and imperialism."[61]

Lominadze, in a lengthy first-anniversary article appearing in The Communist International, noted that all the disputes within the Comintern on "the question of Canton" had been finally resolved by the Sixth CI Congress.[62] He acknowledged his own and others' "political mistake" in initially viewing the uprising as the beginning of a new revolutionary upsurge and of advocating in the succeeding months the organization of armed uprisings on as large a scale as possible. While Lominadze was obviously determined to present the "record" of the Commune as strongly as possible, it is nevertheless equally clear that he was writing under the auspices of and within the strict confines of the Comintern's new political guidelines on China.[63]

The question of proletarian hegemony in the revolution, he wrote, could not be determined "automatically"; the Chinese working class had to demonstrate its capability in action. "The Canton rising proved to be that activity. It was a decisive historical test, in which the Chinese proletariat finally assured to itself the role of the sole leader and director of the Chinese revolution."[64] He further underlined the Commune's political significance:

> The Canton rising connotes a transition to a higher stage
> of the revolution, first and most of all owing to the form
> of revolutionary government which it established (the So-
> viet Government), then owing to the new disposition of
> class forces (the proletarian hegemony in the struggle
> of the masses against the bloc of bourgeoisie, land-
> owners and imperialists), and finally owing to the his-
> torical initiative of the proletariat in organizing a mass
> revolutionary struggle, which is the prototype of imminent
> revolutionary battles on a much greater scale than that of
> December 10th to 12th, 1927.[65] (Italics added.)

Conceding "the great errors committed by the leaders of the rising," Lominadze asserted that "these errors were not in the fundamental political line, which was absolutely sound during the Canton days." The slogans, the establishment of the Soviet, the decrees issued and the policy in relation to "the imperialists, the bourgeoisie and the petty bourgeoisie were all unimpeachably sound," and in these respects "the Canton rising is an excellent example of how the Chinese Communists ought to proceed in the future."[66] The Communist International, Lominadze concluded, "proudly takes on itself all the responsibility for the great Canton Commune."[67]

As the rural soviet areas (and most importantly, those under Mao and Chu Te in the Kiangsi-Fukien-Hunan area) expanded in size and in the armed forces under their control in the years after 1928, both the Comintern and the CCP Party Center in Shanghai (now under Li Li-san's control) gave increasing attention to the need to bring the rural movement under firmer central party leadership and guidance. However, a clear divergence developed between the Comintern's overall view and long-term strategy, and the apparent effort of Li Li-san to utilize the new situation for his personal goals of political aggrandizement over the soviet areas and the entire Chinese Communist movement during 1929 and 1930.[68] The Comintern apparently sought to encourage and support the growing soviet movement while simultaneously bringing it under firmer political control from an urban-oriented and rooted Party Center responsive to Comintern directives and guidance. Thus the "proletarian" outlook and links of the rural movement could be retained and reinforced pending the hopefully not too long delayed general revolutionary upsurge, at which time rural and urban components would again coalesce.[69] By 1930 these objectives began to call for the organization of a central soviet government to unify the scattered rural areas, under the direct supervision of the Party Center, and serving as the nucleus for the future national revolutionary government. Again, the symbolism of the Canton Commune played its part.

During the first part of 1930 the Party Center in Shanghai under Li Li-san made plans for convening a preparatory conference of soviet delegates, which in turn would arrange for a formal soviet congress to establish a central soviet government, presumably to be located in the largest and most important of the soviet areas, the Kiangsi-Fukien base led by Mao and Chu. These preparations, however, apparently became enmeshed in Li Li-san's personal political ambitions and in the strategy he was evolving for a "final" urban labor-led revolutionary confrontation on a national scale in which the rural-based Red armies would be harnessed to the drive to take over major urban centers. In Li's calculations, the new soviet government would be created only when it could be located in a major industrial center such as Wuhan and be under his direct political control.[70] Though Li was presumably bound by the overall framework of Comintern directives, the latter were often ambiguous and generalized in referring to the "beginning" of a new revolutionary upsurge, in the varied uses and connotations of "upsurge" itself, and in the constant stress on the ultimately crucial role of the major urban centers and the workers' movement in such an upsurge. But beyond this interpretive problem, Li's 1930 policies appear to have deliberately diverged in significant ways from Comintern guidelines.[71]

The soviet delegates' conference, which convened May 31, 1930, in Shanghai (and which was boycotted by the Mao forces) was transformed by Li into a "First Soviet Congress," and he sought to avoid for the time being a specific call to organize a central soviet government.[72] Whereas Li envisaged a revolutionary "high tide" (kao-ch'ao) calling for an immediate rural-urban insurrectionary strategy culminating in an urban-based revolutionary government and the move to a socialist Chinese October,[73] the Comintern focused on the strongly developing rural soviet movement (which "unevenly" contrasted with continued urban weakness), emphasized the agrarian revolution linked to a strongly proletarian line in the rural area, and attempted to strengthen efforts to activate and politicize the urban workers' movement. The primary objective remained the formation of a "democratic dictatorship of workers and peasants" under a party leadership and policy line that would ensure proletarian political hegemony, and thus the more carefully phased and protracted but nonetheless clearly projected transition to the Chinese October.[74] As the Comintern described the current phase in July 1930, "the agrarian question lies at the centre of the Chinese revolution. The revolution develops in the form of peasant wars [sic] led by the proletariat."[75]

Leaving aside the factor of personal political rivalries within the CCP at this time, these divergences involved basic strategic and political questions of timing and direction, which were in turn dependent upon assessments of the "stages" of revolution, the balance of Chinese revolutionary forces, rural and urban, of the overall "revolutionary situation" in China and the world, and of the imminence of a new "high tide."[76] Li saw the revolution moving towards its proletarian socialist stage and developing rapidly on a national--indeed international scale.[77] In line with this outlook and his personal power objectives vis-à-vis soviet area leaders, Li evidently denigrated the longer-term importance and intrinsic interests of the rural soviet movement. The Comintern, on the other hand, took a more gradualist position in pointing towards the same objectives, with the rural movement remaining strategically primary for a certain period and with revolution initially spreading on a provincial-regional basis rather than a national scale.[78] Meanwhile it was imperative to keep the rural revolution properly "programmed," if indeed it was to stay on course and develop according to plan. From the Comintern's standpoint, and that of the post-Li Li-san leadership of the CCP, the essential issue was to be precisely how the expanding rural movement and its indigenous leadership and armed forces could be placed within a genuinely proletarian-oriented political framework, while at the same time continuing the increasingly difficult effort to activate the urban struggle as the key both to national revolutionary victory and to the character of the revolution itself.

A June Inprecorr article discussing the May 1930 delegates' conference (erroneously referred to at the time as a "First Congress") seemed to reflect the overall Comintern view. It noted that after the

1927 break with the KMT the Chinese revolution had entered "a new phase of the bourgeois-democratic revolution, the phase of the 'peasant war' under the leadership of the proletariat," directed against imperialism, "the feudal regime," and "the counterrevolutionary bourgeoisie," and moving towards a "revolutionary democratic dictatorship of the proletariat and the peasantry in the form of soviets as the preliminary condition for the development into the socialist revolution." This soviet stage was, as usual, linked to the Canton Commune, and seen as a "continuation of the workers and peasants struggle."[79]

In the "towns" (not the major cities), the article continued, "there is without doubt a steady rise of the working class movement, although this is taking place more slowly than the corresponding activity of the peasants in the villages." It emphasized, however, that the CCP, "well aware of the fact that only the proletariat in alliance with the masses of the peasantry can decide the fate of the Chinese Revolution, is at present conducting tremendous activities in the great industrial centres. Taught by past experiences," the writer went on, "the Party is also taking over the leadership of the peasant insurrections in order to connect up the struggle of the urban proletariat with the 'peasant war.'" Thus, in the present stage of "the peasant movement and the 'Soviet revolution,'" convening a soviet delegates' conference was "urgently necessary."[80] The central focus seemed clearly on the "peasant war" and on its proper urban links and direction.

The continuing uses of the Canton Commune link was rather strikingly manifested in the question of an appropriate date for convening a founding congress to establish a central soviet government in 1930. The Li Li-san-dominated May delegates' conference had finally, and apparently reluctantly, agreed to issue a call for such a congress,[81] setting the date for November 7, 1930--the Bolshevik Revolution anniversary. One could surmise that Li, looking towards the imminent implementation of his climactic insurrectionary strategy, wished to link the congress with this appropriate international "October" symbol. The Comintern, on the other hand, with its concept of a more protracted, proletarian-led "peasant war" which it was determined to set on an eventual socialist course insisted instead on the Commune anniversary date, December 11.[82] Thus, the Central Preparatory Commission for the National Soviet Congress meeting on September 12, 1930--at a time when Li Li-san was coming under increasingly strong Comintern criticism--postponed the convocation of the National Soviet Congress from November 7 to December 11, and at the same time called for the preparatory commission to move its work to the soviet areas. [83]

But with the political downfall of Li Li-san in late 1930 and the successive launching, from December 1930 through September 1931, of the KMT's first three anti-Communist encirclement campaigns, [84] the convening of a soviet congress was postponed, finally meeting, ironically, on November 7, 1931, in Juichin, Kiangsi, in the central soviet areas. The enlarged Fourth Plenum of the CCP Central Committee in January 1931 totally repudiated the Li Li-san leadership and policies and marked the ascension of the so-called Russian returned student group (the "Twenty-Eight Bolsheviks") led by Ch'en Shao-yü (Wang Ming) and Ch'in Pang-hsien (Po Ku) to party control. [85] The Plenum, hewing to Comintern guidelines, underscored the importance it attached to the political consolidation of the soviet areas in its criticism of the Li Li-san leadership for having "completely neglected the task of establishing a strong Soviet base, and [having] completely neglected the establishment of a strong Soviet political regime."[86] A Central Bureau of the Soviet Areas, which became the most important party organ in the base areas, was created by the CCP leadership shortly after the Fourth Plenum, under the secretaryship of Hsiang Ying, a CCP leader of proletarian background who had served as head of the underground ACFL during 1929-1930. [87]

The Comintern and the new CCP leadership clearly wished to move as expeditiously as possible in setting up a central soviet government, [88] and thus now selected the November 7 anniversary date--the party Central Committee in fact at first hoped to convene a founding congress by August 1, the Nanchang uprising anniversary associated with the founding of the Red armies. [89] But that the CI-CCP leadership continued politically to link the new soviet regime with the Canton Commune was reflected in the date officially set for holding the Second Soviet Congress--December 11, 1933, the sixth anniversary of the Commune, [90] though because of various delays, largely relating to the KMT's fifth encirclement campaign then underway, it did not in fact meet until late January 1934. [91] The launching of the official organ of the new soviet republic (Hung-se Chung-hua [Red China]) on the December 11, 1931, fourth anniversay of Canton--a point prominently noted in the first issue[92]--served further to underscore the symbolic link to the Commune, as did a leading anniversary article on the uprising in that inaugural issue. [93]

The symbolism attached to the dates of these soviet congresses is intriguingly illustrated in the puzzling "confusion" seemingly prevailing among the Maoist leadership in the immediate post-Kiangsi period (1936-1937) on the actual date of the First Congress. Mao Tse-tung, in his autobiographical interview with Edgar Snow in 1936, told Snow that the "First Soviet Congress was called on December 11, 1931"[94]; on the other hand, Chu Te told Agnes Smedley in 1937 that this congress, first scheduled by the party's Fourth Plenum for August 1, 1931 (the Nanchang anniversary), "had to be postponed, first to November 7th and then to December 11th. December 11th was the anniversary of the Canton Commune."[95] Finally, Nym Wales (Helen Snow), in her book on her four-month stay in Yenan in 1937, during which she talked "nearly every day with one or another of the extraordinary Communist leaders," wrote:

> I had the greatest difficulty determining the exact date of this first Soviet Congress. The date has often been given as November 7, 1931 (anniversary of the October Revolution in Russia), but nearly everyone I talked with gave me December 11 as the correct day--commemorating the anniversary of the Canton Commune. It seems probable that the congress was called for November 7, but that the delegates did not all arrive in time, so the later date was decided upon.[96]

One may speculate that the CI-CCP in 1931 would indeed have preferred the Canton anniversary date for the First Soviet Congress, and used this date as a reckoning point in setting the original date for the second congress. It is probably more likely, however, that Mao, now in the ascendancy and beginning to dissociate himself from the policy lines prevailing during the Kiangsi Soviet era (policies later excoriated by the Maoist leadership as the "third 'left' line"),[97] sought in some obscure fashion to indicate this by linking the 1931 congress, which ushered in this period in the soviet area, with the symbolism of the Commune-initiated democratic dictatorship and its strongly asserted concepts, policies and strategies of proletarian hegemony.

As the new CCP leadership in 1931 turned more directly to the task of "consolidating" the expanding soviet areas and armies as the CCP-led revolutionary center,[98] a political line emerged which, in the context of unquestioned priority to the soviet movement, tried to avoid "submersion" by the peasant movement, domination by a "peasant mentality," and the danger of "de-proletarianizing" the Chinese Communist movement.[99] It was thus seen as particularly important, precisely in this period of close integration of the central party apparatus with the rural movement, to articulate the party's proletarian features and outlook more distinctly and sharply than ever, and also to avoid "overreacting" to Li Li-san's "adventurism" by turning to a "rightist" line of "retreat."[100] This called for a strong "Bolshevik" political and organizational line in the soviet areas, a continuing activist labor line in the major urban centers,[101] and reemphasis on the importance of capturing cities to reforge the rural-urban revolutionary link and as the best assurance of labor dominance in the soviet movement.[102] However, this military strategy was now framed within the context of the soviet bases, and aimed primarily to "round out," connect and expand these areas by taking adjacent smaller cities and possibly the Kiangsi provincial capital of Nanchang, in what became the Party Center's "forward and offensive" strategy for winning "preliminary successes in one or more provinces."[103]

In line with these strategies, the CCP leadership was determined, both for its intrinsic political importance within the soviet areas and with an eye to the eventual inclusion of the major cities in the unfolding revolutionary process, to retain and promote the policy of organizing and supporting labor through an anticapitalist, struggle-oriented defense of worker interests.[104] In essence, all this was a strategy of "external proletarianization"--and leadership--of the rural struggle.[105] It differed decisively from the later Maoist model of "internal proletarianization" which, while bringing Marxist-Leninist perspectives to the peasant revolution, sought the party's and the army's "proletarian" roots precisely through immersion in the "sea" of "people's [peasant] war."

A March 1931 Comintern article on the Canton Commune focused its attention on the rural-urban link and on the importance of the peasant struggle to the success of the urban revolution, with all this calling for effective activist CCP labor leadership.[106] It concentrated on the "lessons" of the Commune still pertinent for current CCP urban work: the failure effectively to mobilize the workers in support of the insurrection, the weak political work among the "yellow unions," and the lack of coordination with peasant revolts which could have diverted attacking forces and given the Commune time to consolidate its position. Clearly meant as a guide to current and projected revolutionary strategy in China, it stated:

> [The uprising] was unable to mobilize all the masses
> who were prepared to struggle, it could not organize
> and utilize all the forces and means of struggle which
> were at its disposal. It could not practically strengthen
> the proletarian revolt in the city by a peasant war in
> the surrounding villages, and in spite of the great cour-
> age . . . of its defenders, it was crushed. [107]

The article proclaimed the "creative" role of the Canton proletariat in "discovering" the political form for a worker and peasant
bloc, the Russian-invented soviets through which the leading role of
the proletariat could be most easily exerted. It thereby demonstrated
"the universal character of the Soviets as a form of revolutionary
power not only for industrially developed countries, but also for the
economically backward colonies." Thus, "the flag of the Soviets,
stained with the blood of the communards of Canton, is raised high
in China by the millions of workers and peasants of the Soviet districts. It is the flag of the Chinese Red Army, and under this flag
gather the warriors and the detachments of the future colonial October Revolution. This is the tremendous and historical world importance of the Canton Commune."[108]

An _Inprecorr_ anniversary article on the Commune, in the wake
of the establishment of the Chinese Soviet Republic in November 1931,
again stressed its role as the proletarian link to the developing soviet
movement. The Commune, the author wrote, "created the first troops
of the Red Guard. Under the leadership of the Communist Party and
the Communist International, they have become the powerful Red Army
of the workers and peasants, . . . the army of the Chinese revolution."
The four years that have elapsed since the Commune unfurled the soviet
flag "have shown that there is only one way open to the workers and
peasants, the way of the Soviets, of the Canton Commune."[109] Clearly,
in the context of the central importance of the newly established soviet
government, the effort was made to link it politically with the course
charted by the Canton Commune, whose proletarian leadership creden-
tials and internationalist character were continuously emphasized. [110]

FOOTNOTES

1. Huang P'ing, "Canton Uprising and Its Background," p. 161; [Ch'en] Shao-yü, "Report on the Canton Uprising," p. 126. Ch'en (Wang Ming) emphasized: "As we all know, Su Chao-cheng is a CCP Central Committee member and a famous leader of the Chinese labor movement" (ibid.).

 Su Chao-cheng had apparently left Canton for the Hai-lu-feng area in an unsuccessful effort to round up peasant armed forces there to rush to the aid of the Canton uprising. Song of Ariran, p. 169. Chang T'ai-lei was delegated to act as chairman of the Council of People's Commissars during Su's absence. Its other members were: Huang P'ing (Internal and Foreign Affairs), Yang Yin (Counterrevolutionary Liquidation), Chou Wen-yung (Labor), P'eng P'ai (Land), Ch'en Yü (Justice), Ho Lai (Economics), Chang T'ai-lei (Army and Navy), Yün Tai-ying (Secretariat), Yeh T'ing (Commander-in-Chief), Hsü Kuang-ying (Chief of Staff). [Ch'en] Shao-yü, "Report on the Canton Uprising," pp. 125-126.

2. Shinkichi Eto, "Hai-lu-feng," pp. 172-173. Eto notes that "'Hai-lu-feng soviet' was not a designation of a specific government office. In place of such an office, the Tung-Chiang Special Committee of the Chinese Communist Party was the actual centre for the integration of these soviets" (p. 172).

3. [Ch'en] Shao-yü, "Report on the Canton Uprising," p. 153.

4. Handbill distributed December 11, and "Soviet Administration's Message to the People" (December 11, 1927). Huston Report, enclosures 1 and 2.

5. "Soviet Administration's Message to the People." Other sources (Ch'en Shao-yü and Afanasiev), in summarizing this portion of the program, use the phrase "t'u hao, lieh shen" (local bullies and evil gentry), which Huston may have translated as "rich farmers."

6. "Soviet Administration's Message to the People." A further manifesto apparently qualified "all capitalists" to just the "big capitalists." Huang P'ing, "Canton Uprising and Its Background," pp. 158-159.

7. Buber-Neumann, War Theaters of the Comintern, p. 221.

8. See Introduction, n. 13.

9. "Significance and Lessons of the Canton Uprising," pp. 276-278.

10. "The Chinese Question After the Sixth Congress" (October 4, 1928
    Problems of the Chinese Revolution, p. 172. "One of the detach-
    ments of the proletariat was drawn into a struggle which obviously
    held out no hope," Trotsky wrote, "and made easier for the enem
    the annihilation of the vanguard of the working class" (ibid.).

11. "Canton Insurrection," p. 151.

12. Ibid., p. 130. It might be added that, given the characteristics
    of the Commune pointed to by Trotsky, the Comintern leadership
    (if so minded) could have easily disavowed and condemned the
    uprising as a "Trotskyist" action of the ultraleft elements in the
    CI and CCP.

13. See Introduction, n. 13.

14. For a detailed and illuminating discussion of the policy debates,
    and of the theoretical underpinnings of the "extreme left" position
    as represented by Ch'ü Ch'iu-pai, Neumann and Lominadze, from
    the Fifteenth CPSU Congress in December 1927 through the Sixth
    Congresses of the CCP and the CI, June-September 1928, see
    Richard C. Thornton, The Comintern and the Chinese Communists
    1928-1931 (Seattle, 1969), pp. 3-22.

15. "Historical Significance of the Canton Rising," Communist Inter-
    national, V: 2 (January 15, 1928), 34. Lominadze, in finally
    and fully repudiating his position during the Sixth CI Congress,
    stated that before the ECCI Ninth Plenum he had made the
    "serious mistake" of considering the Canton rising "to be the
    beginning of a new upsurge of the Chinese revolution. Events
    have disproved this position. . . . My mistakes consisted in
    that, proceeding from a false estimate of the situation, I con-
    tinued after the Canton uprising to hold that the course for an
    immediate armed uprising was just as necessary as before the
    Canton uprising." Cited in Thornton, The Comintern and the
    Chinese Communists, p. 15.

6. Inprecorr, VIII: 76 (October 30, 1928), 1399-1400; and "The Chinese Question in the Plenum of the E. C. C. I. , " Inprecorr, VIII: 8 (April 15, 1928), 195.

7. See, for example, Inprecorr, VIII: 76, 1399-1400; and VIII: 78 (November 8, 1928), 1474-1477.

8. Inprecorr, VIII: 76 (October 30, 1928), 1399-1400.

9. For the gist of the rightist position as revealed in the exchanges between "Comrade Pepper" and his leftist opponents Lominadze, Ch'ü Ch'iu-pai, and others at the Sixth CI Congress, see Inprecorr, VIII: 53 (August 23, 1928), 933; VIII: 76 (October 30, 1928), 1399- 1400; VIII: 78 (November 8, 1928), 1474-1477; VIII: 81 (November 21, 1928), 1529. The political infighting associated with the 1928 debates on Canton was strikingly manifested in the treatment of the uprising in the well-known Comintern treatise, Armed Insur- rection, first published in 1928 in Germany (see Introduction, n. 3). The chapter on Canton was apparently written under the guidance of Red Army General Staff elements later purged by Stalin (Wollenberg, "How We Wrote Armed Insurrection, " pp. 18-20); and while it hewed to the overall Ninth Plenum line on Canton it strongly underlined the inherent weaknesses and mistakes of the insurrection and stressed the decisive importance of objective factors (associated with a receding revolutionary wave in China) in the defeat. Neuberg, Armed Insurrection, pp. 126-129. In a preface to the original edition by the "publishers" (now seem- ingly identified as the heads of either the propaganda or organi- zation departments of the Comintern [Wollenberg, p. 20]), "A. Neuberg" (the ostensible author of the treatise) was sharply taken to task for drawing "the false conclusion" from the Com- intern assessment of Canton as a rearguard action "that 'the indispensable social conditions, without which the victory of an armed insurrection is impossible, were not present to a suffi- cient degree in Canton'" (Appendix: "Some Prefatory Remarks by the Publishers," Neuberg, Armed Insurrection, pp. 264-265).

10. Lominadze, for example, complained at the Sixth CI Congress that one of the rightist critiques of Canton had said "everything except the word 'putch' [sic]. " Inprecorr, VIII: 53 (August 23, 1928), 933.

21. See n. 15, above; and Inprecorr, VIII: 76 (October 30, 1928), 1420; VIII: 68 (October 4, 1928), 1252-1253; VIII: 72 (October 17, 1928), 1308-1309; also sources in n. 19, above.

22. Pepper, at the Sixth CI Congress, cited the "ten quite weighty critical remarks" contained in the Ninth Plenum resolution regarding mistakes made in the Canton uprising. He hastened to add, however, in line with the Comintern position, that it "would of course be ridiculous to say that these critical remarks mean so much as to say that the uprising in Canton was a putsch." Inprecorr, VIII: 78 (November 8, 1928), 1477.

23. "Resolution on the Chinese Question," pp. 321-322. The resolution had been presented jointly by the delegations of the CPSU and the CCP, with Stalin as one of the coauthors. By the Sixth CI Congress this concept was carefully reformulated into the statement that the Chinese revolution was in a bourgeois-democratic stage "which unavoidably must grow over into the proletarian [stage]." Cited in Thornton, The Comintern and the Chinese Communists, p. 17.

24. Its uncompleted tasks were "the agrarian revolution and the abolition of feudal relations," and the antiimperialist struggle for unity and independence, with its political class character that of the dictatorship of the proletariat and the peasantry. "Resolution on the Chinese Question," p. 321.

25. Ibid.

26. This concept of a revolutionary situation embracing only a portion of China led later to the formula of an "initial victory in one or several provinces." Schwartz, Chinese Communism, pp. 111-112.

27. The Sixth CCP Congress subsequently carefully applied the "adventurist" (putschist) label only to the post-Canton insurrectionary policies of the Ch'ü Ch'iu-pai leadership. "Political Resolution [of the Sixth National Congress of the CCP]," Documentary History, pp. 139-140.

28. "Resolution on the Chinese Question," p. 322. The resolution's full assessment of Canton was as follows: "The Canton insur-

rection, having been a heroic attempt of the proletariat to organize a Soviet Government in China, and having played an enormous role in the development of the workers' and peasants' revolution, has nevertheless revealed a whole series of blunders made by the leaders: insufficient preliminary work among the workers and peasants, and among the enemy forces; a wrong appraisal [approach] to the working class members of the yellow unions; inadequate preparation of the Party organization and the Young Communist League for the insurrection; complete ignorance of the national Party centre of the Canton events; weakness in the political mobilisation of the masses (absence of broad political strikes, absence of an elected Soviet in Canton as an organ of insurrection), for which the direct leaders who are politically responsible to the CI (Comrade N [presumably Neumann] and others) are partly to blame. Despite all these blunders, the Canton insurrection must be considered an example of greatest heroism of the Chinese workers, who have now the right to claim their historical role as leaders of the great Chinese revolution" (ibid.).

29. A CI commentary on the Ninth Plenum Chinese resolution thus declared that the Canton revolt had "demonstrated the great revolutionary maturity of the Chinese proletariat." "The Chinese Question in the Plenum of the E.C.C.I.," p. 197.

30. The Sixth CCP Congress resolved this "contradiction" through the formulation that the Commune was a "rearguard fight" of a receding revolutionary wave, though at the same time it ushered in the soviet stage of the revolution. But how the program of the Commune fitted in with this earlier revolutionary stage was not explained.

31. Thornton, The Comintern and the Chinese Communists, p. 41. The September 1928 Political Resolution of the Congress specifically noted that "The Sixth Congress of the CCP entirely accepts the resolution of the Ninth ECCI Meeting on the China question, which also is the basis of this resolution" (Documentary History, p. 155).

32. Thornton, The Comintern and the Chinese Communists, p. 58.

33. A 1933 Comintern source stated: "The Party's principal base, the source of its strength permitting it to lead the soviet move-

ment, is of course the basic proletarian centers of the country. From here, from the underground organization, the party directs the soviets, giving them political directives, recruiting their cadres from among the workers, etc." Soviets in China, cited by Charles B. McLane, Soviet Policy and the Chinese Communists (New York, 1958), p. 25. McLane describes this source as "the Comintern's most authoritative review of the soviet movement" (ibid.); I have elsewhere in this study cited this source in its 1934 German-language edition.

34. In noting this dual aspect of the policy line of the post-1928 soviet period--a primary focus on a strategy of rural revolution placed within a political context which sought to retain and reinforce an urban standpoint--it is significant that later Maoist evaluations of the Sixth CCP Congress have consistently endorsed the congress' basic position on the continued bourgeois-democratic nature of the revolution and its support of the strategy of rural armed struggle, while increasingly criticizing its concept of the overall urban-rural revolutionary relationship.

35. The Sixth CCP Congress' "Resolution on the Peasant Movement" called for the "consolidation of working-class leadership among the peasantry [as] a prerequisite to the success of the agrarian revolution . . . the liaison between the peasant movement and the workers' movement must be tightened and proletarian members should be drawn into the peasant movement and its leading organs." On the village level itself, the "main task of the village Party headquarters is to consolidate the leading role of the working class in the peasant movement," and thus village party organizations "should be composed of proletarian and semi-proletarian elements." Documentary History, p. 164.

Comintern functionary Otto Kuusinen, in a report to the Sixth Congress of the Comintern, stated: "One cannot be satisfied with the present position of the C.C.P. of China. . . . The Chinese Communists themselves say that the majority of the membership is not drawn from working class but from peasant circles. (Interjection by Piatnitsky: Eighty per cent!) This social composition of our Chinese brother Party is of course abnormal. This Party must certainly work very hard so as to prepare and train for itself cadres drawn from the working class, . . . Apart from the necessary organizational consolidation of the Party, it has to pay special attention to its trade union work. . . . Such are in my opinion the most important immediate tasks of the C.P. of China which must on no account be underestimated now." "Comrade Kuusinen, 'The Revolutionary Movement in the Colonies,'" August 14 session, Inprecorr, VIII: 68 (October 4, 1928), 1232.

36. Pavel Mif, Comintern China specialist and key figure behind the Russian-returned youthful CCP leadership of the early 1930s, delineated this rural proletarian line at the Fifteenth Congress of the CPSU in December 1927: "in China the agrarian revolution can only reckon on the help of the village poor, and must take up the struggle against the kulaks [rich peasants], the landowners, and the bourgeoisie." Only an "unwearying fight" for proletarian hegemony under the democratic dictatorship formula could lead to victory, he added. Inprecorr, VIII: 1 (January 5, 1928), 29.

Thornton points out that some softening in policy towards the rich peasants and the urban petty bourgeoisie emerged in the Sixth CCP Congress documents, reflecting a compromise by the Stalin forces with the right-wing represented by Bukharin, in order to defeat the "extreme left." However, by mid-1929 the Comintern had moved back to the original (Ninth Plenum) line of rigid antagonism to the rich peasants and petty bourgeoisie. The Comintern and the Chinese Communists, pp. 24-29. However, though in the Sixth Congress documents the specific objective of the agrarian struggle was declared to be the elimination of the landlord class, with a proviso against intensifying the struggle against the rich peasants, the leftist view was in part also reflected in the additional warning that this proviso did not mean that "the class struggle against the rich peasants and the semi-landlords is to be abandoned." Ilpyong J. Kim, The Politics of Chinese Communism. Kiangsi Under the Soviets (Berkeley, 1973), pp. 107-108. Kim observes that "Consequently, the issue of rich peasants became extremely ambiguous, at best" (p. 108).

37. The Sixth CCP Congress' Political Resolution noted that while the rural soviet bases and armies then in being "will become an ever more important element in the rising tide," these rural soviets and the emerging urban struggles did not yet constitute such a rising tide, though "such a prospect is possible"--in which case

the important role of urban leadership and the rising tide of the
proletarian masses "will show their decisive power and will decide how to turn the slogan 'all power to the council of workers',
peasants', and soldiers' deputies' [i.e., soviets] into a slogan
of direct action." Documentary History, p. 142. "Full attention
should be paid to the labour movement," the resolution added,
"especially to industrial workers. Only thus can the leadership
of the working class over the peasantry be strengthened" (p. 150).

38. Neuberg, Armed Insurrection, Appendix, p. 283. As noted, this
preface to the book was apparently written by the propaganda or
organization departments of the Comintern. See n. 19, above.

39. Inprecorr, VIII: 50 (August 16, 1928), 894. Ch'ü's speeches to
the Sixth CI Congress were reported under the pseudonym "Comrade Strakhov."

40. Documentary History, p. 134. According to the congress' analysis
the first stage of the revolution had been the period of CCP-KMT
united front, the second that of the left-KMT (the Wuhan period),
ending with the defeat of the Nanchang uprising.

41. Chang Kuo-t'ao observes in his memoirs that this dual characterization of Canton as a rearguard battle which opened the soviet
stage of revolution was "obviously . . . contradictory." Rise of
the CCP, II, 79.

42. Documentary History, p. 139. This "rearguard" character of
the Commune was not taken into account by the party leadership,
the resolution added, which continued to pursue policies which
underappraised "the degree of failure suffered by the revolution"
(pp. 139-140).

43. "Theses on the Revolutionary Movement in the Colonies and
Semi-Colonies," Sixth CI Congress, Inprecorr, VIII: 88 (December 12, 1928), 1660.

44. From Sixth CI Congress' "Appeal to the Workers and Toilers of
China," in Kantonskaia Kommuna, p. 213.

45. "Resolution on the Chinese Question," p. 321.

46. "The Programme of the Communist International" (September 1, 1928), Inprecorr, VIII: 92 (December 31, 1928), 1762.

47. One should contrast the 1928 Comintern formulation with Lin Piao's famous 1965 thesis regarding the "encirclement" of the "cities of the world" by the "rural areas of the world": "Taking the entire globe, if North America and Western Europe can be called 'the cities of the world,' then Asia, Africa and Latin America constitute 'the rural areas of the world.' Since World War II, the proletarian revolutionary movement has for various reasons been temporarily held back in the North American and West European capitalist countries, while the people's revolutionary movement in Asia, Africa and Latin America has been growing vigorously. In a sense, the contemporary world revolution also presents a picture of the encirclement of cities by the rural areas. In the final analysis, the whole cause of world revolution hinges on the revolutionary struggles of the Asian, African and Latin American peoples who make up the overwhelming majority of the world's population. The socialist countries should regard it as their internationalist duty to support the people's revolutionary struggles in Asia, Africa and Latin America" (emphasis added). Lin Piao, Long Live the Victory of the People's War (Peking, 1965), pp. 48-49.

In Lin's macrocosmic projection of the Maoist revolutionary strategy in China, the "rural areas" emerge politically and strategically as the revolutionary vanguard and focal center. Though the Lin statement (as well as the Mao strategy) clearly bears a resemblance to the strategic outline for China adopted by the CCP and the CI in 1928, the long-term revolutionary initiative, as well as the standpoint in the formation of policy and strategy, becomes "rural" rather than "urban." The "cities" remain significant, but as the passive targets of an already basically victorious "rural" revolutionary wave.

The CCP has by now completely replaced the orthodox concept of a proletarian-led world revolution with a "three worlds" formula. China is now linked to the "third world" of underdeveloped and semiindependent countries whose peoples comprise the world revolutionary vanguard in waging struggles against the hegemony and exploitation of the "first world" (the USSR and USA), with the other developed nations constituting an intermediate "second world." See, for example, Teng Hsiao-p'ing's speech to the special session of the United Nations General Assembly on problems of raw materials and development, Peking Review, XVII: 16 (April 19, 1974), 6-11.

48. The key role of the proletariat in the "more developed" ex-colonies or semicolonies, such as China, was posited on the thesis that capitalist relations had already been developing in such areas. This contrasted to the rejected views of the proponents of the "Asiatic mode of production" and to some versions of the world "rural district" theory which sought to deny any significant capitalist development in China. See Thornton, The Comintern and the Chinese Communists, pp. 20-22, for a discussion of these issues at the Sixth CI Congress.

49. "The Chinese Question After the Sixth Congress," p. 172. Trotsky stated that China had entered an "interrevolutionary period . . . [of] a painful, chronic and lasting character" (ibid., p. 174).

50. "Significance and Lessons of the Canton Uprising," pp. 278-279.

51. Inprecorr, VIII: 76 (October 30, 1928), 1420. "It has today become a banality that the Canton uprising is no putsch," Neumann declared. "But the positive side is, and this the Communist International must keep in mind in the future: The Canton Insurrection is of tremendous significance for colonial uprisings. It signifies the erection of the Soviet power for the first time in such a country" (ibid.).

52. N. Fokin, "In Memory of the Organizer of the Canton Rising--Comrade Chang Ta Lai," Communist International, V: 6 (March 15 1928), 156.

53. "First Anniversary of the Canton Revolt," p. 1696.

54. Ibid.

55. See Chapter 2, n. 8. Included are articles by Lozovsky, Ch'ü Ch'iu-pai (under the pseudonym Wei T'o), Teng Chung-hsia, Ch'en Shao-yü, Lominadze and Huang P'ing. Huang P'ing's article appeared also in Soviets in China and has been so cited

in this study. Lominadze's article commemorating the first anniversary of the Commune appeared originally in Communist International and I have cited it from that source. While these articles served also to document and elaborate on the Ninth Plenum's listing of the errors and weaknesses of the Commune, they all closely adhered to and strongly underscored the CI's positive assessment of Canton. The 1930 edition of Canton Commune was itself evidently based on a Russian edition of the same title, published in Moscow and Leningrad in 1929, and which included documentary materials as well as articles. Cited in Kantonskaia Kommuna, p. 213.

56. "Report on the Canton Uprising," pp. 101-102.

57. Ibid., p. 186. Teng Chung-hsia similarly declared that "the red flag of the Soviets will be unfurled over all of China, all of Asia, and the entire world!" "Canton Uprising and the Tactics of the CCP," p. 65.

58. "Report on the Canton Uprising," p. 154.

59. Ibid., p. 197.

60. "Lessons of the Canton Uprising," pp. 2, 13-14.

61. "Canton Uprising and Its Background," p. 165. Ch'ü Ch'iu-pai, in his contribution to the Canton Commune collection, reiterated the points he had made at the Sixth CI Congress, stressing again Canton's significance in demonstrating and asserting proletarian leadership of the emerging peasant war. Wei T'o, "Kuang-chou pao-tung yü Chung-kuo ko-ming" (October 1928) [The Canton uprising and the Chinese revolution], pp. 32-33.

62. Lominadze, "Anniversary of the Canton Rising," pp. 135-142.

63. This is also attested to by the inclusion of Lominadze's article in the Canton Commune collection. See n. 55, above.

64. Lominadze, "Anniversary of the Canton Rising," p. 136.

65. Ibid., p. 138.

66. Ibid., p. 140.

67. Ibid., p. 142. The ECCI's first anniversary theses on the Commune had also specifically endorsed the political program of the Canton Soviet, and had declared that despite its brief life, "the new revolutionary authority [of the Canton Soviet] succeeded in showing itself as the real authority of the oppressed masses of the country." "First Anniversary of the Canton Revolt," p. 1696.

68. See Thornton, The Comintern and the Chinese Communists, for a detailed recent analysis of the Comintern-Li Li-san-soviet area relationship during the 1929-1931 period. According to Thornton, Li's goal of personal political aggrandizement led him into policies which conflicted sharply with Comintern objectives.

69. This longer-term perspective was kept clearly in view during the Kiangsi period. See, for example, Soviets in China, p. 73. McLane notes that during the Kiangsi period "Soviet [Russian] writers did not always take it for granted that the Chinese soviets would develop, ideologically and politically, in a manner satisfactory to Moscow." Soviet Policy and the Chinese Communists, p. 34.

70. Thornton, The Comintern and the Chinese Communists, pp. 111-116, 124-125.

71. Thornton, in his recent study of the 1928-1931 period, in which he presents a full unfolding of the Li Li-san line, as contained in internal CCP documents from late 1929 to mid-1930, states that "no Comintern instruction, including the resolutions of the Sixth Congress of the CCP, can be interpreted to suggest that Li Li-san's policies had the approval of or were indeed ordered by Moscow." The Comintern and the Chinese Communists, pp. 116-117; also pp. 104-115, 121-136. For an earlier, contrary view, see Schwartz, Chinese Communism, pp. 127-128.

72. Thornton, The Comintern and the Chinese Communists, pp. 140-141, 151. See Victor A. Yakhontoff, The Chinese Soviets (New York, 1934), pp. 130-132, for subsequent Comintern criticisms of some of the policies of this delegates' conference.

73. The fully formulated Li Li-san line was contained in a June 11, 1930, CCP Politburo resolution, "The New Revolutionary Rising Tide and Preliminary Successes in One or More Provinces," in Documentary History, pp. 184-200. See also Hsiao Tso-liang, Power Relations within the Chinese Communist Movement, 1930-1934 (Seattle, 1961), pp. 24-28, for a comparison of important points in this document with the key July 23, 1930, Comintern policy directive. See n. 74, below.

74. The basic Comintern guidelines in this period were contained in the "Resolution on the Chinese Problem" of July 23, 1930, and further delineated in a November 16, 1930, letter from the ECCI to the CCP Central Committee. Both documents are summarized at length in Hsiao, Power Relations, pp. 24-31, 74-77. See also Thornton, The Comintern and the Chinese Communists, pp. 168-175, 203-208, for analyses of these two key directives. Jane Degras, ed., The Communist International (London, 1965), III, 115-120, provides lengthy translated excerpts of the July resolution (erroneously dated June 1930) and of the November 16 letter (pp. 137-141).

The July resolution stated, "The Soviet movement confronts the party with a task of cardinal importance, to organize and direct the activities of a central Soviet government." For this to be accomplished effectively, it was necessary to create "a real Red Army . . . in the most secure areas, an army wholly subordinate to communist party leadership and able to serve as the pillar of the Government. It is therefore essential to concentrate attention on forming and strengthening the Red Army so that in future, when the military and political circumstances present the opportunity, it will be able to capture one or several industrial and administrative centres." Degras, Communist International, III, 116. The November letter, which followed the collapse of the Li Li-san strategy, reinforced the call for the establishment of a soviet government on the territory of the base areas, to be buttressed by a CCP-led worker-peasant Red Army. Thornton, The Comintern and the Chinese Communists, p. 207.

It seems, on the evidence now available, that the main thrust of Comintern policy and "in the future" projections for urban takeovers were not endorsements of the immediate Red Army-led insurrectionary upheavals of the Li Li-san strategy. Indeed, the Red armies themselves were still a highly inadequate instrument (not to mention the urban workers' movement), not only militarily but also politically and organizationally from the Comintern's point of view. A Comintern analysis of these weaknesses, as outlined in the November letter to the CCP, is cited in Thornton, The Comintern and the Chinese Communists, pp. 206-207. The task of establishing some form of unified Red Army organization and command was only hastily begun in June 1930 on orders from Li Li-san. See James P. Harrison, "The Li Li-san Line and the CCP in 1930," part 1, China Quarterly, no. 14 (April-June 1963), p. 144.

75. ECCI, July 23, 1930, "Resolution on the Chinese Question," in Degras, Communist International, III, 120. Thornton, The Comintern and the Chinese Communists, p. 169, more correctly translates the last sentence as "a peasant war" rather than "peasant wars."

76. Thornton, The Comintern and the Chinese Communists, pp. 168-172, 204-205.

77. June 11, 1930, CCP Politburo Resolution, Section V, Documentary History, pp. 192-194.

78. The July 23, 1930, ECCI resolution stated that in the current stage of the Chinese revolution the workers and peasants were "carrying out the tasks of the bourgeois-democratic stage, . . . in direct struggle against [the bourgeoisie]." This revolution also "prepares the prerequisites for proletarian dictatorship and the socialist revolution," and through the "noncapitalist road of development . . . for the gradual and steady transition of the Chinese revolution, by a series of intermediate stages, into the socialist revolution." Degras, Communist International, III, 118-119.

79. Kuo, "On the First Congress of the Chinese Soviets," Inprecorr, X: 28 (June 12, 1930), 509.

80. Ibid.

81. Thornton, The Comintern and the Chinese Communists, p. 151.

82. Citing a Russian source on the proceedings of the May delegates' conference, Thornton notes: "The Russian commentary on the documents asserts that the congress was to be held on December 11, not November 7, and that the Chinese had erred. The Russians wanted the congress to coincide with the anniversary of the Canton revolt, the Chinese believed it should coincide with the anniversary of the Russian revolution." Ibid., n. 7, p. 141.

83. Hsiao, Power Relations, p. 43.

84. Jerome Ch'en, Mao and the Chinese Revolution (London, 1965) pp. 166-171.

85. Hsiao, Power Relations, pp. 115-116. Pavel Mif, former rector of Sun Yat-sen University in Moscow and at this time Comintern delegate in China, apparently played a key role at the Fourth Plenum, both on policy issues and in ensuring the ascendancy of his young "protégés"--the Wang Ming group--to party leadership. Mif, through his position as head of the China section of the Comintern's Far Eastern Department, and through his close relationship with the new CCP leadership continued to play a significant role in CCP affairs throughout the 1931–1934 Kiangsi period.

86. "Resolution of the Enlarged Fourth Plenum of the CC, CCP," Documentary History, p. 210.

87. Klein and Clark, Biographic Dictionary, I, 322. Nym Wales in 1937 referred to Hsiang Ying as the "No. 1 'proletarian' of the Chinese Communists" (Inside Red China; cited in Biographic Dictionary, I, 323). Hsiang was elected one of the two vice-chairmen (with Chang Kuo-t'ao) of the Chinese Soviet Republic in November 1931, as well as Commissar of Labor. He apparently was later replaced as secretary of the Central Bureau by Chou En-lai. Dieter Heinzig, "The Otto Braun Memoirs and Mao's Rise to Power," China Quarterly, 46 (April-June 1971), 279; see also Hsiao, Power Relations, pp. 150-151. But Hsiang remained influential throughout the Kiangsi period in political and military affairs, and is generally considered to have been in opposition to the Mao group. Klein and Clark, Biographic Dictionary, I, 322-323.

The Central Bureau of the Soviet Areas, of which Mao was a member, became the top party authority in the soviet areas (including control of party organizations in the army), and was only disbanded with the basic shift of the Party Center's operations from Shanghai to Kiangsi, probably in late 1932 or early 1933. Heinzig, pp. 278-280; Hsiao, Power Relations, pp. 161-162; and Kim, Politics of Chinese Communism, p. 63.

Only some of the top party leaders attended the November 1931 First Soviet Congress, and the Party Center's shift to Kiangsi seems to have been gradually accomplished over the next year or so. The Central Committee apparently retained an office in Shanghai even after the move to Kiangsi, and through this office maintained communications with CI headquarters in Moscow until mid-1934. Heinzig, p. 284; Tien-wei Wu, Mao Tsetung and the Tsunyi Conference: An Annotated Bibliography (Washington, D.C., 1974), p. 42.

88. "Letter of the ECCI Presidium to the CCP" (July 1931), summarized in Hsiao, Power Relations, pp. 155-156.

89. Derek J. Waller, The Kiangsi Soviet Republic: Mao and the National Congresses of 1931 and 1934, China Research Monograph No. 10 (Berkeley, 1973), p. 25; Agnes Smedley, The Great Road (New York, 1956), p. 294. The setting of the earlier November date may also have been influenced by the need to take advantage of the respite afforded by the calling off of the KMT's third encirclement campaign in late September, due to the crisis created by the Mukden Incident and the Japanese occupation of Manchuria See Ch'en, Mao and the Chinese Revolution, pp. 169-170. The removal of Li Li-san and the repudiation of his moves to "merge" the bourgeois-democratic and socialist stages of the revolution may also have defused the November 7 date of its earlier implications.

90. Inprecorr, XIII: 54 (December 8, 1933), 1229-1230.

91. Hsiao, Power Relations, pp. 266-267.

92. Red China (Juichin, Kiangsi), December 11, 1931, p. 1. Ch'en Ch'eng collection, reel 16.

93. Chou I-li, "Chi-nien Kuang-chou pao-tung" [Commemorate the Canton uprising], ibid. Chou I-li, a member of the Central

Executive Committee of the Chinese Soviet Republic, was chief
editor of Red China. Waller, Kiangsi Soviet Republic, p. 47.
The article linked the initial raising of the soviet banner by the
Canton uprising with the establishment of the new soviet republic.

94. Snow, Red Star Over China, p. 164.

95. Smedley, The Great Road, p. 294.

96. Nym Wales, Inside Red China (New York, 1939), p. 346n.

97. "Resolution on the History of Our Party," pp. 186-190.

98. For an example of the central importance now attached to the
rural armed struggle, see the detailed and informative two-part
article by G. Sinani, '"The Red Army of the Chinese Revolution,"
Communist International, VIII: 15 (September 1, 1931), 450-456;
VIII: 17 (October 15, 1931), 527-537.

99. Involved also, by late 1931, was the notion of a new "revolutionary crisis" and a stronger antiimperialist line in the wake of
Japan's Manchurian aggression. "The Revolutionary Crisis in
China and Tasks of the Chinese Communists," Communist International, VIII: 20 (December 1, 1931), 658.

100. All these positions (which adhered to the basic Comintern guidelines of 1930-1931) were outlined in Wang Ming's major ideological
treatise of this period, originally published in Shanghai in early
1931, The Two Lines (Liang t'iao lu-hsien); republished in Moscow, March 1932, with a postscript added; in 1940 a Yenan edition was identical to the Moscow edition except for a new title,
Struggle for the More Complete Bolshevization of the Chinese Communist Party. Hsiao, Power Relations, pp. 202-203; and pp. 203-
207 for summary based on the Yenan edition. The Chinese text
of Wang's book, cited hereafter as Struggle for Bolshevization, is
in Hsiao Tso-liang, Power Relations within the Chinese Communist Movement, 1930-1934, Vol. II: Chinese Documents (Seattle,
1967); hereafter cited as Hsiao II.

101. This too was linked to the support of the soviet areas. In
listing the "triple task" of the CCP, a March 1931 Comintern
article put the formation of a regular Red Army and a Soviet

government as the first two tasks, the third being "The further unleashing of partial economic struggles of the proletariat in all the big industrial centres, their further revolutionizing, [and] linking up these proletarian struggles with the struggle for the defence of the Soviet districts." V. Kuchumov, "The Struggle for the Bolshevization of the Communist Party of China," Communist International, VIII: 6 (March 15, 1931), .164.

102. In his 1932 postscript to Struggle for Bolshevization, Wang Ming discussed the 1930 "Changsha incident" at some length, arguing that while the Changsha occupation was an "adventurist action," it was nevertheless of "historical significance." The principle at stake was not whether central cities (chung-hsin ch'eng-shih) should be taken but whether overall conditions and the strength of the Red Army were appropriate to the task. The "International and Party line" called for the Red Army gradually to prepare and strengthen itself to become powerful enough to occupy key cities, and only under conditions of a favorable position of strength relative to the enemy should important cities be attacked. "Postscript," I, B-2, "The Question of the Evaluation of the Changsha Incident" ("Kuan-yü Ch'angsha shih-pien ku-chi wen-t'i") Struggle for Bolshevization (Hsiao II, 569-570). The above views were essentially those of the July 23, 1930, ECCI resolution, and presumably now served as a corrective for those who would use the attack on Li Li-san to "distort" the correct "Leninist" position on the necessity of occupying cities. Ibid., p. 570.

103. Hsiao, Power Relations, pp. 207-210, for a summary of CCP policy directives of mid-1932 outlining these military policies. A key Comintern article of December 1931 listed among the main tasks of the Chinese Communists, "to fight for the expansion of Soviet regions, for the formation of unbroken stretches of Soviet territory." "The Revolutionary Crisis in China and the Tasks of Chinese Communists," p. 658.

104. In the hinterland Soviet Republic this became in great part the attempt to support agricultural labor interests, largely against the rich peasant (kulak).

105. The ECCI Eleventh Plenum summed up these points in August 1931: "The hegemony of the proletariat and the victorious development of the revolution can be guaranteed only on condition that

the Chinese Communist Party becomes a proletarian party not
only in its political line but in its composition and the role
played by the workers in all of its leading organs." Stressing
the central role of the agrarian revolution, it noted that proletarian leadership of the revolutionary movement was "being reinforced." The CCP as "the party of the proletariat . . . is the
ruling party of Soviets, the organizer and commander of the
workers' and peasants' Red Army, and sole leader of the workers
and peasants. The hegemony of the proletariat is being consolidated in the rudiments of state power and constitutes an incipient
and transitional stage on the way to the dictatorship of the proletariat." Carrère d'Encausse and Schram, Marxism and Asia,
pp. 246-247. Though equating the leadership of the proletariat
with that of the party, it was based on the premise of a genuinely proletarianized CCP. It thus looked to the establishment
of Soviet power in "the large proletarian centres" as a key
means of making "the hegemony of the proletariat many times
stronger" by "radically improving the Communist Party's social
composition, . . . [and] creating numerous leading proletarian
cadres for the Soviets and the Red Army" (ibid., p. 247).

106. G. Sinani, "The Importance and the Lessons of the Canton Commune," Inprecorr, XI: 13 (March 11, 1931), 256-257.

107. Ibid., p. 257.

108. Ibid., p. 256.

109. S. C. Lin (Shanghai), "Canton Commune, a Beacon-Light in the
Fight for the Soviets," Inprecorr, XI: 65 (December 24, 1931),
1135. The new organ of the soviet republic, Red China, in its
December 11, 1931, Canton anniversary article, also pointed to
the Canton antecedents of the Red Army. See n. 93, above.
The link of Canton Red Guard with Soviet Red Army underscored
the determination to "proletarianize" the latter. The 1931 Comintern account of the Red Army already referred to (n. 98, above)
stated that "the task of reinforcing the Red Army with the proletarians of the biggest factories of Shanghai, Wuhan, Hong Kong,
Canton and other cities is one of the most important tasks facing
the Party in the realm of military development." Sinani, "Red
Army of the Chinese Revolution," Part 2, p. 531.

110. These points were reiterated in a fourth anniversary article in
     Pravda, which linked the triple concepts of proletarian hegemony,
     the soviet political form, and the "democratic dictatorship" for-
     mula with "the slogans of the Canton Commune." E. Iolk, "The
     Fourth Anniversary of the Canton Commune," _Pravda_, Decem-
     ber 13, 1931; cited in O. Edmund Clubb, _Communism in China._
     As Reported from Hankow in 1932 (New York, 1968), p. 98.

PROLETARIAN HEGEMONY AND THE KIANGSI SOVIET

The Chinese Soviet Republic, proclaimed at the First National Soviet Congress in Juichin, Kiangsi, in November 1931 was viewed as the political expression and instrument of the "proletarian-led peasant war" as it moved on towards national power. The constitution adopted by the First Soviet Congress declared: "It shall be the mission of the Constitution of the Chinese Soviet Republic to guarantee the democratic dictatorship of the proletariat and the peasantry in the Soviet districts and to secure the triumph of the dictatorship throughout the whole of China." The dictatorship, through implementation of its program and goals, aimed "to promote the class consciousness and solidarity of the proletariat, and to rally to its banner the broad masses of poor peasants in order to effect the transition to the dictatorship of the proletariat."[1] Worker deputies were to be elected through the factories rather than their places of residence, with special electoral advantages granted to workers.[2]

It would be the purpose of the Soviet government "to improve thoroughly the living conditions of the working class" through labor and social legislation, and also to grant workers "the right to supervise production."[3] It called for radical improvement of the living conditions of the peasants through a land law confiscating the land of all landlords and distributing it among the poor and middle peasants, "with a view to the ultimate nationalization of land." The Soviet regime would restrict the development of capitalism and move towards "the socialist order of society." It opposed "bourgeois and landlord democracy, but is in favour of the democracy of the workers and peasant masses. It breaks down the economic and political prerogatives of the bourgeoisie and the landlords, in order to remove all obstacles placed by the reactionaries on the workers' and peasants' road to freedom."[4] The constitution deprived "militarists, bureaucrats, landlords, gentry, capitalists, rich peasants, monks, and all exploiting and counterrevolutionary elements" of electoral rights and political freedoms.[5]

The land law adopted by the First Soviet Congress was sharply "class struggle" oriented, and based on the poorer peasantry and the rural semi-proletariat.[6] The law called for the confiscation of all land and properties of the landlords and other big landholders, as

well as for the confiscation of the land and "surplus" properties of
the rich peasants, though the latter could be given allocations of
poorer land on condition that they cultivate it with their own labor
power. The strong rural proletarian line was reflected in the dec-
laration that "the hired farmhand union, the coolie union, and the
poor peasant corps" were to be "indispensable bodies," and the "solid
pillars of the land revolution launched by the Soviets."[7] The subsequent inaugural issue of Red China, the organ of the new central
soviet government, listed as one of the important tasks of the newspaper to point out and correct defects and mistakes in the work of
the soviets at all levels, and especially to remedy the past "incorrect
class line" (fei chieh-chi lu-hsien) in the land revolution.[8]

The establishment of a hired farmhand union and a poor peasant
corps had been called for in the important July 1930 Comintern resolution on the Chinese question.[9] The provisional regulations for the
farmhand union, adopted in February 1931, declared its purposes to
be to "practice the class struggle, resist all oppression and exploitation, and fight for the liberation of the working class," and "to participate in all struggles for the land revolution and for the consolidation and expansion of the Soviets."[10] The union was to exercise
a leadership role in all struggles and "to rally the poor and middle
peasants" around it.[11] Significantly, the hired farmhand union and
poor peasant corps apparently first began to function during the implementation of the anti-rich peasant policy (following the First Soviet
Congress) at the beginning of 1932, and only became "dynamic political forces at the grass roots level" in mid-1933, with the launching
of the sharply class-struggle-oriented Land Investigation Movement.[12]
The accentuated rural proletarian policy line was also reflected in
a Comintern resolution on the peasant problem which circulated in
the soviet areas in February 1933.[13] In Ilpyong Kim's summation:
"The primary task of the CCP in the soviet areas, as outlined in
this document, was to establish farm-labor unions parallel to the
ordinary labor unions composed of the industrial proletariat, and
the poor-peasant corps, like the existing peasant associations, were
to be under the leadership of the labor unions."[14]

The proclaimed goals and methods of the Land Investigation
Movement of the second half of 1933, and again in the spring of 1934,
reflected most sharply the rural class war line which focused principally on the "proletarian" struggle against the rich peasants--the
"capitalists" of the countryside.[15] The drive was aimed in good part

at "uncovering" landlords and rich peasants who had "disguised" themselves as poor or middle peasants, with the labor unions in the rural districts taking the lead "in this great and fierce class struggle. "[16] A Communist report from the northeastern Kiangsi soviet region thus declared: "A precise class differentiation is taking place now as a result of the agrarian revolution, and the class struggle in the countryside is assuming ever more naked forms. The kulaks, who have always tried to represent themselves as middle peasants and even as poor peasants, are being exposed by the toiling population. "[17]

Though this drive was launched and implemented under Mao's direction in his capacity as Chairman of the Council of Commissars, it clearly mirrored the CI-CCP class guidelines of the Kiangsi period, and was in fact launched at a time when Mao's own political power was probably at a relatively low point.[18] Nevertheless, in his executive capacity Mao was apparently able to soften somewhat the drive's impact through his directives carefully defining rural class status.[19] When the drive was renewed in March 1934 under Chang Wen-t'ien (Lo Fu), a returned student leader, and Mao's replacement as Chairman of the Council of Commissars after the Second Soviet Congress in January of that year, the Mao directives were castigated as having impeded the drive by stressing technical problems of class definition rather than the political imperatives of class struggle.[20] By mid-1934, however, with the soviet region in its last extremity, Chang Wen-t'ien reversed his position and denounced the "ultraleft" character of the March policies.[21] Since Mao had apparently gradually succeeded in winning over Chang to his side in the CCP leadership struggle, which grew in intensity in this closing phase of the soviet period, Chang's shift presumably reflected this development.[22]

The labor law of the new soviet regime (adopted by the First Soviet Congress) was notable for its elaborate complexity and its preoccupation with worker rights and interests which were often irrelevant to or inapplicable in the circumstances of the rural soviets. But this law did serve to assert the Soviet Republic's strong defense of labor interests, underscored its worker-oriented outlook, and the determination and expectation of moving towards a more solid and congenial labor base through a return to the cities. The labor code had no less than 75 articles, and covered collective agreements and contracts, working hours (a basic eight-hour day), rest time, sick leave, holidays (including the anniversary of the Canton Commune) and paid annual vacations, wage policies (with a minimum to be set

by the Commissariat of Labor), special provisions protecting women,
adolescent and child labor, health and safety regulations, and work-
men's compensation.[23] The trade unions, organized under the ACFL
(now an underground organization based in Shanghai), were given rights
to negotiate and implement collective agreements, to conduct strikes,
to supervise application of the labor code, to participate in the management of state and cooperative enterprises, and to have a controlling voice in private enterprises. There were elaborate social insur-
ance provisions, including free medical aid, disability, sickness and
old-age benefits, unemployment relief, funeral and poor relief.

Thus, beyond its "anti-feudal" goals, the "democratic dictatorship" focused on direct defense of worker and rural proletarian-poor
peasant interests along class struggle lines, with capitalists and rural
exploiters as the targets. A "unique" feature of the present stage
of the Chinese revolution, the Comintern account, Soviets in China,
stated, is that while it continues "as a bourgeois-democratic and anti-
imperialist revolution, it turns its dagger simultaneously against the
national bourgeoisie, and against the rich peasants in the village."[24]
The bourgeoisie were viewed as political and economic adversaries
in the struggle to advance worker interests and hegemony in line with
and linked to the continuing longer-term goal of activating, organizing
and leading the industrial proletariat on an increasingly national scale
as the primary political force in the transition to socialism and proletarian dictatorship. Meanwhile, by helping the workers in the soviet
areas to organize and by leading them in the struggle to improve their
conditions, Soviets in China declared, "the role of the workers in
creating and building up the Soviets, and in the entire Soviet movement,
is strengthened, without which there can be no talk of the hegemony
of the proletariat in the peasant agrarian revolution."[25] Yakhontoff,
citing "orthodox Communist" sources, wrote in his 1934 book on the
Chinese soviets that though the large cities "are not Sovietized, they
harbor large numbers of Communists and are the centers of their
work outside of the Soviet areas. The records of the Chinese Soviets,"
he continued, "indicate that the progress of the movement is linked
with the increasing influence of the urban proletariat and the growth
of the leadership offered by the latter to the rural masses."[26] He
underlined the role of soviet area labor policies in this process,
noting that while the Red trade unions in the cities worked to build
influence among urban labor in preparation for an ultimate uprising,
"the most effective influence on the working masses outside the Soviet
areas comes not from the Red Trade Unions but from the rumors

penetrating into the factories and shops about the better living conditions of their brethren in the Soviet districts. "[27]

Bela Kun, a leading Comintern functionary, commenting on the constitution and policy lines of the Soviet Republic, noted that "the bourgeoisie must bear the burden of all taxation" in the soviet areas, and declared that the Soviet Republic's labor legislation, "although it must take into consideration the more primitive industrial conditions, surpasses everything which the Social-Democratic Party and the Social-Democratic governments of the highly-developed capitalist countries extolled to the skies during the post-war boom. "[28]

The strongly activist role the trade unions were expected to play in the soviet areas was spelled out in a 1932 resolution on the Chinese labor movement, passed by the eighth session of the Central Council of the Red International of Labor Unions (RILU).[29] Declaring that the Chinese labor movement was "experiencing a new upsurge," the resolution dwelt at length on overall developments and CCP labor policies and activites in the non-soviet areas of China. Turning to the soviet zones, it stated that the "Trade Unions of Soviet China serve as the most important mass prop of the revolutionary-democratic dictatorship of the working class and the peasantry. " By the "widely developed struggle for their direct economic interests, drawing the working masses into the building up of the Soviet State and the Red Army," the resolution continued, "the trade unions create the connection between the proletarian vanguard, . . . and the broad masses of the workers. "[30]

Though declaring that the trade unions must overcome "all narrow craft and 'trade unionistic' tendencies" in participating in the "general struggle for the realization of the anti-imperialist and agrarian revolution in China," the resolution stressed that the unions "must at the same time most resolutely develop work to defend day-to-day economic interests of the working class. " All workers in the soviet areas must be organized, including "agricultural proletarians [and] semi-proletarians," though these latter groups should not include peasants except in cases where the sale of the peasant's labor power is his major source of income. The leading trade union organs must be "proletarianized" so that their "predominating majority" be composed of "worker militants who have come to the fore during the course of the class struggle. "[31]

The "fundamental task" of the soviet area trade unions was "to gain the complete and universal realisation of the workers' chief demands, provided for by the Soviet labour legislation." In addition, the unions must fight for workers' demands not included in the labor law, such as wage increases, closed shop arrangements, housing priorities for workers, etc. Among the most important tasks of the unions was aiding the Red Army, strengthening its proletarian base, organizing workers' detachments, etc. The resolution emphasized the need for close links with and assistance to the labor movement in the KMT areas, while the latter was called upon to give top priority to assisting actively the soviet movement. [32]

The proclaimed intent in the Kiangsi period sharply to accentuate and protect labor interests, which in that rural context meant in good part the interests of agricultural labor and of artisans and other employees of small enterprises and shops, [33] clashed with the economic concerns and well-being of a broad spectrum of the peasantry and of the small entrepreneurs and merchants. [34] The strong emphasis on labor struggle and welfare, and the difficulties in carrying out such a policy, were reflected in a report, in the wake of the passage of the November 1931 labor law, criticizing the sluggish implementation of that law, which the report attributed to the continued existence of a "rich peasant mentality" at local soviet levels. [35] Other articles and reports in 1932 and early 1933 also castigated various soviet area party committees and unions for an insufficiently aggressive labor-struggle approach, considered the key to "class consciousness" and proletarian leadership. [36] But in view of the growing imperatives--economic, political and military--for the soviet regime to develop and maintain broad mass support, the labor law was often impractical and unenforceable, [37] and the policy of encouraging extremely sharp worker struggle tactics and demands proved increasingly harmful. [38]

These pressures and concerns were apparently reflected in the growing concurrence between Mao and some among the dominant party leadership (notably Chang Wen-t'ien) in the latter part of 1933, on the need for more widely based and positive economic construction and mobilization policies, [39] and led also at that time to the promulgation of a revised labor protection law which specifically exempted (on the consent of the laborers involved and of the trade unions) middle and poor peasants and small handicrafts industry hiring auxiliary labor, from the provisions of the law. [40] But aside from certain other minor changes and clarifications, the basic provisions and class standpoint of the labor law remained essentially intact. The continued strong affirmation of worker class interests was exhibited, for example, in Mao's January 1934 report to the Second Soviet Congress (see below), while a rural-proletarian, anti-rich peasant line was strongly manifested in the Land Investigation Movement of 1933-1934, though the latter was interlaced, as already noted, with Mao-supported mass mobilization objectives. In all, it seemed that the "contradictions" between a proletarian-oriented class war line and the imperatives and realities of a protracted rural peasant war were becoming increasingly compelling. But the Kiangsi base was already becoming militarily untenable, and it would remain for a new CCP leadership, and building on the rural revolutionary experiences of the soviet areas, under the different conditions of a national war of resistance, to approach these problems from a vantage point in which "proletarian leadership" and the strategies and policies for achieving it would gradually take on a strikingly different character.

The main policy lines of the later Kiangsi period were enunciated by Mao Tse-tung in his major report to the Second National Soviet Congress, held in Juichin, Kiangsi, in January 1934.[41] Though Mao was reporting to the congress in his role as Chairman of the Central Executive Council of the Soviet Republic, he spoke in the shadow of the dominant "Bolshevik" Party Center, and to a congress which apparently further confirmed his subordinated role. Mao's report thus essentially adhered to the guidelines laid down by the Central Committee (now headquartered in Kiangsi) at its Fifth Plenum, held just prior to the Second Congress.[42] Working within the political framework of a worker-peasant dictatorship as a stage towards "the socialist proletarian dictatorship" of the future,[43] Mao listed among the "urgent tasks" of the soviet government the promotion of the class struggle of the workers and the agrarian revolution of the peasants. He noted the provision of the soviet electoral law which "guarantees the leading position of the workers in the worker-peasant alliance."[44] The soviet regime, he declared, was not democratic for the exploiters--the "landlords and bourgeoisie who have been knocked down [overthrown] by the revolutionary masses."[45] In an exposition of soviet labor policy, Mao stated that the soviet area, "based on the class character of its political power," and its task of arming the masses to fight a revolutionary war, "must initiate class struggles of workers, defend their everyday interests, develop their revolutionary initiative, . . . and turn the workers into active leaders for the revolutionary war and pillars for the consolidation and development of Soviet power." The "basic principle" of Soviet labor policy, he continued, "is to protect the interests of the workers and to consolidate and develop the Soviet power," with "strong class trade unions" as the foundation of this power.[46] Mao cited detailed statistics indicating generally sharp increases in wages for workers and farm hands in the soviet areas since the adoption of the labor law. After only two years, Mao summed up, "the Soviet Labour Act has been generally observed in all towns and all villages." In the course of this period, he added, "the capitalists and the kulaks attempted to resist the Act. But the active struggles of the working masses, together with the close superintendence [supervising] of the Soviet, have frustrated them."[47]

Reflecting the increasing Communist emphasis on a broadened national antiimperialist appeal in the face of the mounting Japanese threat, Mao called on the soviets to aid "every anti-imperialist struggle of the workers, peasants and petty bourgeoisie," though he also urged simultaneously supporting "in every way possible the revolutionary struggle of the workers against capitalists and of the peasants against the landlords."[48] It was a "united front from below" concept along the class lines of the soviet period.

In a section on economic policy in the soviet districts, Mao stressed the theme of economic construction in agriculture, industry and trade, and noted the predominance of small-scale private and cooperative enterprises and the pragmatic need to encourage and promote their economic activities. (In fact, "big capitalists," against whom labor-struggle techniques and the entire panoply of the labor code might be applied, were notable for their absence in the rural soviets.) It is precisely this brief portion of Mao's 1934 report, and only this portion, which appears in the Selected Works.[49] It may also be noted that in a major December 1947 speech, at a time when the CCP-led forces were once more engaged in all-out civil war against the KMT, and at a time when the CCP realistically anticipated an early return to the major urban centers, Mao cited the "ultra-leftist" errors in labor policy during the Kiangsi soviet period as an example in warning against similar policies in the later period.[50]

It is apparent that Mao had some significant input into the policies pursued in Kiangsi after 1931, particularly in the increasing emphasis on economic construction priorities, broader mass mobilization strategies, and more careful concern for the interests of middle peasants and small producers. But whatever the inner political dynamics of leadership relationships and policy formulations and implementation

n Kiangsi, Mao clearly functioned within the constraining limits of
he overall proletarian line set by the dominant CI-CCP policy makers.
Thus in his 1969 memoirs of his experiences in the Chinese Communist
movement, Otto Braun ("Li T'e," the German appointed by the Comin-
ern as military adviser to the Central Committee of the CCP in 1933)
wrote of this period that while Mao evidently already held opinions that
he rural villages had replaced the working class as the vanguard of
he revolution, "these opinions were not known to us. Therefore there
were no serious clashes between us. Indubitably, here lay the germ
or the future development of the CCP. In fact, in all the discussions
of the following years the tacit bone of contention was which line would
dominate: the international-Marxist or the petty-bourgeois nationalist."[51]

Pavel Mif, the Comintern mentor of the post-1931 CCP leadership,
emphasized the continuing thread of proletarian revolutionary leadership
n China in a December 1932 anniversary article on the Canton Commune.[52] Delineating the role of the Chinese workers during the 1922-
927 period, he wrote that this had paved the way for the hegemony of
he proletariat, "the decisive prerequisite for the victorious development of the Chinese revolution." But, he added, "only the Canton
Commune won and secured for the proletariat the role of hegemony,
he role of organizer and leader of the Chinese revolution." Again,
e stressed the uprising's larger significance for "the subsequent
development of the revolutionary struggles in the colonial East," and
declared that the decrees issued by the Commune "proclaimed a new
ra for the whole colonial world."[53]

A Canton fifth anniversary address by Teng Fa (then head of the
arty's reputedly anti-Mao Political Security Bureau),[54] published in
he Kiangsi Soviet organ, Red China,[55] hailed the great revolutionary
ignificance of Canton in pioneering the way for the Chinese soviet
movement. He cited the usual factors held responsible for the failure
f the Commune, exhorted the soviets to profit from the experiences,
essons and resolute proletarian spirit of the uprising, and pointed to
ts "proletarian Communist party" leadership of the peasants and rev-
lutionary soldiers. Teng linked the commemoration of the Canton
nsurrection with an enumerated list of key military and political pol-
cies for the soviet area--essentially the "class line" policies of the
ominant "Bolshevik" party leadership of that time. He included the
forward and offensive" military line, the emphasis on the hired farm-
and union and the poor peasant corps in implementing the 1931 soviet
and law, the encouragement of worker class struggles in carrying out

the labor law, the reinforcement of proletarian leadership, the expansion of the Red Army and the strengthening of its military and political training, and the intensification of class struggles and antagonisms to ensure soviet victory and the liquidation of counterrevolutionary factions and activities in the soviet zones.[56]

The Comintern's Soviets in China summed up the standard points on Canton in 1934, in the context of a strongly underlined assertion of the proletarian line for the soviet areas and for the Chinese revolution generally. "Red Canton" was again hailed as "the vanguard of the colonial revolution in Asia"; the soviet political form and the proletarian-peasant democratic dictatorship were as usual directly linked to its worker-initiated origins in the Commune.[57] While this same account endorsed the Hai-lu-feng soviet as having been "a guiding star" for the south China peasant movement, with special praise for its sharply class-war-oriented agrarian policies, it criticized Hai-lu-feng's failure effectively to overcome, in its mass work, the "local peasant limitations" characteristic of all peasant movements. The account specifically noted that little attention had been paid to the important tasks of improving the living conditions of the workers and defending their immediate economic interests. "The leading role of the proletarian party was weakened by an enormous influx of petty bourgeois elements. . . . Frequently, entire villages entered the party." All this weakened the Hai-lu-feng soviet and in the last analysis led to its defeat.[58] Clearly, there was a lesson in this for the current rural soviet movement. Adherence to a genuinely proletarian mobilization line (linked to the symbolism of Canton) was vital if inherent "peasant limitations" were to be avoided. It was Canton, Soviets in China thus declared, which became the beacon for the split and dispersed revolutionary elements, and whose forces served as organizers and leaders of the emerging soviet movement in south China.[59]

The above-mentioned Comintern report emphasized the key role of the January 1931 CCP Fourth Plenum (and the subsequent First Soviet Congress) as a "turning point" in the development of the soviet region's labor movement. The soviet organs had since that time more firmly undertaken the task of organizing the workers and leading them in struggles to improve their conditions--the key to labor's strengthened role in the soviets and to the achievement of proletarian hegemony in the peasant revolution.[60] Through the various phases in "the struggle for the economic disarmament of the bourgeoisie"[61] (in which the working masses in the great industrial centers were major participants), the role and consciousness of the proletariat would be strengthened for the transition to the coming socialist revolution and the dictatorship of the proletariat.[62]

Wang Ming, the youthful Moscow-based CCP ideological spokesman, focused on the question of proletarian leadership under conditions of the "uneven development" of the Chinese revolution, in the 1932 postscript to The Two Lines. This work, written in 1931 as an anti-Li Li-san polemic served, particularly in its 1932 version, as a general theoretical framework for the party's "Bolshevik" leadership during the 1931-1934 years.[63] Wang Ming noted the existence within the party of "differences in interpretation or understanding" on the key issue of the uneven development of the workers' and peasants' movements in China.[64] This uneven quality, however, had been characteristic of the revolutionary movement since the early 1920s, with first workers, then peasants coming to the fore. At present, in many rural areas where the peasants are a majority, the soviet system has been developed, while the workers' movement in the major cities has not kept pace. But this does not mean, Wang Ming stressed, that the revolutionary character of the Chinese peasantry is greater than that of the urban workers or that the worker is "backward" compared to the peasant. Nor does it mean that the Soviet power and Red Army in China represent a so-called pure peasant revolutionary movement without working-class participation and leadership.[65]

"Some individual comrades among us," he continued, may be disregarding the power of the working class while overly exaggerating the independent role of the peasantry. Such comrades are attempting to construct a theory of the special revolutionary character of the peasantry in colonial and semi-colonial countries, thus raising the peasants to first place in the revolution and relegating the workers to the position of assistants. In essence, they thus deny the possibility of a noncapitalist path of development for such revolutions and project instead a future of "peasant capitalism." In similar vein, they attempt to equate the entire national question with the peasant question--in a distortion of Stalin's pronouncements on the national problem.[66]

The peasants, Wang Ming maintained, whether in a capitalist or a colonial country, are basically petty bourgeois in character and are incapable of an independent role or ideology. But since the peasants are laborers as well as small property owners, they are able to unite with the proletariat and, under the latter's leadership, to play a revolutionary role. Without the proletarian movement there would be no such thing as the Chinese Soviet Red Army. Wang Ming here pointed to the role of the Canton working class in the 1927 uprising in first raising the Soviet flag and securing proletarian leadership of the Chinese revolution. This leadership was then specifically confirmed in the government-structured policies and objectives outlined in the constitution of the First Soviet Congress in 1931, in the role of the CCP in the soviet areas, and in the strong worker nucleus in the Red Army. He pointed also to the substantial number of workers in the soviet areas and their growing proportion in CCP organs, to the numerous towns under soviet control, and to the proletarian leading core in the key mass organizations in the soviet districts.[67]

At the same time, Wang Ming stressed the significance of the CCP-led workers' movement in the central cities, which on the one hand helped provide the best cadres for the soviet areas, while on the other giving direct support to the soviets through strikes and other supportive actions--which also represented first steps to armed uprisings. The interaction of all these forces and struggles contributed to the victorious development of the soviet areas and attested to the leading position of the proletariat. The main task now, in both non-soviet and soviet areas, was further to reinforce this leading role.

Nevertheless, he concluded, the importance of the peasantry-- a very great force in the revolution--should in no way be denigrated. But recognition of this should not lead to a denial of proletarian leadership and to talk about a pure peasant movement.[68]

Wang Ming's theoretical premise that the struggle against the capitalists was of equal importance to that against feudal forces and imperialists, and his stress on the importance of capturing key cities, were clearly central to the concept of the indispensable role of a genuinely activist and effective proletarian revolutionary vanguard. Only a CCP which could foster, organize and closely identify with such a vanguard and with its specific class interests and struggles[69]--both in the cities and the rural soviet areas--could ensure the triumph of the proletarian-internationalist position under the conditions of a semi-colonial peasant struggle. Chinese experience had shown, Wang Ming stressed in a subsequent December 1933 report to the ECCI Thirteenth

Plenum, that "Soviet power is a world system," suitable not only for revolution in capitalist countries but also in colonial and semi-colonial ones.[70] The assertions of proletarian hegemony linked to the democratic dictatorship formula, and the very role of the Canton Commune itself, were therefore by no means merely semantic or ritualistic devices designed to obscure the reality of a peasant-based and rural-centered revolution. They were significant and meaningful efforts to place this revolution within the Communist movement's orthodox theoretical and strategic framework as a vitally necessary stage, but whose future course would depend on the nature and quality of its Communist-cum-proletarian leadership, as measured in ideological, political, organizational and economic terms, and which would determine in turn the eventual balance of the worker-peasant, urban-rural, international-national relationship in the revolutionary process. It was only in the subsequent Maoist redefinition of the notion of proletarian leadership in all its ramifications that "semantics" presumably came into play.

Two articles that appeared in successive issues of Communist International early in 1935 cast significant light on many of the strategic and political questions raised for "semi-colonial countries" by the Chinese pattern of an armed uprising to establish soviet bases in overwhelmingly peasant interior regions of a country.[71] Though written in this larger context, the articles were clearly concerned with the specific lessons of the Chinese revolutionary experience itself. The first article, by V. Myro, deliberately differentiated between the revolutionary strategy followed by the Bolsheviks in Russia of concentrating on the takeover of the major industrial and political centers as the key to revolutionary success (a strategy also applicable in western Europe), and an approach which followed the example of the Chinese soviets, where the initial concentration was on the outlying districts, a strategy generally suitable to the colonial and semi-colonial countries.[72] As for the conditions necessary for establishing such inner bases, using China as his example Myro listed "a high level in the development of the peasant movement" and the inability of the weak Kuomintang state apparatus to exercise effective nationwide control. As "absolutely necessary" additional elements for the success of this interior strategy, he specified the existence of a revolutionary upsurge "at least in some regions of the country," as well as "a certain coordination" between "the levels of upsurge attained by the working class movement and the peasant movement," and the leadership of the Communist Party.[73] The most "optimal" location for such a base would be an economically depressed area where a peasant

insurgent movement already existed, situated away from the major
arteries of transportation and communication and from centers of
foreign interests and power, and comprising a relatively extensive
and self-sufficient territory.[74]

Myro advocated a flexible and mobile military strategy: "The
main thing is not the maintenance of the territory but the preservation
of the armed cadres of the revolution." It would be "a big mistake"
to hold a base area "at all costs" in the face of superior enemy
forces. "In the last analysis, however, if the political line pursued
by the leaders of the Soviet movement is correct," enemy offensives
will in fact be successfully repulsed and a stable base area established.
Referring again to the Chinese example, the author stressed the importance of small-scale partisan warfare in the initial stages, leading ultimately to the building of a firm territorial base under the control of
a powerful Red Army.[75] Basically, it would appear, the article
outlined in emergent form what came to be some of the key Maoist
strategic principles of revolutionary war.[76]

The second article, cryptically signed "Li," was a lengthy rejoinder to Myro and was specifically so identified, and apparently
ended the debate. Li expressed agreement on "the main question,"
that is, the desirability of a strategy of establishing interior bases
which "will be of immense (and perhaps of decisive) importance for
the development of the revolution on a national scale."[77] He argued,
however, that the soviet movement in China was not the result of a
localized revolutionary upsurge but the culmination of a long-term,
multistage national revolutionary movement, in the course of which
proletarian leadership had superseded that of the bourgeoisie. The
Canton Commune, he declared, "was the completion of a whole
series of heroic struggles of the retreating revolution. And at the
same time it gave the banner of the Soviets to the new stage of the
revolution."[78] The soviets and the Red Army became a mighty
force only in the context of the new national revolutionary crisis in
late 1929 and early 1930. This crisis was brought about not only
by the soviet movement itself but by the failure of the Kuomintang
to establish and consolidate "a national bourgeois centralized government," and by the new wave of the labor movement in which "the
working class assumed the role of leader of the new revolutionary
upsurge."[79]

"Notwithstanding the fact that the Soviets arose and became consolidated in peasant districts," Li declared, "they were from the very

beginning not peasant Soviets but <u>workers</u>' and peasants' Soviets; a form of the <u>revolutionary democratic dictatorship of the proletariat and peasantry.</u> " Despite the "undisputed and colossal revolutionary importance of the peasantry, " proletarian leadership of the soviets was crucial to victory and ultimate socialism, and this "must determine the <u>political line</u> of the Communist Party, and the entire system of its practical measures. " Thus the leading role of the proletariat must be an all-pervasive one in the soviet areas and not merely restricted to the question of establishing a "proletarian kernel in the revolutionary army. "[80]

Li stressed the importance of establishing soviet bases in the more advanced (from an economic and class struggle point of view) heart of China, where these factors could come into maximum play. He attacked the "Northwestern Theory, " which he attributed to the "opportunistic leaders" of the CCP during the critical summer of 1927, and which proposed to concentrate the main Communist forces in Shansi, Kansu and Inner Mongolia in China's northwest.[81] This region, he maintained, neatly fitted the description of an "optimal" base area as laid down in the Myro article. This strategy was rejected by the CCP at that time, and instead the party concentrated its activities in south and central China. "<u>The success of the Soviet movement was decided by the battles in Canton and Changsha, by the concentration of the work of the Communist Party in the industrial districts of Shanghai and Wuhan, by the work of the Party among the proletariat.</u> "[82]

Li summed up: "In preparing and in the very process of the struggle for Soviet power and Soviet districts, <u>the center of gravity in the work of the Communist Party must remain work among the proletariat in the large industrial centers.</u> " The stronger the Communist Party's position among the proletariat and the stronger the latter's struggles in the major industrial centers, the more successfully will the struggle for soviets develop and the more stable will the soviet districts be "even if we do not succeed at the outset in establishing Soviet power in the big cities occupied by imperialist troops. " At the same time, "the struggle for Soviet power (including the struggle in the inner, i. e. , peasant districts as a rule) demands that the proletariat win <u>the leading role in the movement</u>'' and that the Communist Party exercise a monopoly of leadership.[83] Thus, from the perspective of a national revolutionary struggle, agrarian revolution in the countryside must be linked to the overall antiimperialist movement (an increasingly dominant theme) and to the proletarian struggle in the cities directed against both the foreign and domestic bourgeoisie.

Yet it was precisely to the isolated and marginal rural area in the northwest, criticized by Li, that the Red Army forces under Mao were retreating on the Long March at just this time, following Mao's assumption of party leadership at the Tsunyi Conference in January 1935, events which proved to be a decisive watershed in CCP history.

FOOTNOTES

1. Constitution of the Chinese Soviet Republic (November 7, 1931), in Documentary History, p. 220. All the key documents adopted by the First Soviet Congress were introduced by the CCP Central Committee, with their contents presumably predetermined by the Party Center. Hsiao, Power Relations, pp. 171-172. Something of a balance of power in the central soviet area was reached at this congress between the Mao-led "real power" forces and those linked to the returned student-led Party Center. Though Mao was elected Chairman of the Central Executive Committee and also of the Council of People's Commissars operating under this committee, the basic policy lines were largely determined by the Party Center. It is clear that Mao suffered further serious declines in political and military influence over the next two years, culminating in his apparently much-reduced power position as a result of the Second National Soviet Congress in January 1934. Rue, Mao in Opposition, pp. 238-265.

A recent analysis of the soviet congresses of 1931 and 1934 concludes that while the Mao forces were able to win control of the soviet government created by the November 1931 congress (though not of the party apparatus in the soviet areas), by mid-1933 Mao "had lost effective control over the government, a situation which was formalized by the Second Congress." Waller, Kiangsi Soviet Republic, pp. 112-114. On the other hand, Kim maintains that at the January 1934 Congress Mao "was in full command of the government bureaucracy and its policy-making processes." Politics of Chinese Communism, p. 72. Kim's view accords with his thesis that Mao had already developed the substance of his "mass line" principles and strategies during the Kiangsi period. The issue of Mao's exact status is essentially marginal to my study, which focuses on the actual policies proclaimed and pursued by the dominant CI-CCP leadership, with some indication in this chapter of the problems encountered in implementing them under the conditions of the soviet area. See also n. 22, below.

2. Documentary History, p. 221.

3. Ibid.

4. Ibid., pp. 222-223.

5. Ibid., p. 220, with corrections by Hsiao, Power Relations,
    p. 178. A November 1933 Mao report on a model hsiang-level
    soviet government in Kiangsi stated that landlords and rich peas-
    ants were classified into two groups: those who could vote and
    those who could not, with the classification based on political
    attitudes and behavior rather than on the extent of their previous
    property holdings. Kim, Politics of Chinese Communism, p. 176.
    This modified policy, Kim observes, "exemplified an administra-
    tive policy based on Mao's concept of 'mass line'" (ibid.).

6. See Hsiao Tso-liang, The Land Revolution in China, 1930-1934
    (Seattle, 1969), pp. 186-191, for the English text of this law.
    Hsiao notes that the law was clearly based on Comintern direc-
    tives from mid-1929 on (p. 54). While the record is apparently
    complex and inconsistent, it seems that Mao's land policies from
    early 1930 on were on the whole not as unyielding on the question
    of allotting some land to surviving landlords or their dependents,
    and in supporting equal rather than poorer land allotments to dis-
    possessed rich peasants (pp. 20-22). See also Hsiao, Power Re-
    lations, pp. 164-165, for summary of the Political Resolution of
    the First Party Congress of the (Central) Soviet Area (November
    1931), which condemned these earlier Mao policies as a "rich
    peasant line." Hsiao (p. 164) notes that this congress marked
    the "successful penetration" into the central soviet area by the
    returned student party leadership.

    Kim notes that the November 1931 land law, in exempting middle
    peasants from land redistribution if the majority of them so de-
    sired reflected a Maoist input into the law. He adds, however,
    that its harsh and discriminatory provisions regarding the rich
    peasants clearly conflicted with the more lenient rich peasant
    policies Mao had been following since early 1930. Politics of
    Chinese Communism, p. 114. I would question whether this
    law truly represented, as Kim contends, a "compromise solu-
    tion" on the peasant problem, since it clearly conformed in its
    key provisions to the rural proletarian class war line of the new
    CCP leadership.

7. Hsiao, Land Revolution, p. 190.

8. "Fa k'an tz'u" (Introductory remarks), Red China, December 11,
    1931, p. 1.

9. Kim, Politics of Chinese Communism, p. 127.

10. Hsiao, Land Revolution, Document 27 (February 1931), p. 170.

11. Ibid., p. 173. The more broadly based poor peasant corps (or associations) included (aside from poor peasants) hired laborers, manual workers, coolies, handicraftsmen and apprentices. Its tasks were to fight for the interests and liberation of "the poor and miserable laboring masses in the rural districts," to "carry out the land revolution . . . , practice the class struggle, and resist all oppression and exploitation," and they were to "ally with the middle peasants and support them in their opposition to all oppression and exploitation." Ibid., Document 28 (February 1931), p. 175.

12. Kim, Politics of Chinese Communism, p. 129.

13. "Resolution on the Chinese Peasant Problem," cited in ibid., p. 128.

14. Ibid. The resolution also stresses voluntary, not coercive, re-cruitment of poor peasants and rural workers into the poor peasant corps (ibid.). Pavel Mif wrote in 1934: "The trade unions and groups of the poor play a tremendous role in the consolidation of the Soviet regime, . . . It would have been quite unthinkable to correctly carry out the redivision of land or to fight all the maneuvers of the kulaks, without these organizations." "Only the Soviets Can Save China," Communist International, XI: 11 (June 5, 1934), 375.

15. The drive was thus marked by an extremely harsh and discriminatory land allotment policy towards the rich peasants. Kim, Politics of Chinese Communism, p. 142.

16. Hsiao, Land Revolution, Document 60 (June 1, 1933), pp. 198-202; and Document 63 (June 20, 1933), pp. 205-208.

17. Cited in Mif, "Only the Soviets Can Save China," p. 373.

18. See n. 2, above.

19. Hsiao, Land Revolution, Documents 96 (June 17-21, 1933), and 101 (October 10, 1933), pp. 254-282. Hsiao notes (p. 110) that

these directives were issued by "cabinet order over the signatures of Mao and his deputies, but not by order of the Party, then controlled by the Russian Returned Students."

By his stress on the mass mobilization aspects of the drive and by his attempt to shield a broader class spectrum of the peasantry from its struggle impact, Mao exhibited, as Kim argues, a "mass line" outlook in contrast to the "class line" standpoint of the dominant returned student group. Politics of Chinese Communism, p. 142. On the whole, however, it appears that mass mobilization strategies in Kiangsi functioned well within the confines of the overall "class line" guidelines of the Party Center. Kim thus (somewhat understatedly) acknowledges that in the Land Investigation Movement "Mao did not ignore completely the programs of class struggle based on the 'class line' concept put forward by the returned student leaders" (pp. 142-143).

20. Hsiao, Land Revolution, p. 110; and Document 106 (March 15, 1934), pp. 282-285.

21. Ibid., pp. 122-124; and Document 117 (June 25, 1934), pp. 285-290.

22. Wang Ming, in a work published in Moscow after his death in March 1974, stated that Mao's success in "usurping the party's supreme command of the army at the [1935] Tsunyi conference was mainly due to the so-called Mao-Chang alliance. That is, he gained the support of Chang Wen-t'ien and Wang Chia-hsiang [another Russian-returned party leader]." Moscow radio, May 28, 1974, Daily Report, Soviet Union, FBIS, May 30, 1974, pp. C7-8. See also Heinzig, "The Otto Braun Memoirs and Mao's Rise to Power," p. 285. Chang Wen-t'ien had apparently begun to compromise with Mao in the fall of 1933 on the issue of economic construction policy in the soviet area. Kim, Politics of Chinese Communism, pp. 10-11, 102-103; Shanti Swarup, A Study of the Chinese Communist Movement (London, 1966), pp. 160-167. Mao seems to have won substantial support at that time in asserting the imperatives of more pragmatic attention and approaches to this area of soviet work. Kim, pp. 102-103. This was reflected in Mao's report to the Second Soviet Congress in January 1934, although the overall line of that report, as well as the new phase of the Land Investigation Move-

ment under Chang's direction in the spring of 1934, indicated the continued dominance of the proletarian class line. Thus, Chang Wen-t'ien, in pushing the policy of mobilization through economic construction in August 1933, insisted that "The Soviet government must legislate and implement the labor-protection law in order to prevent capitalist exploitation, and improve the living conditions of the working class in order to arouse·their consciousness and spirit of unity, as well as to persuade the workers that they themselves ought to participate in the management of their own government" (cited in Kim, pp. 101-102).

3. For the English text of. the 1931 labor law, see Yakhontoff, Chinese Soviets, pp. 224-235. The Chinese text of the law ("Lao-tung fa") is in Hsiao II, 440-443.

4. Soviets in China, p. 117.

5. Ibid., p. 89.

6. Yakhontoff, Chinese Soviets, p. 183. Yakhontoff also observed, citing its program, that "Orthodox members of the Party believe that the Canton Commune, . . . contributed much to the cause of Communism in China" (p. 81).

7. Ibid., p. 161.

8. Fundamental Laws of the Chinese Soviet Republic (New York, 1934), Introduction by Bela Kun, p. 4.

9. "Tasks of the Revolutionary Trade Union Movement in China" (Resolution of Eighth Session of R.I.L.U. Central Council), Inprecorr, XII: 10 (March 3, 1932), 189-193.

0. Ibid., p. 192.

1. Ibid., p. 193.

2. Ibid. In a similar vein, Wang Ming in December 1933 described "the twofold task" of the Chinese revolutionary movement to be the military and political "consolidation of the territorial base, on the one hand; and the wide development of the revolutionary mass struggle, especially the strike struggle, of the workers in

Kuomintang China, on the other." <u>Revolutionary China Today</u> (Moscow, 1934), p. 42.

33. Liu Shao-ch'i reported to the Second Soviet Congress in January 1934 that three trade unions had been established in the soviet area: "the Trade Union of Agriculture, the Trade Union of Shop-employees and Handicraftsmen, and the Trade Union of Stevedores." He stated that over 90 percent of the workers in the soviet areas were in the trade unions. "The Trade Union Movement in Soviet Areas During the Past Two Years," pp. 3-4.

34. In his January 1934 report, Liu Shao-ch'i, describing the advances made by workers in the soviet areas in accordance with the provisions of the labor law, acknowledged that "extreme 'left' mistakes" had been committed in 1932. Strikes had been staged in six cities at the end of that year, as a result of which "wages were increased and various special demands were met without restriction, with the result that the small entrepreneurs could not bear the burden and fell into a miserable plight." But since mid-1933, he added, "such mistakes were generally rectified." <u>Ibid.</u>, p. 7.

35. Kim, <u>Politics of Chinese Communism</u>, p. 38. This January 1932 report of the party's Kiangsi Provincial Committee to the Party Center in Shanghai on the southwest Kiangsi soviet area complained, in Kim's summation, that the labor law "was just beginning to be put into effect, but only in the industrial plants and printing shops owned and operated by the provincial soviet government, and it was not even implemented by the <u>hsien</u>-level government. The reason for this error was simply that the local government continued to maintain a rich-peasant mentality" (<u>ibid.</u>).

36. Swarup, <u>Study of the Chinese Communist Movement</u>, pp. 159-160.

37. See Isaacs, <u>Tragedy of the Chinese Revolution</u>, App., pp. 345-347; Roy, <u>Revolution and Counter-Revolution in China</u>, pp. 631-633; and Swarup, <u>Study of the Chinese Communist Movement</u>, pp. 159-165, for documentation and discussion of the problems and controversies regarding labor policies during the 1931-1934 soviet period.

38. Wang Ming in his December 1933 report to the ECCI Thirteenth Plenum also stated that "individual trade union members failed to take into account the military and economic situation in the Soviet districts and therefore put up demands which were not only absolutely impossible of fulfillment but were sometimes even harmful." Revolutionary China Today, p. 63. See also n. 34, above.

39. Kim, Politics of Chinese Communism, pp. 102-104; Swarup, Study of the Chinese Communist Movement, pp. 164-168.

40. Hsiao, Power Relations, pp. 277-278. Chinese text of the October 15, 1933, revised law is in Hsiao II, 747-756. The new law stated that for the exempted categories, special regulations would be issued through the Central Executive Committee of the government. It further provided for temporary exemptions in special emergencies relating to war, famine or other disasters, and also contained more elaborate provisions than the 1931 law in relation to apprentices. Hsiao II.

41. The English text of the major portion of Mao's report to the Second Congress is in Yakhontoff, Chinese Soviets, pp. 249-283, reprinted verbatim from Chinese Workers' Correspondence (Shanghai, March 31, 1934). An improved, though much reduced, version is in Documentary History, pp. 226-239. See Hsiao, Power Relations, pp. 270-273, for a comparison of these two versions with the original Chinese text. Since the sections omitted from the Yakhontoff text are not directly relevant to the issues under review here, I have used this text, indicating certain corrections.

42. See Hsiao, Power Relations, pp. 264-265, for an analysis of "Instructions of the Fifth Plenum to the Party Corps of the Second National Congress," a document adopted by this Central Committee plenum meeting in Juichin, January 1934. Hsiao states that Mao's report was drafted on the basis of these instructions, though he also notes a few differences between Mao's report and the resolutions, the most significant perhaps being Mao's position that the socialist revolution would follow the nationwide completion of the bourgeois-democratic revolution, while the Fifth Plenum talked of socialist revolution after the earlier stage had been carried out in important parts of the nation. Ibid., pp. 272-273.

98

43. Yakhontoff, Chinese Soviets, p. 256.

44. Ibid., pp. 258-259. The electoral law of the Soviet Republic had set the percentage of worker representatives to the Soviet Congress at a minimum of 35 percent. Liu Shao-ch'i, "The Trade Union Movement in Soviet Areas During the Past Two Years," p. 8.

45. Yakhontoff, Chinese Soviets, p. 261.

46. Ibid., pp. 263-265.

47. Ibid., p. 266. Mao added that in dealing with independent producers and middle peasants who violated the law in connection with their farmhands and other employees, "the method of convincing them with frank explanations has been used" (ibid.).

48. Ibid., p. 282.

49. "Our Economic Policy" (January 23, 1934), SW, I, 141-145.

50. "It is absolutely impermissible," Mao stated, "to repeat such wrong ultra-Left policies towards the upper petty bourgeois and middle bourgeois sectors in the economy as our Party adopted during 1931-1934 (unduly advanced labour conditions, excessive income tax rates, encroachments on the interests of industrialists and merchants during the land reform, and the adoption as a goal of the so-called 'workers' welfare,' which was a shortsighted and one-sided concept . . .)." Mao also criticized "the wrong ultra-Left policy, which was carried out in 1931-1934, of 'allotting no land to the landlords and poor land to the rich peasants.'" "The Present Situation and Our Tasks" (December 25, 1947), SW, IV, 168, 164.

51. "Von Schanghai bis Jänan" [From Shanghai to Yenan], Horizont (East Berlin), No. 26 (1969). Braun's death was reported in 1974.

52. Pavel Mif, "The Fifth Anniversary of the Canton Commune," Inprecorr, XII: 57 (December 22, 1932), 1227-1228.

53. Ibid.

54. Waller, Kiangsi Soviet Republic, p. 105. This bureau later reportedly kept Mao under house arrest for a time (ibid.). See also William W. Whitson, The Chinese High Command: A History of Communist Military Politics, 1927-71 (New York, 1973), p. 56. Teng Fa, of proletarian origin, had been active in the Canton-Hong Kong labor struggles of the mid-1920s, and participated in the 1927 Canton uprising. At the time of his death in an April 1946 plane crash, he was head of the trade unions in the Communist base areas. Klein and Clark, Biographic Dictionary, II, 817-819.

55. "Chi-nien Kuang-chou pao-tung, hsüeh-hsi Kuang-chou pao-tung ching-yen ho chiao-hsün" [Commemorate the Canton uprising, study the Canton uprising's experiences and lessons], Red China, December 11, 1932, p. 2. Teng Fa spoke on November 27 at Huich'ang in the central soviet area.

56. Ibid.

57. Soviets in China, pp. 12-13.

58. Ibid., p. 14.

59. Ibid., pp. 41-42. In Yenan in July 1937, in the course of an ideological exposition to Nym Wales on the stages of the Chinese revolution, Chang Wen-t'ien (then party secretary general) veered from the former orthodox formulas on the Canton Commune. While he described the Commune as "the last battle in the retreat of the revolution," he failed to link it with the succeeding soviet stage of the revolution, noting instead that the soviet form was first used in Hai-lu-feng in the last months of 1927. Chang also stressed that "the problem of the Chinese Soviet movement was how to complete [the] bourgeois tasks and not how to change to the stage of proletarian revolution. Only should the Soviet movement be victorious in the whole of China would the problem of transforming to the Socialist Revolution arise." Wales, Inside Red China, pp. 234-238. See also n. 42, above, for indications of a divergence between Mao and the returned student group in early 1934 on this latter issue.

60. Soviets in China, p. 89.

61. The anticapitalist and antirich peasant thrust of this stage of the Chinese revolution was particularly stressed by Soviets in China, p. 117.

62. Ibid., pp. 119-120.

63. See Chapter 3, n. 100.

64. Struggle for Bolshevization, Postscript, I: A-3: "The Question of the Uneven Development of the Chinese Revolutionary Movement" ("Kuan-yü Chung-kuo ko-ming yün-tung fa-chan pu p'ing-heng wen-t'i") (Hsiao II, 559-563). The above summation is based on this section; for a briefer summary, see Hsiao, Power Relations, pp. 204-205.

65. Struggle for Bolshevization (Hsiao II, 559).

66. Ibid., pp. 559-560.

67. Ibid., pp. 561-562.

68. Ibid., pp. 562-563. A fully articulated Maoist rejoinder to these views of Wang Ming was contained in a 1958 history of the CCP. It describes post-Fourth Plenum (1931) CCP policy as follows: "In their [CCP leaders'] understanding of Chinese society and Chinese revolution, they tended to exaggerate the relative importance of capitalism in Chinese society and to regard the Chinese revolution . . . as a democratic revolutionary movement somewhat socialist in nature. They regarded the participants in this revolution as a socialist force (an army of middle and poor peasants under the leadership of the proletariat). . . . They thus exaggerated the significance of [the] workers' movement and neglected the decisive function of peasants in the Chinese revolution. They were afraid to admit that the peasants' movement had surpassed the workers' movement, and that the Soviet movement was actually the peasants' movement. . . . They emphasized the significance of the workers' struggle by strikes, . . . [and] stubbornly regarded the urban areas as revolutionary centers and placed emphasis on the capture of central cities and armed uprisings in the urban areas as a means to achieve victory in one or several provinces. Thus they underestimated the function of revolutionary wars and revolutionary bases and denied the signifi-

cance of encircling the urban areas by the rural areas." Wang
Shih et al., A Brief History of the CCP (Shanghai, 1958), p. 144;
translated in JPRS, 8756 (Washington, DC, 1961), pp. 108-109.

69. I do not mean to imply that the revolutionary political role assigned to urban labor by the CCP necessarily brought an appropriate response from the Chinese labor movement, then mostly
organized in the "yellow unions" under the KMT and focusing
primarily on immediate economic issues alone. The split between the returned student group and the "labor union faction"
under Ho Meng-hsiung at the 1931 Fourth Plenum, to some extent reflected these divergences--the latter group being more
concerned with careful organizational work centering on everyday
issues rather than with the more "revolutionary" and highly politicized approach of the CCP leadership.

70. Revolutionary China Today, p. 54.

71. V. Myro, "The Struggle to Establish Inner Soviet Regions in the
Semi-Colonial Countries," Communist International, XII: 4 (Feb-
ruary 20, 1935), 151-159; and Li, "The Conditions for Estab-
lishing Soviet Districts in the Interior in Semi-Colonial Countries"
(A Reply to Comrade Myro), Communist International, XII: 5
(March 5, 1935), 222-239.

72. Myro, pp. 152-153.

73. Ibid., pp. 153-155.

74. Ibid., pp. 156-157.

75. Ibid., p. 159.

76. See Mao Tse-tung, "Problems of Strategy in China's Revolutionary
War" (December 1936), SW, I, 179-254.

77. Li, "Conditions for Establishing Soviet Districts," p. 222.

78. Ibid., p. 229.

79. Ibid.

80. <u>Ibid.</u>, p. 234.

81. This "Northwestern Theory" was proposed by Borodin in 1927, and apparently called for the CCP temporarily to retreat to the remote northwest area then under the control of General Feng Yü-hsiang, to whom the Communists still looked for support. However, this "theory" did not envision the creation of an independent armed force but rather a reliance on Feng's power. Stuart Schram <u>Mao Tse-tung</u> (New York, 1966), p. 97.

    For a detailed account of the locally-led, Communist-directed, peasant-partisan soviet movement which did emerge in the early 1930s in northern Shensi, prior to the arrival of the Mao-led forces in 1935, see Mark Selden, <u>The Yenan Way in Revolutionary China</u> (Cambridge, 1971), pp. 42-78.

82. Li, "Conditions for Establishing Soviet Districts," p. 237.

83. <u>Ibid.</u>, pp. 238-239.

THE MAOIST VERSION OF PROLETARIAN HEGEMONY:
THE ANTI-JAPANESE AND CIVIL WAR YEARS, 1936-1948

The Continuing Influence of the Proletarian International Line,
1937-1940

Questions of proletarian hegemony, the urban-rural relationship,
and the character of Communist revolutionary leadership assumed a
new context as Chinese developments moved towards a national front
of resistance to Japan in the 1935-1937 period. The united front
guidelines of the Comintern's Seventh World Congress in 1935; the
basic interests and anti-Japanese policies of the Chinese Communists;
the security needs of the Soviet Union, reflected in a growing rap-
prochement with the Nanking government;[1] and the rising tide of
anti-civil war and patriotic resistance sentiment throughout China
in the face of mounting Japanese aggression--all contributed to the
emergence of the new united front between the Kuomintang and the
Communist Party.[2] Relinquishing its anti-KMT political and social
revolutionary policies, the CCP sought to immerse itself again in the
mainstream of Chinese political life as a potent force in the struggle
against Japan.[3]

But the standpoint of the still-influential "Internationalists" in
the party's ruling circles, led by Wang Ming, diverged significantly
from that of the now increasingly dominant Maoist leadership of the
party. Wang Ming returned to China in late 1937 from Moscow,
where he had spent the past six years, arriving in Yenan by December. He had served as the CCP's representative to the Comintern
and was also a leading Comintern figure, having been elected a member of the ECCI Presidium at the 1935 Seventh World Congress. He
had played a leading role in formulating and publicizing the CCP's
united front overtures and initiatives since 1935. On his return to
China he became head of the party's United Front Work Department
and of the CCP's Yangtze Bureau, and served as the party representative at the temporary national capital at Hankow during most of
1938.[4] Through these roles Wang in 1938 developed an important
political base of power in the Yangtze area, which was at that time
reflected in the pages of the New China Daily (Hsin-hua jih-pao), the
Communist paper published in Hankow (and later in Chungking) under
the united front arrangements with the KMT, and also in the Yangtze

103

Bureau's influential role in the Communists' New Fourth Army, organized in December 1937 to wage guerrilla war against the Japanese in the vicinity of the great cities of the lower Yangtze valley.[5] Wang Ming's continuing prestige in the CCP during the early wartime years was also indicated in his second-place listing, after Mao, on the twenty-five-member preparatory committee set up in December 1937 for the convocation of a CCP Seventh Congress.[6] His still-powerful status was also evident in the effusive and elaborate welcome accorded him by Mao and other CCP leaders on his return by special plane flight from Moscow to Yenan at the end of 1937.[7]

Wang, emphasizing the overriding importance of national unity under Chiang Kai-shek, focused principally on the party's new role as spokesman and organizer of a national political constituency (seen again very much in urban and labor terms), functioning under the aegis of the National Government and seeking to promote a more broadly based and united political front for all-out resistance to Japan.[8] While stressing the need to retain the party's separate identity and organizational base and its ultimate commitment to a proletarian socialist China, Wang clearly viewed the latter objectives as a future and distant stage of development, distinct from the party's support and participation in the "bourgeois-nationalist" anti-Japanese war.

Thus, writing in the wake of the outbreak of hostilities between Japan and China in July 1937, Wang Ming acclaimed the role of the Chinese Communists as being in "the front ranks in defense of the national existence and independence of China," but added that "between the bourgeois nationalists and the Communists there is and always will be an impassable boundary." Though firm defenders of China's national interests, "we [the Communists] remain true revolutionary internationalists and consistent proletarian fighters."[9] And while supporting the creation of a "united Chinese democratic republic, . . . the Chinese Communists are on no account, not for a moment, converted into bourgeois democrats, nor cease to be consistent supporters of the Soviet [power] and socialism."[10] Wang also carefully noted that "not all those active in the anti-Japanese struggle can become Communists. . . . Communists are not only fighters in the national-revolutionary movement but also consistent fighters for the emancipation of the working class and the whole of working mankind, i.e., for the dictatorship of the proletariat, Soviet power and Communism."[11]

Wang Ming appeared to play down the territorial (rural) base strategy in favor of a nationwide Communist effort focused primarily on the cities and the workers. He stressed, for example, the key importance to the Chinese resistance war of heavy industry (quoting Stalin on this point), and on the significance of holding key cities, communication lines, and vital natural resource areas.[12] Even in urging a national effort to draw the peasants into the anti-Japanese struggle, he denigrated, in this regard, the overall impact of the territorially restricted peasant base areas: "The Chinese Communists appreciate the fact that in spite of their wealth of experience in work among the peasants, the Communists, apart from the districts where the Red Army has been or is to be found, have in general done extremely little to organize the peasantry." In mounting a nationwide anti-Japanese struggle, Wang maintained that the party must "in the first place" devote tremendous efforts "to the education and organization of the working class millions." He pointedly noted in this regard that the party's work among the trade unions and workers in the main centers of the country "was extremely weak in the previous period."[13] He stressed "the necessity of re-educating the old Party cadres in accordance with the new tasks," adding:

> The majority of the present cadres of the Communist Party of China were trained and steeled in the civil war. Many of them are of peasant origin. They have had experience of armed struggle against the Kuomintang and its armies, but many of them have had no experience whatsoever of the struggle for the masses in circumstances where there is no Soviet government or Red Army nor have they even any idea of the working class movement in the big towns. Therefore the education of the old Party cadres to suit the new conditions and methods of work is by no means an easy job.[14]

A task of equal importance, he continued, was the training and promotion of new cadres, "first and foremost from among the workers." Many such leaders have emerged from the anti-Japanese movement and the strike struggle, and from among them the party "can and must draw fresh forces and new reserves, its new fighting cadres who . . . possess experience of struggle and work."[15]

These views essentially reflected continuing emphasis, under the new conditions of the united front and the resistance war, on the notion of building for the CCP an urban proletarian constituency and organizational base on a national scale. In this view, the CCP,

while retaining and reinforcing its proletarian features and its ideological commitment to eventual Communist goals, would now basically
defer to and participate in a democratized KMT-led resistance struggle. In this "bourgeois-led" collaboration, not only socialist objectives but also CCP-proletarian hegemony were relegated to a distinctly
separate and future stage. [16]   In mid-1938, for example, Wang Ming
declared in Hankow that China needed the Kuomintang, since the
"Communist Party represents the working class; it does not claim
to, and cannot, represent the whole people. For a considerable
time to come China needs a party representing many other classes
--merchants, intellectuals, landlords. "[17]

Wang Ming reinforced the above themes in a major 1938 May
Day policy statement in the New China Daily. [18]   In order for the
working class effectively to fulfill its "vanguard role" in the resistance struggle, Wang called on the workers to take an increasingly
active role in the war. He urged unemployed workers and staff
(many of whom had left their jobs in Japanese-occupied centers) to
join the armed forces in large numbers, particularly the modern
military branches (air, tank, armored vehicle, etc.), where their
former work experiences and skills could be readily adapted for
service in these more technically demanding units. Wang was obviously referring here to recruitment into the KMT armies, in line
with his views on the crucial role of the modern national armed
forces in the war (and of an elitist labor role in those forces), and
his tendency to minimize the role of rural, guerrilla-style struggle.
To strengthen labor's leading role, Wang also stressed the importance of establishing a new, powerful and united national labor organization. He underlined the massive potential of organized labor in
China, declaring that the Chinese proletariat included not only some
three million industrial workers, but also nine or ten million handi-
craft workers, over a million staff (administrative, professional,
clerical) personnel, and ten to fifteen million village (hired farm)
workers. All were bona fide members of the proletariat and should
be included in a nationally organized labor federation. The focus
was clearly on the national scene, with Wang Ming asserting the
viability and importance of a CCP policy which was primarily oriented
towards building the party's key political base through the organization and mobilization of a broad national labor movement within the
parameters of the KMT-led resistance war.

The Yangtze Bureau-influenced New Fourth Army in the early
wartime period carefully operated within the KMT administrative

purview and in overall coordination with Nationalist guerrilla forces in the lower Yangtze area.[19] They did not implement the CCP's rent and interest reduction policies, nor did they attempt to establish Communist base areas.[20] Yeh T'ing, commander of the New Fourth Army until his capture in the KMT's January 1941 attack on the head-quarters of that army, stated in a 1938 Hankow interview that indus-trial workers from Shanghai comprised more than half of the nearly one thousand students enrolled in the army's Military and Political Academy--the source of the army's future officers and political work-ers.[21]

Following the important Sixth Plenum of the CCP's Central Committee in November 1938, which marked the beginning of the final eclipse of the "internationalist" forces in the CCP leadership, a CCP administrative reorganization restricted Wang Ming's authority to a new South China Bureau responsible only for the (increasingly minor) CCP interests in the KMT areas. Liu Shao-ch'i[22] was dis-patched to take control of New Fourth Army forces moving north of the Yangtze, with a full reorganization of this entire army under a new Central China Bureau headed by Liu, taking place after the January 1941 New Fourth Army incident.[23] Under Liu's direction, from late 1939 on, the New Fourth followed a much more activist strategy, promoted peasant mobilization through rent and interest reduction campaigns, and began establishing local Communist admin-istrations.[24]

The continuing influence of the proletarian line in the CCP in the first years of the resistance war was manifested not only in the outlook of the Wang Ming-controlled Yangtze Bureau of the party, but also to a lesser extent in labor policy articles and directives emanating from the Yenan party center itself.[25] It was exhibited at that time in the seeming tendency in the economically backward Shen-Kan-Ning Border Region to favor the miniscule worker forces in the few state-run enterprises as a special "proletarian core" in that rural base area. The head of the labor unions (and also direc-tor of state-run mines and factories) in the Border Region in that period was Liu Ch'ün-hsien, a former Wusih (near Shanghai) young woman textile factory worker and labor movement activist who had married Po Ku (Ch'in Pang-hsien) in Moscow in 1928,[26] and who was herself (as was of course Po Ku) one of the "twenty-eight Bol-sheviks" who took over the CCP leadership in 1931.[27] In a May Day article she contributed from Yenan to the Hankow New China Daily in 1938, she strongly emphasized the great economic, political and cultural advances made by the virtually all-unionized workers in the Border Region through their "past struggles," detailing a wide range of welfare benefits, good working conditions (including the eight-hour day, six-day week), and substantially increased wage levels.[28] She also underlined the important role of the unions (under the new conditions of labor-capital conciliation) in defending labor's interests in contract negotiations. Nym Wales describes a 1937 visit she made accompanied by Liu Ch'ün-hsien to a small state textile factory in Yenan staffed by women workers. "The factory girls all wore Red Army uniforms and red-starred caps, had bobbed hair, and considered themselves leading a 'proletarian revolution,'" she recounts.[29] Nym Wales was told that while wages in this poor and backward area of the northwest were not nearly as high nor factory conditions as good as they had been under the Kiangsi Soviet, they were still much higher than the average income of the local population.[30]

An internationalist-oriented Communist account of a visit to Yenan in late 1937, in describing the working conditions of the elite printing workers there, stressed that their income was at least double that of the highest government and party officials in the Border Region.[31] A decade later, in 1948, leading Maoist ideological spokesman Ch'en Po-ta, in quite evident reference to this earlier period, pointedly criticized the "mistakes" on the question of wages "in certain old liberated areas in the past," adding that wages and working conditions at that time had been set "excessively high," and that state-run factories had even required heavy governmental subsidies in order to continue operations under these policies, a procedure supported by "certain comrades" as being "in the interests of the workers."[32]

The Wang Ming line, in seeking closer Communist identification and links to urban labor, also strongly emphasized and endorsed the need substantially to improve the livelihood of workers in the KMT areas. Yet at the same time, this was placed within the conciliatory framework of the commitment to the national united front, with overriding priority on a collaborative policy in support of the "bourgeois" (KMT)-led resistance war. The championing of labor's cause and interests thus tended in the last analysis to rely on an ineffectual "persuasion" approach--an appeal to both the KMT government and to intransigent capitalists to alleviate the workers' badly exploited and inflation-ravaged situation in the interests of greater productivity and unity for the war effort.[33] And finally, after the KMT loss of most of the main cities, the internationalist position underlined the need for a much more activist CCP role in the Japanese-occupied industrial centers--viewed as still "the strongholds of the proletariat" in China.[34]

But the emerging realities of China's wartime situation and the corresponding growing dominance of the Maoist position and standpoint soon fatally undermined the remaining influence of the proletarian international line. The loss of the major cities to the Japanese and the virtual ending of the united front with the KMT by the beginning of 1941 underscored the impracticalities of a CCP political strategy strongly geared to the activation of a nationwide mass labor movement. At the same time, it had become abundantly evident that the CCP locus of power resided in the expanding and autonomous Communist base areas increasingly guided by a more fully articulated and independent Maoist military-political strategic line. The Mao-led cheng-feng ideological-political-economic rectification and struggle movement of the early 1940's, brought to a head by the pressing need more fundamentally to resolve the critical concerns and problems facing the rural base areas in those years,[35] was to mark the final eclipse of the Wang Ming-Po Ku group in the policy-making circles of the CCP.[36]

The Maoist Redefinition and Reassertion of Proletarian Hegemony

In the initial wartime years, a divergent Maoist strategy and political-ideological formulation emerged which reflected Mao's long-held though previously often submerged independent revolutionary outlook and rural mass line vantage point. While adhering to the united front policy, and also acknowledging Kuomintang national leadership and support of the goal of a "united democratic republic," the Maoist line focused first of all on an independent, if initially somewhat nationally coordinated, military strategy of establishing, consolidating and expanding rural, peasant-based anti-Japanese liberated areas. The CCP was thus able to develop parallel centers of political and military power outside the parameters of Nationalist government influence and authority, but which did not yet directly challenge that authority. The rapid loss by the Nationalist armies of the major coastal cities and communications lines and of north China and the lower Yangtze valley, the tendency of the Kuomintang to move increasingly away from earlier expectations of a broadened and more popularly based government and war effort, and the growing strains in the new "united front from above" between the Kuomintang and the CCP clearly reinforced and facilitated the development and effectiveness of the Maoist strategy.

The initial CCP call for a democratic republic eventually focused on the Communist-led rural base areas themselves as prototypes and nuclei for such a republic--increasingly seen as emerging under direct CCP leadership of a multiclass coalition through the political formula of "new democracy."

Through new democracy Mao thus asserted his own concept of "proletarian hegemony" during a transitional stage to socialism. It marked a distinct departure from the democratic dictatorship of the Kiangsi period, when the Comintern-guided CCP had sought to give the concept of proletarian hegemony over the agrarian revolution a concrete class content and meaning, and it diverged as well from the new united front line of the Wang Ming group. The latter, while seeking as before to link the CCP with genuinely proletarian forces and interests, at the same time abandoned the goal of proletarian-CCP hegemony for the duration of the "bourgeois"-led national resistance war.

The Maoist strategy now redefined proletarian hegemony in essentially rural terms; though linked as before to the leading role of the CCP and its armed forces, such leadership was now directly and unequivocally joined to the political, military and social mobilization of the broad masses of the peasantry in support of the national and popular goals of the resistance war. [37] And while a confiscatory land policy had been abandoned for the wartime united front, it was replaced by social and economic reform measures (such as rent and interest reduction) through which the poor peasant base could be consolidated without seriously undermining broader rural support. Thus Communist leadership could be effectively asserted over the entire multistage revolutionary process beginning with the wartime national democratic phase, linked by the concept of "liberation," with its many-faceted connotations. And in building the base of support for this leadership role, the CCP now had little need for a specifically worker-linked "proletarian" outlook or class identification (urban or rural), which would have been largely irrelevant and even counterproductive.

Thus the national democratic goals of the resistance war were not juxtaposed to those of a later, proletarian-led struggle for socialism, but became the means for building the "proletarian hegemony" necessary to move towards Communist goals. But in the process of so doing, the content and meaning of proletarian leadership, the mix of class forces, the political-organizational base and ideology of the party and the role of the army, as well as the ultimate rural-urban, peasant-worker relationships in Chinese Communism, all under-went transformation--the consequences of the new rural vantage point and strategy.

In Communist moves towards a united front, Mao had already declared in late 1936 that "concerning the labor-capital problem" the soviet districts had "formulated the minimum conditions for the im-provement of the living conditions of the workers," and that labor-capital agreements had been concluded "in accordance with the prac-tical situation" in the various enterprises.[38] All "unnecessary strikes and sabotage" were avoided, "former laws providing for superinten-dence and management of enterprises by workers have been repealed," and workers were "advised not to press demands beyond the capacity of the enterprise." As for nonsoviet China, Mao stated that "though we support the improvement of the living conditions of the workers, we similarly do not willfully intensify the anti-capitalist struggle." The struggle against imperialist aggression would benefit both workers and capitalists, and while "imperialism is intensifying its aggression, neither the capitalists nor the workers can expect the improvement of their respective conditions. The joint interests of capitalists and workers are built on the foundation of struggle against imperialist aggression."[39] In time these views were to evolve into the theme of mutual benefits and joint interests of labor and capital and to be-come dominant in Maoist labor and urban policies through the later wartime period and in the subsequently renewed all-out civil war with the KMT as well. Though this early Mao formulation on the "labor-capital problem" seemingly reflected overall CCP policy at that time, as I have already noted, the proponents of the proletarian line continued to retain for the party a stronger labor orientation and interest than Mao himself presumably intended in this statement. At any rate, when Mao acted to assert full ideological-political supremacy in the CCP after 1940, he specifically criticized the party's labor pol-icies of the early wartime period and moved away from a stance which had continued to accord labor a specially favored status in the base areas.[40]

In May 1937 at a National Conference of the CCP in Yenan, Mao discussed the Communists' united front slogan for a "democratic re-public," describing it as "a new type of republic" which would once again be comprised of a four-class bloc (proletariat, peasantry, petty bourgeoisie, and "democratic sections of the bourgeoisie") for the period of "the national and democratic revolution."[41] In the face of the Japanese threat, he said, "the bourgeoisie has been compelled to seek an ally in the shape of the proletariat just as we are seeking an ally in the shape of the bourgeoisie." As to the longer-term perspectives of the revolution, Mao stated that "a condition of the struggle to achieve the victory of socialism is that we absolutely take our stand at the head of the democratic revolution. . . . The efforts we are expending today lead to the great aims of tomorrow. Anyone who loses this great aim ceases immediately to be a Communist, but anyone who disregards the tasks of today is also no Communist." To "pass from the situation wherein the bourgeoisie predominates to the situation where the proletariat will do so," Mao continued, "will be a lengthy process of struggle." And "our present alliance with the revolutionary section of the bourgeoisie is precisely the necessary bridge for the future passage to socialism."[42]

In a June 1937 interview presaging his new democracy formula, Mao further stated that since the bourgeoisie of a semi-colonial country was weak and incapable of exercising leadership, "the proletariat must take it up." The "democratic republic" in China was thus "different from the bourgeois-democratic republic of history. It is the united front of the proletariat, the peasants, and part of the bourgeoisie in the form of a republic." While affirming the need for the continued existence of capitalism during a transition to socialism, Mao added that "the leadership of the proletariat makes it possible to transform war into socialist revolution."[43]

Mao thus projected the oncoming resistance war as an _integral_ phase of a continuous Chinese revolution, in the course of which the "proletariat" would continue to compete with the bourgeoisie for national leadership. But as the Maoist political strategy developed further to new democracy, the competition for leadership no longer implied or called for a direct break with the bourgeoisie, but rather for taking the "national bourgeoisie" (a grouping increasingly dissociated from the Kuomintang leadership) itself under the mantle of CCP leadership. In the unfolding of this strategic doctrine, the urban working class was clearly no longer required to play its former role as the revolutionary cutting edge in achieving "proletarian hegemony" and national Communist power. One might note here that Otto Kuusinen, the veteran Comintern functionary and a leading figure in Soviet Russian party circles up to his death in mid-1964, stated in an interesting speech to the February 1964 Plenum of the Central Committee of the CPSU: "Even during the period prior to the accession to power [i.e., 1949], the leaders of the Communist Party of China did not pay due attention to the proletarian stratum within the party's ranks, and did little work among the urban proletariat. And later the Chinese leaders complained that, for example, in such an important working class centre as Shanghai, 'the Kuomintang was more influential than the Communist Party, and blamed the workers for this.'"[44]

Similarly, meaningful distinctions between "bourgeois nationalist" and "proletarian internationalist" standpoints were largely erased as the party moved to take direct leadership of a rural-based "liberation war." A mid-1938 Central Committee propaganda outline, while still at that time carefully proclaiming the CCP to be "the Marxist-Leninist Party of the Chinese working class," also declared that as a result of the party's work in the resistance war "the comrades of our Party have demonstrated that they are indeed the vanguard of the Chinese nation and the Chinese people."[45]

This standpoint was strongly reinforced in Mao's major report to the Sixth Plenum of the CC, CCP in November 1938.[46] "The Communists are internationalists. Can they be at the same time patriotic nationalists?" Mao queried. "They can and should be according to historical conditions. . . . Our nationalism is actually a manifestation of internationalism in time of national revolutionary war."[47] Mao further developed this theme at the close of the report:

A Communist is a Marxist internationalist, but Marxism must take on a national form before it can be applied. There is no such thing as abstract Marxism but only concrete Marxism. What we call concrete Marxism is Marxism that has taken on a national form, Marxism applied to the concrete struggle in the concrete conditions prevailing in China, and not Marxism abstractly used.[48]

Mao then addressed himself to the need for "the Sinification of Marxism," "a problem that must be understood and solved by the whole Party without delay." Underscoring this, Mao added, "We must put an end to writing eight-legged essays on foreign models."[49] In these and immediately succeeding passages, with their strongly implied criticism of "foreign models," of "dogmatism," and of "empty and abstract refrains," Mao clearly moved towards the post-cheng-feng formal definition of the "Thought of Mao Tse-tung" as "the integration of the universal truth of Marxism-Leninism with the concrete practice of the Chinese revolution."[50]

On this "nationalist-internationalist" question, it is interesting that Owen Lattimore, reporting on his 1969 and 1970 visits to the Soviet Union, where he met many of the Soviet experts on China and the Far East and was able "to sit down right along with discussions with them," states that "on the level of research, one can find that the Russians are working very, very seriously, analyzing what they think is an important problem, namely, that a revolution based on the peasantry instead of on an industrial proletariat is always in danger of diversion into what they call 'bourgeois, great power chauvinism.'"[51]

The strategic outlines for an emerging Communist leadership of the rural-based resistance struggle, with this struggle seen as a broadly inclusive and protracted revolutionary transitional stage to a socialist China, was sketched out by Mao in December 1939 in his major treatise, "The Chinese Revolution and the Chinese Communist Party," and further elaborated in the following month in his more publicized work, "On New Democracy."[52] Mao stressed the pivotal importance of the rural base areas and their vanguard role in the overall, long-term revolutionary struggle. "Since China's key cities have long been occupied by the imperialists and their reactionary Chinese allies," Mao wrote in the 1939 work, "it is imperative for the revolutionary ranks to turn the backward villages into advanced, consolidated base areas, into great military, political, economic and cultural bastions of the revolution from which to fight their vicious enemies who are using the cities for attacks on the rural districts, and in this way gradually to achieve the complete victory of the revolution through protracted fighting." Thus, "victory in the Chinese revolution can be won first in the rural areas" through a protracted struggle consisting mainly of "peasant guerrilla warfare led by the Chinese Communist Party."[53]

Mao of course added that "stressing work in the rural base areas does not mean abandoning our work in the cities and in the other vast rural areas which are still under the enemy's rule." To do this would isolate the base areas and the revolution would suffer defeat; moreover, "the final objective of the revolution is the capture of the cities, the enemy's main bases, and this cannot be achieved without adequate work in the cities."[54] But Mao at the same time cautioned the party against being "impetuous and adventurist in its propaganda and organizational work in the urban and rural areas which have been occupied by the enemy and dominated by the forces of reaction and darkness for a long time"; rather, the party "must have well-selected cadres working underground, [and] must accumu-

late its strength and bide its time there."[55] The character of the
"transitional stage" of the revolution and of the CCP's long-term
class strategy were clearly undergoing significant alterations. As
Mao told André Malraux in 1965, "We made the Revolution with peasant rebels; then we led them against the cities ruled by the Kuomintang."[56]

In its present stage, Mao stated in his 1939 essay, the Chinese
revolution is "a new special type" of bourgeois-democratic revolution:
"We call this new type the new democratic revolution and it is developing in all other colonial and semi-colonial countries as well as in
China."[57] It "clears the way for capitalism [though on a restricted
basis] on the one hand and creates the prerequisites for socialism
on the other" and is "a stage of transition between the abolition of
the colonial, semi-colonial and semi-feudal society and the establishment of a socialist society." The new democratic revolution results
in "a dictatorship of the united front of all the revolutionary classes
under the leadership of the proletariat"; its prototype is "the anti-
Japanese democratic political power established in the base areas."[58]
The Communists' wartime united front goal of "a democratic republic"
must thus be based on "a revolutionary alliance of the workers, peasants, urban petty bourgeoisie and all others who are against imperialism and feudalism. Only under the leadership of the proletariat [i.e.,
the CCP] can such a republic be completely realized."[59]

In "On New Democracy" Mao further noted that the new democratic republic would differ both from the capitalist republics of the
West and the socialist republic of the Soviet Union. The former,
"bourgeois dictatorships" of "the old democratic form," are already
out of date, while the Soviet type of dictatorship of the proletariat
"will be established in all the capitalist countries and will undoubt-
edly become the dominant form of state and governmental structure
in all the industrially advanced countries."[60] But this latter form,
"for a certain historical period," is unsuited to the revolutions in
the colonial and semi-colonial countries, for whom the form of the
new democratic republic must be adopted. "This form suits a certain historical period and is therefore transitional; nevertheless, it
is a form which is necessary and cannot be dispensed with." Thus
in addition to the first two types of republics there is now a third:
"republics under the joint dictatorship of several revolutionary
classes."[61]

Though Mao vaguely stated that the Soviet form will "in the future . . . be the dominant form throughout the world for a certain period," he avoided portraying the new democracy as specifically transitional to the Soviet form of proletarian dictatorship, and he quite clearly linked the suitability of the Soviet model to the advanced capitalist countries.[62] This is in marked contrast to the role assigned earlier to the revolutionary democratic dictatorship of workers and peasants, itself a formula directly linked to Soviet experience and to the goal of proletarian dictatorship. Mao instead projected a multiclass dictatorship (which "at certain times and to a certain extent" included the national bourgeoisie) under the CCP,[63] not as a revised version of the earlier formula but as a distinctively new revolutionary track in which the transitional forms--structure, strategy, policies and class forces--would significantly shape the ultimate form of the Chinese socialist model.

Thus the CCP's focus was now on the central and long-term role of the rural liberated areas and on building Communist political-military power ("proletarian leadership") almost entirely on a broadened peasant base. The party's proletarian character and socialist mission were no longer considered directly linked to or dependent upon a workers' struggle movement which would in turn inevitably generate and accentuate labor-capital conflict. The CCP was thus able to assert direct and continuous leadership over both a multistage and a multiclass revolutionary process.[64]

In a key 1962 speech (unpublished at the time), Mao noted that "the laws governing the Chinese revolution," based upon "the objective world of China," had only been fully recognized and formulated after some two decades of revolutionary practice which included both victories and defeats. "It was during the War of Resistance Against Japan that we began to formulate the party's mass line and a series of specific policies appropriate to the situation," Mao stated; and it was only with the rectification [cheng-feng] movement of the early 1940's that the entire party reached a full understanding on "the question of how to promote democratic revolution in China."[65] "This objective world of China, generally speaking," Mao added, "was recognized by China, not by those comrades of the Communist International in charge of the China problem." These latter "comrades," Mao continued, "did not at all understand Chinese society, Chinese nationality, or the Chinese revolution."[66]

An East German (pro-Soviet) 1969 analysis of Maoist economics, for its part observed that "already in the 1940s" there had been serious conflicts between the "internationalist, Marxist-Leninist" and the "petty-bourgeois" (Maoist) factions of the CCP, "with regard to the question of the role of the working class in the liberation movement and in the socialist construction, [and] with regard to the question of the attitude toward the proletarian international movement."[67]

It was precisely on the above issues that Liu Shao-ch'i (who became the party's leading proponent and interpreter of Maoist ideology in the wake of the cheng-feng movement) had pinpointed the significance of the "Thought of Mao Tse-tung" in 1947. "Mao Tse-tung's great accomplishment," he told Anna Louise Strong, "has been to change Marxism from a European to an Asiatic form."[68] European Marxism focused on the industrial worker as the key to socialism and communism, he added, but China had comparatively few such workers among its hundreds of millions. Liu then pointed to a "little devil" (presumably a budding young peasant soldier) who, he said, "has been brought up and trained in this special, highly military Communist organization of ours. . . . China has only a few industrial workers to be the foundation of communism but we have millions of kids like this." Liu continued, "They fight now for the 'new democracy' but if in the future it is time to build socialism, they will be ready to build it. If it is time for communism, they will be ready for that also." Such people, he noted, "are not only no less disciplined and devoted, but in fact perhaps even more disciplined and devoted than the industrial workers."[69] An indigenous rural "proletarian" vanguard (the peasant transformed) could thus carry the multistage revolution through to eventual communism. Thus, just as the role of the Canton working class in the Commune of 1927 had been continuously pointed to in the pre-Yenan period as the "historically significant" evidence that the proletariat in the colonial and semi-colonial countries could play its leadership role as part of the developing world socialist revolution, so the CCP now specifically pointed to the revolutionary role of the politicized peasant as a unique characteristic of "Asiatic" Marxism.

In an inner-party directive at the close of 1940, Mao summed up a series of new Central Committee directives on a broad range of basic issues which in effect delineated a more clearcut Maoist policy line on the united front, military strategy, class alignments, and labor, tax, land, economic, and cultural-educational policies.[70] Mao not only rejected the standpoint of the internationalist faction,

but now characterized the line they had followed in the Kiangsi Soviet
as "ultra-left," specifically citing, among other issues, their labor-
capital and agrarian policies. Mao declared the CCP's united front
policy to be one of "independence and initiative," combining elements
of both "alliance and struggle" with a military strategy which stressed
independently waged guerrilla warfare and the maximum expansion of
the Communist armies. Mao defined the party's policy for the KMT
and Japanese-occupied areas (in effect, the party's urban policy) as
one of developing "the united front [i.e., a coalition of class forces]
to the greatest possible extent," while having "well-selected cadres
working underground for a long period, to accumulate strength and
bide our time." He outlined in this regard a sophisticated class
strategy which, while isolating the "anti-Communist die-hards,"
sought to build the broadest possible CCP class base.[71] Taken in
all, these party directives clearly signaled a more decisive break
with the Wang Ming-Po Ku line both of the Kiangsi Soviet era and
of the subsequent early united front years.

In the interests of promoting self-sufficiency in the Communist
base areas, Mao stated that capitalists should be encouraged to come
into these areas and start enterprises. "Private enterprise should
be encouraged and state enterprise regarded as only one sector of
the economy."[72] While Mao acknowledged the need to spur the workers' resistance-war enthusiasm by improving their livelihood, he immediately added that "we must strictly guard against being ultra-Leftist;
there must not be excessive increases in wages or excessive reductions
in working hours." Under present conditions, Mao continued, the
eight-hour day (a sacrosanct plank in previous CCP labor policy and
laws) could not be "universally introduced" in China, and the ten-
hour day should be permitted in certain branches of production, with
a flexible approach on this issue generally. He emphasized that once
a labor-capital contract was concluded, "the workers must observe
labour discipline and the capitalists must be allowed to make some
profit." "Particularly in rural areas," Mao concluded, "the living
standards and wages of the workers should not be raised too high,
or it will give rise to complaints from the peasants, create unemployment among the workers and result in a decline in production."[73]

The rectification (cheng-feng) movement initiated in 1941-1942
espoused a more fully committed and self-reliant rural-peasant vantage point in the Border Region. It promoted a wide range of village-
focused and decentralized economic policies which struck at bureau-

cratism in the state structure and emphasized a broader mix of private, cooperative, and household enterprises in addition to the state-run sector.[74] The movement included as well, the "rectification" of union, party, and management cadres in the state factories and of the factory workers, with "counterrevolutionary" and "destructive" elements among all these groups coming under severe attack.[75] There was a particularly strong thrust in this regard against "economist" attitudes and "antiquated" policies, such as an emphasis on high wage incentives, the uncritical support of the demands of "backward" workers, and the use of adversary labor struggle tactics against management.[76]

The avowed determination in the course of the rectification campaign to inculcate a "new labor attitude" was highlighted by the launching of a major movement in the Border Region in the fall of 1942, centered around a model worker (Chao Chan-k'uei) who epitomized all the newly extolled labor virtues.[77] In acclaiming this model worker, the CCP's Liberation Daily in Yenan declared: "He is completely different from the slackers who only seek high wages, demand preferential treatment, and work erratically and half-heartedly. . . . Every time rewards are given he steps back, regarding it to be a result of collective effort, with no achievements of his own to speak of." The article added that though Chao Chan-k'uei--the model worker-- "is a highly skilled veteran worker, . . . he lacks the bad habits of the average veteran worker."[78]

Cheng-feng thus also marked a move away from policies which attempted, even in the uncongenial environment of the rural base areas, to maintain, as a specially favored constituency, a state-run industrial sector with its related bureaucratic structure and proletarian underpinnings.[79] Gunther Stein, reporting on his 1944 visit to the Shen-Kan-Ning Border Region, noted that "the workers in the industries of the Communist-controlled regions apparently do not claim a right to greater influence on public affairs than other classes. . . . Their professed solidarity with the peasantry from which they came," he added, "has nothing artificial about it. None of the factory workers to whom I spoke about labor problems referred to their class as 'proletarian.'"[80]

In striking contrast to the new labor policy was the manner in which the CCP heightened and politicized its implementation of the rent and interest reduction policy in the base areas in this same period. As the rent and interest reduction campaign moved into high gear, it took on the qualities of a "struggle" movement and was clearly intended to activate and organize the masses of poorer peasantry, raise their political consciousness, and consolidate CCP power in the villages of the expanding liberated areas. [81] But while this campaign in effect escalated the "anti-feudal" struggle, it carefully avoided a hostile stance towards capitalist forces, industrial or agricultural. In its basic January 1942 directive on this campaign, the CCP simultaneously affirmed its recognition of "the capitalist mode of production [as] the more progressive method in present-day China," and applied this specifically to policy towards the rich peasants (though rent and interest payments due the latter were also to be reduced): "They are the capitalists in the rural areas and are an indispensable force in the anti-Japanese war and in the battle of production. . . . The policy of the Party is not to weaken capitalism and the bourgeoisie, nor to weaken the rich peasant class and their productive force, but to encourage capitalist production and ally with the rich peasants, on condition that proper improvements are made in the living conditions of the workers." [82]

A mid-1942 Central Committee directive on the staff and workers' movement in the southeast Shansi base area explained at some length why wages were of necessity low in the backward rural areas under wartime conditions, when compared to those in more economically advanced enemy-occupied urban areas. And in discussing agricultural hired labor, it spelled out the approach implicit in the January 1942 document cited above. It thus criticized the militant "worker struggle" attitude of union activists, which it stated rendered such union people undesirable to those hiring agricultural labor. Such activists hold excessive meetings and slow down production, and they sometimes use union authority to bully others, make excessive demands, etc. Harmonizing labor-capital relations and increasing agricultural production were the keys to improved livelihood. Where necessary, the government would mediate to further the principle of benefits to both labor and capital (lao-tzu shuang-fang-ti li-i) and to benefit "all levels and classes." [83]

In the course of cheng-feng, party ideologues such as Ch'en Po-ta and Liu Shao-ch'i carefully dissociated such orthodox Communist labels as "proletarian," "Bolshevik," and "Marxist-Leninist" from the now discredited line of the internationalist faction of the party, and applied them instead to the Maoist policies, now summed up as the "Thought of Mao Tse-tung. "[84] The new "proletarian" outlook, with its strongly nationalist-populist content, had thus been largely separated out from a particular labor class interest and vantage point. [85] But the semantic ambiguities and internationalist Marxist-Leninist ideological underpinnings of the Maoist line[86] reflected continuing "contradictions" and ambivalences which would increasingly manifest themselves after 1949 with the return to the cities, the cementing of close Sino-Soviet ties, and the initiation of high-priority programs of state-sponsored industrialization.

The famous Maoist summing up of party history, adopted on the eve of the CCP Seventh Congress in April 1945, avoided any direct reference to or assessment of the major Communist-led uprisings of the second half of 1927, including Canton. [87] In so doing, it presumably sidestepped any direct challenge to the original Comintern-endorsed appraisals of these events. The resolution specifically cited the 1927 CCP November Plenum as marking the dominance in the party leadership of "a 'Left' line of putschism," though any connection between this November line and the December Canton events was left ambiguously unstated. [88] This oblique approach seemed in keeping with the 1945 resolution's dual purpose: to assert and articulate the Maoist line of "concrete" Chinese revolutionary practice as opposed, most particularly, to the standpoint of the internationalist faction, and to affirm the Maoist place within the orbit of "universal" Marxism-Leninism. [89]

In any event, insofar as the Yenan period was concerned, the symbolism of Canton, particularly as an armed uprising against the KMT, was clearly inappropriate during the national war of resistance --both from the standpoint of the Maoist and the internationalist forces in the CCP. [90] In postliberation China, however, as issues of the worker-peasant, urban-rural relationship reemerged in the new context of socialist construction, the Canton Commune once again seemingly came to play its symbolic political role in both Chinese and Soviet commentaries.

Class Strategies in the Civil War, 1946-1948

The continuing ambivalences in the now supposedly "integrated" Maoist-Marxist-Leninist line of the CCP was manifested in the notion, still strongly held within the party, that the cities were destined to play an ultimately central role as the revolutionary struggle moved towards final victory. In its April 1945 resolution on party history, the CCP had stated that the time had come "to place work in the Japanese-occupied cities on a par with work in the Liberated Areas," in preparation for the shift in "the center of gravity of our work to the cities. This will be a change of historic significance for our Party, which shifted the center of its work to the countryside with so much difficulty after the defeat of the revolution in 1927. . . . When the Japanese-occupied cities are liberated by the people," the resolution continued, "and a unified democratic coalition government is really established and consolidated, the rural base areas will have accomplished their historical task."[91] Thus the city was again juxtaposed to the countryside. The rural bases had played their crucial leading role, but the time was approaching for the cities to assume their natural and appropriate central place for the period of national political power and economic construction ahead.

Yet it soon became evident that the party no longer looked upon this projected shift to the cities either as a restoration of the pivotal revolutionary role of the worker or as the means for ensuring proletarian political hegemony over the revolution's culminating phases. On the contrary, the civil war years after 1945 only served further to reinforce the primary revolutionary position of the countryside and the peasant, while the cities were approached on a multiclass, united front basis in which the theme of urban class conflict remained muted. It is true that in the initial postwar period, in 1945-1946, as the CCP gained control of many small and medium sized urban centers in the wake of the Japanese surrender, a latent "old-proletarian" line towards these new labor constituencies apparently surfaced in some areas, leading to (subsequently criticized) "left adventurist" tendencies in Communist labor policy which again inordinately stressed worker interests and demands.[92]

But the Maoist Party Center consistently maintained its labor-capital line and avoided any notion of anti-capitalist worker struggles. While supporting "appropriate" or "proper" (shih-tang--the standard Maoist qualification since 1940) improvement in workers' livelihood, it continued to place this within the context and confines of the collaborative policy of "mutual benefits for labor and capital" (lao-tzu liang-li). For example, a mid-1946 Yenan dispatch carried the following report from Kalgan (the most important North China urban center held by the Communists at that time): "Increased wages, increased profits and low costs are the outcome of the Labor-Capital Cooperation Policy. now in force in Kalgan, important Communist-led centre of North China. Many private-owned factories in town have speeded up output and netted increased profits after the application of this policy. . . . The employers are to run their factories on a profit basis while the workers must be provided with decent means of living and working conditions and not demand overmuch from the employers, is the common ground of the discussion."[93] And a major <u>Liberation Daily</u> May Day labor policy editorial in 1946 on the tasks of the liberated areas' labor movement reiterated the concept of labor-capital cooperation, stressed the mutual interests of both sides in raising production and the desirability of mutual compromises which took into account the interests of both sides, and pointed to the need to overcome narrowly one-sided "economist" attitudes on the part of labor.[94]

The deepening of the social revolution in the countryside during the 1946-1948 civil war provided the Communists with an even more secure and expanded rural power base. Thus as the CCP began in 1948 to move into the larger urban centers, it was able to stress more than ever its production-oriented united front appeal to the bourgeoisie, to caution against "leftist" labor policies, and to avoid direct revolutionary involvement of urban labor in the liberation struggle.[95]

In February 1948, during the final pre-urban stages of the civil war, Mao stated that even during the 1927-1931 period, when "quite a few" of the national bourgeoisie sided with Chiang Kai-shek, the Communists should have attempted to win over this class politically and to protect them economically, instead of adopting an "adventurist" and "ultra-left" policy towards them. He added that since it was now both desirable and possible to win over the majority of the national bourgeoisie, "we should be prudent in dealing with the economic position of this class and in principle should adopt a blanket policy of protection."[96] Thus in an order issued in April 1948, on the occasion of the Communists securing the city of Loyang, Mao directed that "on entering the city, do not lightly advance slogans of raising wages and reducing working hours," and "do not be in a hurry to organize the people of the city to struggle for democratic reforms and improvements in livelihood."[97] The notion of mounting a workers' struggle in support of the People's Liberation Army was clearly discouraged.

While land policy veered sharply to the left in 1946 and 1947, the Party Center here too sought to avoid the more extreme rural-

proletarian class war line of the Kiangsi period. The confiscatory
land law promulgated by the CCP in October of 1947 thus provided
for land allotments to the landlords, protection of rural commercial
and industrial holdings, and confiscation only of the "surplus" land
and noncommercial properties of the rich peasants.[98] Though again
there were widespread "leftist deviations" at local levels, reminiscent
of the policies of the Kiangsi era,[99] these were sharply criticized
by Mao in his December 1947 report to the Central Committee, in
which he stressed that "there should be no repetition of the wrong
ultra-Left policy, which was carried out in 1931-34, of 'allotting no
land to the landlords and poor land to the rich peasants.'" He also
called for a more careful determination of class status "to avoid the
mistake of classifying middle peasants as rich peasants," and himself
used the more restrictive term, "old-type rich peasants."[100] By
early 1948 the party had taken additional steps to preserve and consolidate its broad peasant base, including the issuance of detailed
definitions of class status which further protected the more prosperous middle peasants from inclusion in the rich peasant category.[101]
Thus despite some reemerging "left" tendencies within the party
during the civil war years, the Maoist leadership carefully eschewed
a proletarian revolutionary line against capitalist forces either in
the countryside or the cities, limiting its targets to the revolutionary
overthrow of rural "feudalism" and the urban takeover of statist
"bureaucrat-capitalism."[102] But rural populist-proletarianism now
faced complex new challenges and accommodations as the party in
1949 at long last shifted its political center to the cities of China.

FOOTNOTES

1. A Sino-Soviet nonaggression pact was signed in August 1937, the result of negotiations which had been in progress for over a year. McLane, Soviet Policy and the Chinese Communists, p. 86. During 1936, Van Slyke has noted, "the Comintern took a much more unconditional position of support for Nanking than did the CCP." Lyman P. Van Slyke, Enemies and Friends: The United Front in Chinese Communist History (Stanford, 1967), p. 64.

2. See Van Slyke, Enemies and Friends, pp. 49-91, for an analysis of united front policy lines of the Comintern and the CCP in this period. See also Lawrence K. Rosinger, China's Wartime Politics (Princeton, 1944), pp. 13-24. To a significant degree, these various pressures and interests were reflected in the complex interplay of forces involved in the resolution of the Chiang kidnapping crisis (the Sian Incident) in December 1936. See Enemies and Friends, pp. 75-89.

3. Ibid., pp. 103-104. See Rosinger, China's Wartime Politics, pp. 96-99, for texts of September 1937 parallel statements on unity by the CCP and Chiang Kai-shek.

4. Klein and Clark, Biographic Dictionary, I, 130-131.

5. Whitson, Chinese High Command, pp. 209-211.

6. CCP Political Bureau, "Resolution on Preparation for Convocation of the Seventh Party Congress" (December 13, 1937), in Kuo, Analytical History, III, 366-367. Wang Ming probably controlled at least four votes in the nine-man Political Bureau Standing Committee after this December 1937 Political Bureau Conference in Yenan. Richard C. Thornton, China: The Struggle for Power, 1917-1972 (Bloomington, 1973), p. 108.

7. "Tang Wang Ming Hui Tao Yenan Shih" [When Wang Ming returned to Yenan], in Sheng-huo tsai Yenan [Life in Yenan], compiled by Lu P'ing (Sian, 1938), pp. 57-66; also see Kuo, Analytical History, III, 326-327.

126

8. See text of Wang Ming's statement to the December 1937 CCP
    Political Bureau Conference, "The Current Situation and Tasks
    in the War of Resistance," in Kuo, Analytical History, III, 360-
    364; Wang Ming, "The New Stage of Japanese Aggression and
    the New Period of the Struggle of the Chinese People," Commu-
    nist International, XIV: 10 (October 1937), 719-736; and Chen
    Shao-yui [sic], "For the Consolidation and Extension of the Anti-
    Japanese National United Front," Communist International, XV: 5
    (May 1938), 461-465. For a recent delineation of Wang Ming's
    united front strategy which stresses his focus on urban anti-
    Japanese national consciousness, see Tetsuya Kataoka, Resistance
    and Revolution in China. The Communists and the Second United
    Front (Berkeley, 1974).

9. Wang, "New Stage of Japanese Aggression," p. 734. Wang was
    presumably still in Moscow when this article was written.

10. Ibid., p. 735.

11. Ibid., p. 735-736.

12. Ibid., pp. 721-722.

13. Ibid., p. 733. In the post-1949 period the CCP leadership offi-
    cially castigated Wang for his allegedly "capitulationist" views
    regarding the CCP role in the united front with the KMT in the
    early wartime years. A 1962 CCP commentary, in listing these
    "errors" of the Wang Ming faction in the wartime period, declared
    that this group "lacked a sufficient understanding of the long dura-
    tion of the war in China and held in contempt the Communist-led
    people's armed forces and their guerrilla fighting as well as the
    role played by our bases behind the enemy lines in the war of
    resistance. On the other hand, they exaggerated the role played
    by big cities and Kuomintang troops and placed the hope for vic-
    tory on the 'regular war' fought by the Kuomintang troops." Hu
    Hua, ed., Lectures on the History of the Chinese Revolution
    (1962), p. 382; cited in Kuo, Analytical History, III, 469. Wang's
    reassertion of his urban-proletarian outlook in these early wartime
    years was reflected in his republication of Struggle for Bolshevi-
    zation in Yenan, March 1940. The Maoist leadership acknowledge
    in 1945 that Wang's treatise had not only represented the "left"
    line in the CCP in 1931, but "was taken by people then, and for

another ten years or more, to have played a 'correct program-
matic role,' . . ." "Resolution on Questions in Party History,"
pp. 187-188.

14. Wang, "New Stage of Japanese Aggression," p. 735.

15. Ibid. In the years after 1937 there was in fact a flow of students
     and intellectuals from the coastal cities to Yenan, motivated
     largely by strong nationalist anti-Japanese sentiments. Schram,
     Mao Tse-tung, pp. 189-190. Though these elements did indeed
     often bring a new urban outlook and skills to the countryside,
     these individuals were themselves integrated into the rural
     environment to serve the needs of the expanding liberated areas.
     Though their skills and training were valued and utilized by the
     Border Region government, it was precisely the urban outlook
     which was "rectified" in conformity with the peasant-based and
     village-centered policies and tasks of the Maoist cheng-feng
     movement of the early 1940s. Selden, Yenan Way in Revolution-
     ary China, pp. 205-206.

16. Wang Ming, "The Struggle of the Chinese People Against the
     Japanese Aggressor, and the Great Socialist Revolution in the
     U.S.S.R.," Communist International, XIV: 12 (December 1937),
     992-1001. Wang acclaimed the fact that there was now "the
     beginning of the establishment of a single state power for the
     whole of China, headed by the Nanking national government.
     Although the composition of the Nanking government," he went
     on, "which still includes pro-Japanese elements, is far from
     satisfying the demands of the serious military situation and the
     desires of the whole of the Chinese people, it is becoming an
     undoubted fact that, following the example of the reorganized
     Soviet regions, all the local authorities in the provinces are
     beginning to subordinate themselves to this government. Thereby,
     the Nanking government is beginning to become a real government
     for the whole of China" (ibid., p. 996). Wang stressed also "The
     beginning of the process of the democratization of the political
     regime and the growth of the mass movement and the mass orga-
     nizations" (p. 997).

17. Cited in Roy, Revolution and Counter-Revolution in China, p. 657,
     from an article by Anna Louise Strong in Asia (August 1938).
     Wang went on to say that it was "Our hope that the Kuo Min Tang

will strengthen itself by getting rid of corrupt officials, reactionaries and traitors" (ibid.).

18. Ch'en Shao-yü, "Chin-nien-ti wu-i chieh yü Chung-kuo kung-jen" [This year's May 1 holiday and the Chinese workers], Hsin-hua jih-pao [New China daily] (Hankow), May 1, 1938, p. 1.

19. Whitson, Chinese High Command, pp. 212-213.

20. Ch'en, Mao and the Chinese Revolution, p. 250; Israel Epstein, The People's War (London, 1939), pp. 262-263. Epstein writes, based on his 1938 experiences with the New Fourth Army and interviews with its commander, Yeh T'ing, that "the New Fourth Army must function within a definite allotted territory, under military and civil administrations that were there before it arrived on the scene. . . . It must depend upon the [Eastern] War Zone headquarters for its general orders, finances, and supplies. . . . Moreover, in its campaign for popular support, it cannot carry out democratic administrative reforms or decree the reduction of the rent and tax burdens borne by the people, as was done by the Border [Region] Government" (pp. 262-263).

21. Epstein, People's War, p. 275.

22. Wang wrote in his 1974 posthumous account that a "Mao-Liu alliance" had been formed at the 1938 Sixth Plenum, on the basis of which Mao was subsequently able to carry out the 1942-1944 rectification movement. Moscow radio, May 28, 1974.

23. Whitson, Chinese High Command, pp. 213, 220-221. Whitson notes that, as a result of the Nationalist attack on the headquarters unit of the New Fourth Army in January 1941, "Ironically, the last Communist unit that still retained some sympathy for the United Front was eliminated by the Nationalists" (p. 220).

24. Ibid., p. 220.

25. For example, Ch'i Hua, "Kung-jen tou-cheng-ti hsien chieh-tuan" [The current stage of the workers' struggle], Chieh-fang [Liberation] (Yenan), May 9, 1937, pp. 19-22; "Chung-Kung chung-yang kuan-yü k'ai-chan chih-kung yün-tung yü wu-i kung-tso-ti chüeh-ting" [CC, CCP decision on promoting the staff-workers movement and May Day work], Liberation, May 1, 1939, p. 6.

26. For autobiographical sketch, see Helen Foster Snow (Nym Wales), The Chinese Communists: Sketches and Autobiographies of the Old Guard (Westport, Conn., 1972), pp. 229-249. Helen Snow has erroneously romanized her name as Liu Chien-hsien.

27. Howard L. Boorman, ed., Biographical Dictionary of Republican China (New York, 1967), I, 386. Po Ku and Liu Ch'ün-hsien were subsequently divorced (ibid.). Liu apparently later lost her important role in the Border Region labor movement. A north Shensi guerrilla fighter from the early 1930s, Kao Ch'ang-chiu later became head of the Border Region Labor Union and Minister of Construction in the Border Region government. Li Kuang, ed., Ti-liu tz'u ch'üan-kuo lao-tung ta-hui [The Sixth National Labor Congress] (Hong Kong, October 1948), Appendix I, pp. 60-61.

28. Liu Ch'ün-hsien, "Pien ch'ü kung-jen-ti chi-nien wu-i lao-tung chieh" [Border region workers' commemoration of the May 1 labor holiday], New China Daily, May 1, 1938, p. 2.

29. Inside Red China, p. 197.

30. Ibid., p. 198.

31. "Yin-shua kung-jen-men-ti sheng-huo" [The life of printing workers], in Life in Yenan, p. 135. The author notes that the more than 100 workers in this Border Region printing factory had come from the major industrial centers of China, and many had been in the Red Army and on the Long March from Kiangsi, and thus represented a concentration of "revolutionary workers" from the entire country (p. 133).

32. "Labor Policy and Tax Policy for Developing Industry," Part 1, NCNA, North Shensi radio, April 26, 1948, in Foreign Broadcast Information Service (FBIS) (Washington, DC), April 27, 1948, p. PPP4.

33. Ch'en Shao-yü, "This Year's May 1 Holiday and the Chinese Workers"; Po Ku, "Chin-nien wu-i ho Chung-kuo kung-jen" [This year's May 1 and the Chinese workers], New China Daily (Chung-king), May 1, 1940, p. 1; Hsü T'iao-hsin, "Ta hou-fang kung-jen tui-yü k'ang-chan-ti kung-hsien chi ch'i sheng-huo" [Regarding

the resistance war contributions of the workers in the great rear (KMT) area and their livelihood], New China Daily, May 1, 1940, p. 4.

34. Wu K'o-chien, "Lun ti-hou chung-hsin ch'eng-shih kung-jen yün-tung-ti kung-tso" [On labor movement work in the central cities in the enemy-occupied areas], New China Daily, May 1, 1940, p. 4. The writer argued against the tendency to "disparage" the workers' movement now that the major cities had come under Japanese occupation.

35. For a discussion of the problems facing the Border Region in the 1941-1942 period and the Maoist response in the policies associated with the cheng-feng movement, see Selden, Yenan Way in Revolutionary China, pp. 177-276.

36. Thornton, The Struggle for Power, pp. 134-137.

37. For a heavily concentrated focus on the role of the nationalist factor in this mobilization, see Chalmers A. Johnson, Peasant Nationalism and Communist Power (Stanford, 1962).

38. Mao Tse-tung, "Reply of the Chinese Soviets to Program of the National Salvation Union, " China Today (New York), III: 4 (January 1937), 42.

39. Ibid.

40. See n. 70, below.

41. Mao Tse-tung, "Tasks of the Anti-Japanese United Front in China, " Communist International, XIV: 11 (November 1937), 826-827. This article is a "somewhat abbreviated" version of Mao's major report and concluding remarks to the conference. Fuller, less oblique, but possibly revised texts of these reports appear in SW, I, "The Tasks of the Chinese Communist Party in the Period of Resistance to Japan" (May 3, 1937), pp. 263-283; and "Win the Masses in Their Millions for the Anti-Japanese National United Front" (May 7, 1937), pp. 285-294. In the SW version Mao more specifically spelled out the developing role of the CCP as the leader of this national-democratic phase of the revolution, in contradistinction to what he termed the eco-

nomically and politically "flabby" bourgeoisie. "Our democratic republic is to be established in the course of national armed resistance under the leadership of the proletariat. . . . Therefore, though it will still be a bourgeois-democratic state socially and economically, yet it will be different from the general run of bourgeois republics because, in concrete political terms, it will have to be a state based on the alliance of the working class, the peasantry, the petty bourgeoisie and the bourgeoisie. Thus, as to the future of the democratic republic, though it may move in a capitalist direction, the possibility also exists that it will turn towards socialism, and the party of the Chinese proletariat should struggle hard for the latter prospect" (I, 275).

42. "Tasks of the Anti-Japanese United Front in China," pp. 829-830.

43. T. A. Bisson, Yenan in June 1937: Talks with the Communist Leaders, China Research Monograph No. 11 (Berkeley, 1973), pp. 58-59. See n. 41, above, for the correspondence between these ideas and the SW version of Mao's May 1937 report to the Yenan party conference.

44. Extracts from Kuusinen's speech (originally published in Pravda, May 19, 1964), in Carrère d'Encausse and Schram, Marxism and Asia, p. 333.

45. Documentary History, pp. 258-259. In mid-1938 Mao delineated the CCP's popular mobilization strategy in establishing base areas: through the anti-Japanese struggle "the people are to be aroused and home guards and additional guerrilla detachments formed. Through these struggles mass organizations of labourers, peasants, youth, women, children, merchants and professionals are to be formed and developed--keeping step with the degree of the people's political consciousness and their heightening sentiment for struggle." Aspects of China's Anti-Japanese Struggle (Bombay, 1948), p. 68; also in SW, II, in somewhat revised form, as "Problems of Strategy in Guerrilla War Against Japan," 79-112.

46. Mao Tse-tung, The New Stage (Chungking, New China Information Committee, n.d.). This report is in SW in somewhat revised and much abbreviated (only the final section) form, entitled "The Role of the Chinese Communist Party in the National War," II, 195-211.

Stuart Schram, The Political Thought of Mao Tse-tung (New York, 1969), includes a substantial extract from the final section of the original Mao report, offering a translation based, he states, "partly on the New China Information Committee translation, with extensive revisions" (p. 171, n. 1). I have utilized and cited all three versions where appropriate.

47. The New Stage, pp. 63-64.

48. Schram, Political Thought of Mao Tse-tung, p. 172.

49. Ibid., pp. 172-173.

50. The SW version spells this out more specifically: "The great strength of Marxism-Leninism lies precisely in its integration with the concrete revolutionary practice of all countries. For the Chinese Communist Party it is a matter of learning to apply the theory of Marxism-Leninism to the specific circumstances of China" (II, 209).

51. Owen Lattimore, "The International Position of China Today," Asia Quarterly (Tokyo), III: 4 (October 1971), 187. On this same issue, Schram notes and corrects (as does the SW version) a deliberate distortion of Mao's clear intent in the sentences of The New Stage translation immediately following Mao's criticisms of "foreign stereotypes" and his call for "a new and vital Chinese style and manner." Whereas Mao stressed the need to give "national form" to "internationalist content," The New Stage version subtly turned this around to stress the danger of separating internationalist content from nationalist form, and inserted the following sentences not found in the original Mao text: "Such a separation leads to telling the backward masses [the peasantry?] what they like to hear, that is the paean of praise about their own country. This is an actual promotion of chauvinism, not the work of internationalists" (p. 75).

Schram speculates that "Po Ku (Ch'in Pang-hsien) may have had something to do with it." Political Thought of Mao Tse-tung, p. 173, n. 1. The New Stage was published in Chungking by the New China Information Committee, probably in 1939. Po Ku, one of the leaders in the CCP's internationalist wing, served in Chungking as a liaison official with the National Government in the 1938-

1940 period, and was a leading member of the CCP's Yangtze Bureau headed by Wang Ming, who was also in Chungking during the latter part of 1939. See Klein and Clark, Biographic Dictionary, I, 199 and 132; and Kuo, Analytical History, IV, 133. One surmises that these leaders reacted to Mao's criticism of "foreign stereotypes" (clearly referring to present and/or past policy differences) and inserted these sentences as a counter-criticism of Mao's strongly independent nationalist position.

52. "The Chinese Revolution and the Chinese Communist Party" (December 1939), SW, II, 305-334; "On New Democracy" (January 1940), II, 339-384. Only the second section of the former essay is entirely attributed to Mao, but this is the only section I will cite. These texts have been checked against earlier (and inferior) translations of the originals, and any substantive differences will be noted. These earlier translations are: The Chinese Revolution and the CCP (Shanghai: China Digest, 1949); and China's New Democracy (New York: New Century Publishers, 1945), originally published in Chinese Culture, January 15, 1941.

53. SW, II, 316-317. The transformation of "backward villages" into "advanced" base areas in no way implied a process of external proletarianization analogous to that of Kiangsi period policies. Also, Mao's statement that "victory . . . can be won first in the rural areas" seemed to be a deliberate paraphrasing of the pre-1935 CI-CCP formula of "victory first in one or several provinces"--a strategic concept specifically linked to the more immediate takeover of cities.

54. Ibid., p. 317.

55. Ibid., p. 318. The earlier text stated: "Again, we can understand, that in carrying out propaganda and organization work of the Communist Party in the reactionary and corrupt cities, towns and rural districts long occupied by our enemies, we must not adopt a line of impatient adventurism, but contrarily we must lie low to prepare ourselves, waiting for the opportune moment." The Chinese Revolution and the CCP (1949), p. 9.

The tendency to view the cities as "reactionary and corrupt" centers, rather than as China's industrial and proletarian heartland and potentially the most advanced centers of revolution, is a striking thread in Maoist thinking. Thus in a speech to the 1969 First Plenum of the Ninth Central Committee, Mao extolled the austerity, self-sacrifice and egalitarianism of the Communist cadres during the years of struggle in the countryside, and then added: "Now we have entered the cities. To enter the cities is a good thing. If we hadn't entered the cities, Chiang Kai-shek would have continued to occupy them. However, to enter the cities is also a bad thing, because it debilitates our Party." "Mao Tse-tung's Speech to the First Plenary Session of the CCP's Ninth Central Committee" (April 28, 1969), Issues and Studies (Taipei), VI: 6 (March 1970), 98.

56. André Malraux, Anti-Memoirs (New York, 1968), p. 369.

57. SW, II, 326. Note the significant shift from earlier CI-CCP commentary which cited the working class role in and the program of the Canton Commune as evidence that the revolution in colonial and semicolonial countries could and would follow the Soviet Russian path to proletarian dictatorship.

58. Ibid., p. 327. The earlier version does not pinpoint the base areas as being such prototypes, referring more generally to "the anti-Japanese democratic regime which should be set up," though the model of the base areas is implied. The Chinese Revolution and the CCP (1949), p. 16.

59. SW, II, 329.

60. Ibid., p. 350. In the 1941 text Mao was less explicit in stating that the Soviet form of republic "is fermenting in the various capitalist countries." China's New Democracy, p. 26.

61. SW, II, 350.

62. This was further spelled out in 1951, in key CCP thirtieth-anniversary statements at that time. One authoritative article by the party's Propaganda Department head declared that "Mao Tse-tung's theory of the Chinese revolution is a new development of Marxism-Leninism in the revolutions of the colonial and semicolonial countries and especially in the Chinese revolution." Thus the "classic type of revolution in imperialist [i.e., advanced capitalist] countries is the October Revolution. The classic type of

revolution in colonial and semicolonial countries is the Chinese revolution." Mao's theory of the Chinese revolution is therefore "a contribution of universal significance to the world Communist movement." Lu Ting-yi, "The World Significance of the Chinese Revolution," NCNA, Peking, June 25, 1951.

McLane notes that the Soviets ignored Mao's On New Democracy and his other major theoretical works written during that same period. McLane states that despite Anna Louise Strong's claim that On New Democracy was published in Moscow in 1940 and hailed as "a new Marxist classic" during the war, "no record of these editions has been found." Soviet Policy and the Chinese Communists, p. 145, nn. 341 and 342.

Benjamin Schwartz has pointed out that though in their initial pre-1948 phase the "People's Democracies" in Eastern Europe contained policy resemblances to Mao's New Democracy program, neither at that time nor later in the various Soviet analyses of the theory of people's democracy "do we find any acknowledgment of Mao's professed theoretical innovations in these matters." "China and the Soviet Theory of People's Democracy" (1954), in Communism and China: Ideology in Flux (Cambridge, 1968), p. 51.

During the 1947-1948 civil war period, in line with the CCP's more direct united front appeal to the urban middle classes, the national bourgeoisie emerged more affirmatively as a component element of the joint dictatorship and were accorded such status in 1949 under the political formula of the "people's democratic dictatorship." See "On People's Democratic Dictatorship" (June 30, 1949), SW, IV, 417.

One may note here a 1927 Stalin comment, following the CCP break with the Wuhan government in July 1927: "The opposition apparently think that blocs with the national bourgeoisie in colonial countries should be long-lived. But only people who have lost the last remnants of Leninism can think that . . ." "China" (extracts from a speech on "The International Situation and the Defence of the U.S.S.R." [August 1, 1927]), in Stalin on China, p. 100.

"Speech to an Enlarged Work Conference of the Central Committee,

136

CCP," in <u>Translations on Communist China</u>, No. 109, <u>JPRS</u>
50792 (June 23, 1970), p. 47.

66. <u>Ibid.</u>, p. 48. Mao commented further that "Regarding this objective world of China, for a long time even we did not clearly recognize it, much less our foreign comrades" (<u>ibid.</u>).

67. Klaus Maehnel, "The Economic Policy of the Mao Tse-tung Clique," <u>Wirtschafts Wissenschaft</u>, No. 6 (East Berlin, 1968), in <u>Chinese Economic Studies</u>, III: 1 (Fall 1969), 53. This source gives a translation of this entire article (pp. 48-69).

68. Anna Louise Strong, "The Thought of Mao Tse-tung," <u>Amerasia</u>, XI: 6 (June 1947), 161.

69. <u>Ibid.</u>, p. 162.

70. "On Policy" (December 25, 1940), <u>SW</u>, II, 441-449. The policies outlined in this <u>SW</u> version of the directive are in accord with Chinese Communist pronouncements of the early 1940s.

71. <u>Ibid.</u>

72. <u>Ibid.</u>, p. 447.

73. <u>Ibid.</u>, pp. 445-446.

74. Selden, <u>Yenan Way in Revolutionary China</u>, pp. 208-276.

75. Teng Fa, "Lun kung-ying kung-ch'ang tang yü chih-kung-hui kung-tso" [On the work of the party and trade unions in the public factories], <u>Liberation Daily</u>, May 1, 1943. Teng Fa was the overall head of labor organizations; this was the text of his closing speech to a Factories Conference in Yenan which marked a highpoint in the labor-industry rectification campaign.

76. <u>Ibid.</u>

77. "Hsiang Mo-fan Chao Chan-k'uei hsüeh-hsi [Learn from model hero Chao Chan-k'uei], <u>Liberation Daily</u>, September 11, 1942. A follow-up editorial on December 22, 1942, called implementation of this movement the current main task of the unions.

78. Ibid.

79. Ch'en Po-ta's 1948 comments concerning these pre-cheng-feng policies have been cited in this chapter.

80. The Challenge of Red China (New York, 1945), p. 177.

81. See Selden, Yenan Way in Revolutionary China, pp. 229-237. Though this campaign was limited to reducing rent and interest while simultaneously guaranteeing their payment, Selden observes that the movement "initiated a more militant effort to break the social and economic grip of the landlords through organized peasant power" (132).

Major Liberation Daily editorial articles appeared during the 1942-1946 period on the rent reduction campaign, emphasizing its importance as a mass struggle movement for activating the peasantry and for helping to create basic level mass organizations as the foundation of the new political power. For example, "Develop the Rent Reduction Mass Movement" ("Fa-chan ch'ün-chung chien-tsu yün-tung"), November 15, 1943.

82. "Decision of the Central Committee on Land Policy in the Anti-Japanese Base Areas" (January 28, 1942), in Documentary History, pp. 276-285. This directive has been attributed to Mao in mainland Chinese sources. Selden, Yenan Way in Revolutionary China, p. 231, n. 27.

83. "Central Committee Directive on the Staff and Workers' Movement of the Southeast Shansi Anti-Japanese Base" ("Chung-yang tui chin-tung-nan k'ang-Jih ken chü-ti chin-kung yün-tung-ti chih-shih"), Liberation Daily, May 1, 1942.

84. See Ch'en Po-ta, Notes on Mao Tse-tung's "Report of an Investigation into the Peasant Movement in Hunan" (Spring 1944) (Peking, 1954); Ch'en Po-ta, Notes on Ten Years of Civil War, 1927-1936 (Spring 1944), (Peking, 1954); and Liu Shao-ch'i, "Liquidate the Menshevist Ideology within the Party" (July 1, 1943), Collected Works of Liu Shao-ch'i Before 1944, pp. 437-447; Liu Shao-ch'i, "On the Party" (May 1945 report to the Seventh CCP Congress), Collected Works of Liu Shao-ch'i, 1945-1957 (Hong Kong, 1969), pp. 9-95.

85. See n. 15, above.

86. This was illustrated in the carefully balanced ideological formulation contained in the new party constitution adopted in 1945 by the CCP Seventh Congress: "The CCP takes the theories of Marxism-Leninism and the combined principles derived from the practical experience of the Chinese revolution--the ideas [thought] of Mao Tse-tung--as the guiding principles of all its work." Documentary History, p. 422.

87. "Resolution on Questions in the History of Our Party," pp. 177-225.

88. Ibid., pp. 181-182. Later CCP commentaries on Canton, written from the Maoist perspective of the late 1950s, would indicate that any adventurism associated with that uprising was primarily related to its urban-centered outlook and strategy, rather than to its notion of taking up armed revolutionary struggle under unfavorable circumstances per se. See Chapter 6 of this study.

89. "Ever since its birth in 1921," the resolution began, "the CCP has made the integration of the universal truth of Marxism-Leninism with the concrete practice of the Chinese revolution the guiding principle of its work, and Comrade Mao Tse-tung's theory and practice of the Chinese revolution represent this integration." The party's great achievements and current unprecedented strength and solidarity, it added, had come about because it "firmly adhered to the correct Marxist-Leninist line and waged a victorious struggle against all erroneous ideas opposed to this line" (ibid., pp. 177-178).

90. As one indication of this, the December 11 Commune anniversary date, which had been one of the prescribed holidays in the labor law of the Kiangsi period, was no longer included among the labor holidays in the Border Region's 1940 collective labor contract regulations. "Shen-Kan-Ning Border Region Standard Regulations for Wartime Collective Contracts" (November 1, 1940), in Compendium of Policies and Regulations of the Anti-Japanese Base Areas: Shen-Kan-Ning Area (K'ang-Jih ken chü-ti cheng-ts'e t'iao-li hui-chi: Shen-Kan-Ning chih-pu) (n.p., n.d.), pp. 258-259.

91. "Resolution on Questions in the History of Our Party," pp. 200-201.

92. See Kenneth Lieberthal, "'Mao Versus Liu?' Policy Towards Industry and Commerce, 1946-49," China Quarterly, 47 (July-September 1971), 494-520, for a recent discussion of these CCP urban policy lines. As I have indicated above, I do not agree with Lieberthal's view that in the early postwar period (1946-1947) the CCP once again acted as "the political party of the workers" (p. 498). I am presently completing a detailed study of CCP labor policy from 1936-1948 in which the points made briefly in this chapter will be greatly amplified and reinforced.

93. NCNA, August 28, 1946, transmitting an August 25 report from Kalgan, in United States Information Service (Shanghai), August 29, 1946, p. 1.

For a contemporary sympathetic journalist's account of CCP labor-capital policies in Kalgan in 1946, see Anna Louise Strong, The Chinese Conquer China (New York, 1949), pp. 139-148. She probably gives an overblown version of the benefits accruing to both labor and capital in Communist-ruled Kalgan, but the policy line followed is clear enough.

94. "The Tasks of the Staff and Workers' Movement in the Liberated Areas" ("Chieh-fang ch'ü chih-kung yün-tung-ti jen-wu"), April 30, 1946, p. 1.

95. The CCP in the civil war years described its struggle targets as imperialism, feudalism (the agrarian revolution), and "bureaucrat-capitalism"--with this last identified with the KMT-run state economic apparatus.

96. "On the Policy Concerning Industry and Commerce" (February 27, 1948), SW, IV, 209.

97. "Telegram to the Headquarters of the Loyang Front After the Recapture of the City" (April 18, 1948), SW, IV, 248.

98. See Frank C. Lee, "Land Redistribution in Communist China," Pacific Affairs, XXI: 1 (March 1948), 30-32, for text of this law.

99. These leftist policies (the "poor-and-hired peasant line") are graphically described in William Hinton, Fanshen (New York, 1966).

100. "The Present Situation and Our Tasks," pp. 164-165. See also the Mao-drafted innerparty directive, "On Some Important Problems of the Party's Present Policy" (January 18, 1948), SW, IV, 181-189. In it, Mao stressed the need to "distinguish between the new rich peasants and the old rich peasants" (p. 184).

101. At the end of 1947 the CCP Central Committee reissued, with modifications, the documents on rural class status which had been drawn up under Mao's auspices in Kiangsi in 1933 during the Land Investigation Movement, and which had become a source of contention between Mao and the party leadership at that time. See Chapter 4, n. 19. In the modified definitions, a middle peasant could receive up to 25 percent of his gross income (instead of 15 percent in the 1933 version) from rent, loans, or the use of hired labor, before being classified as a rich peasant. Chao Kuo-chün, Agrarian Policy of the Chinese Communist Party, 1921-1959 (New Delhi, 1960), pp. 79-80.

102. See in particular the January 18, 1948, directive referred to in n. 100, above.

MAOIST IDEOLOGICAL, CLASS, AND
DEVELOPMENTAL PATTERNS IN POSTLIBERATION CHINA
AND THE NEW SYMBOLISM OF CANTON

The Urban Multiclass and Rural Populist Bases of Maoist
Socialist Construction

The return to the cities as the center of gravity in 1949, the impact of an urban labor constituency, the renewal and reinforcement of the Soviet tie, and the compelling pressures on the CCP to be guided and assisted along the unfamiliar and uncharted path of social-ist industrialization by the example of the Soviet Russian model--all these brought the "rural" and "urban" outlooks and forces in Chinese Communism into a new, uneasy and potentially unstable combination. [1] But the impact of the massive and poor countryside and of the forces and policies which had shaped the Chinese revolution, reflecting as they did to a greater degree the "concrete practice" and "national characteristics" of China ("the objective world of China," as Mao put it in 1962), eventually again came strongly and sharply to the fore, though, in Maoist fashion, often accompanied semantically by a coopting of the ideological formulas of internationalist Communist orthodoxy.

The early 1950s thus witnessed major new trends in party policy which reflected not only the new circumstances and pressures noted above, but also the still strongly held Communist conviction of the unquestioned primacy of accelerated state socialist industrialization, for which the Soviet Russian model remained the standard and guide. [2] These were years marked by initial efforts greatly to expand the urban proletarian component of the party's membership, [3] by an emphasis on production-oriented incentive wage policies and differentials, [4] and by a policy of high priority development of a capital intensive heavy in-dustrial base. [5] Mao was to observe in 1962, in reference to these earlier policies, "Since we were inexperienced we had to imitate the Soviet Union in the field of building the economy, especially in heavy industry in which we imitated the Soviet Union in almost everything and had very few creations of our own. "[6]

Yet at the same time, pre-1949 Maoist patterns also retained a significant place. A nationwide agrarian reform movement carried out from 1950-1952, which carefully focused on "feudal" (landlord) struggle

141

targets,[7] served as a vital key to the Communist consolidation of power, while in the urban centers, labor-capital class collaboration remained a dominant if rather ambiguous theme. And when Mao moved in mid-1955 vastly to accelerate the pace of agricultural cooperativization, the campaign was portrayed not as a new class war against the small minority of rich peasants (the "kulaks" of Soviet terminology) and the more prosperous of the middle peasants, but rather as a broad mass movement of the poorer peasantry (the poor and lower middle peasants) comprising over 70 percent of the rural population.[8] In this approach, the interests of the upper middle peasants were given some consideration, with even the vast majority of the rich peasants admitted into the cooperatives by 1956 as regular or probationary members.[9]

It is also noteworthy that the nationwide move to agricultural cooperatives in 1955-1956 was accompanied by an initial Maoist questioning (as I shall indicate below) of an urban-industrial policy bias which continued largely to prevail through the First Five Year Plan ending in 1957. And in pushing for large-scale socialization of agriculture before its mechanization could be accomplished on any significant scale,[10] Mao asserted his faith in the vast potential of a socialized though backward and poverty-stricken countryside,[11] and also in effect undercut the role which the urban industrial sector was ultimately expected to play in "leading" the peasants to socialism. Whereas the Soviet collectivization drive of 1929-1930 relied heavily on urban worker and party activists sent to lead the villages, the Chinese campaign utilized and built further upon indigenous rural leadership forces.[12] Agricultural socialization in fact preceded and in turn apparently helped accelerate the 1956 nationalization of urban private industry and commerce. The "upsurge" in agricultural cooperation also brought a full return to a policy of massive party recruitment in the countryside and a final tacit abandonment of the post-1949 theme of party proletarianization.[13]

Policy ambivalences within the CCP in the early postliberation years were perhaps most strikingly evident in the handling of the question of the national capitalists (affirmed by Mao in 1949 to be one of the four classes comprising the people's democratic dictatorship) during the wu-fan (five-anti) movement in 1952. In this movement the national bourgeoisie in Shanghai and other cities were struggled against, with the specific target the alleged corrupt and illegal practices of many of the businessmen. At the same time, however,

the pressures generated by the campaign were used to begin the
phased and partially compensatory process of socialist transformation
of private industry and commerce.   In a reflection of the ambivalent
elements in the campaign, the CCP's ideological journal at the time,
Hsüeh-hsi (Study), took a harshly antagonistic "class struggle" line
towards the bourgeoisie in the earlier phases of the campaign, but
suspended publication in April 1952 after carrying in its last issue
Mao's newly published essay, "On Contradiction," together with a
covering article by the journal's editorial board exhorting its readers
to study the Mao essay as a weapon in overcoming "dogmatism and
Party jargon"--sins which the editors confessed to, citing the journal's
recent articles "on the question of the bourgeoisie."[14]   In a subsequent
"self-examination" article on resuming publication in August, the editors
rejected their former approach to the bourgeoisie as an "antagonistic"
class.   Ignoring Mao's precepts in "On Contradiction" had led to "a
failure to understand the character of the national bourgeoisie and the
policy adopted towards them as a whole."[15]   (A major CCP fiftieth
anniversary article in 1971 noted the policy followed in gradually
transforming private enterprise "in accordance with the policy of re-
demption.   Some people, afflicted with impetuosity, found this process
not to their satisfaction and thought the transition period far too long;
they wanted the problem to be solved overnight.   This 'Left' deviation
was overcome relatively quickly through education.")[16]

Thus in the socialist transformation of China's private capitalists,
the state in 1956 adopted a policy of annual dividend payments to the
former owners of such nationalized enterprises.   These interest payments (set then at 5 percent of the assessed value of their invested
capital) were to run for seven years, but the payments were later
extended to 1965, and subsequently apparently beyond that date as
well.[17]   In his fascinating account of the role of "Red capitalists" in
China, based on a two-month 1966 survey of China's industrial establishment, Barry Richman writes that "Under the joint state-private
enterprise setup [the basic form of nationalization adopted in 1956]
numerous capitalists were urged to stay on as managers of their
nationalized firms (usually at their former salaries), but they were
to do so under state direction and party leadership.   In addition to
a party secretary, directors and vice-directors were appointed by the
state to run these firms."[18]   Mao himself, in a recently available
December 1956 talk to private industry and commerce representatives,
pointed to differences from the Soviet pattern in the Chinese approach
to the socialist transformation of the private capitalists.   "We have

reformed all capitalist industrialists and businessmen, eliminating them as a class and taking them all into our fold as individuals." Mao added that the workers did not "understand" the party's policy because "in the past, they have had conflicts with the capitalists in the factory."[19]

A recent analysis of the wu-fan campaign notes· that even during the Cultural Revolution of 1966-1969 there was a relative lack of interest in the bourgeoisie as a class: "While a few capitalists have been held up as objects for condemnation, the majority of them (and there are still ninety thousand in Shanghai alone) have not."[20] It was in fact "neo-bourgeois" elements of the state socialist bureaucracy ("capitalist-roaders") that became prime targets of "class struggle" in the Cultural Revolution.

Benjamin Schwartz in 1954 discerningly examined the significant divergences between the Maoist new democracy--people's democratic dictatorship formula of 1949 and the Soviet concept of people's democracy--used to describe the East European Communist states after World War II. Schwartz noted that people's democracy, particularly in its more fully formulated and mature form after 1948, was closely identified with the Soviet path to socialism, including the policy of bitter class struggle against both the bourgeoisie and the kulaks, and the transition to a dictatorship of the proletariat.[21] (People's democracy would thus appear to have been essentially an updating of the earlier China-applied Comintern formula of the democratic dictatorship of workers and peasants.) Post-1949 Soviet writings, Schwartz added, continued to classify China as a people's democracy in Soviet-defined terms. "However different China's people's democratic development may have been in its earlier phases, in its latter phase there can be only one path of development for any people's democracy--the Soviet path. On its way to socialism, China must be transformed into a 'dictatorship of the proletariat'; it must pass through a period of bitter 'class struggle' against bourgeoisie and kulaks."[22] (Mao was to observe to André Malraux in 1965 that Stalin had known nothing at all about peasants. "There is no sense in confusing your Kulaks with the poverty-stricken people of the underdeveloped countries.")[23]

In the wake of the Khrushchev attack on Stalin at the Twentieth Congress of the CPSU in 1956, the CCP leadership increasingly assumed a more vigorously independent political and ideological stance within the international Communist movement. In that context, the CCP began in

1956 to describe China as also an example of a dictatorship of the proletariat, though with the crucially important ideological proviso that "in China it is a people's democratic dictatorship led by the working class"[24]--still the basic 1949 Mao description of the Peking government. In effect, the CCP affirmed the suitability and orthodoxy of its particular political patterns and policies for the entire socialist stage of the Chinese revolution, thus dispensing with awkward questions of transition and avoiding the ideological and policy implications of the Soviet concept of proletarian dictatorship. At the same time, this formulation gave the Chinese model the advanced status and leadership potential in the Communist world of such a proletarian dictatorship.[25] Thus the same 1956 editorial article pointed specifically to the CCP's wartime successes in winning over the "middle forces" (primarily the national bourgeoisie and urban democratic parties and groupings), in contrast to the Stalin formula of directing "the main blow" at such forces. The article noted that during the 1927-1936 period "some of our comrades crudely applied this formula of Stalin's to China's revolution by turning their main attack on the middle forces."[26]

A 1958 history of the CCP, written for cadre training purposes at a time of strong Maoist ideological resurgence, reinforced these points in its discussion of the Sixth CCP Congress of 1928.[27] "The Congress believed," it stated, "that the national bourgeoisie was one of the most dangerous enemies of the revolution and failed to foresee that they played a revolutionary role to a certain extent and for a certain period." This point was linked to criticism of the congress' continued focus on the primacy of party work in the urban rather than the rural areas.[28] This same history also specifically attempted to equate the CCP's post-1937 political concepts with the orthodox Leninist formulas of the past, with the evident intent of giving these Leninist terms a basically Maoist content. It thus spoke of the people's democratic dictatorship as having gone through "two historical periods": the period of the liberated base areas up to 1949 (the new democratic phase), during which "the people's democratic dictatorship was in the nature of the democratic dictatorship of workers and peasants"; and the period since 1949 when, as it began to perform "socialist tasks," the people's democratic dictatorship was now "in the nature of the dictatorship of the proletariat," though characterized by the fact that "in the struggle for the building of socialim the proletariat continued to maintain the relations of an ally with the bourgeoisie."[29]

The Leninist-proletarian ideological overlays noted above, in fact coincided with a resurgence of Mao thought in China linked to substantively revised developmental policies and priorities. Mao had initiated this process in a key April 1956 report[30] (then unpublished) in which he began to raise the fundamental questions and issues which would, in the course of the often cataclysmic developments of the succeeding decade, move China from its post-1949 Soviet-oriented construction policies. In his report, Mao spoke out for a more balanced agricultural-industrial development program and criticized "some socialist countries" for exploiting the agricultural sector of their economies in favor of industry.[31] At the same time, Mao indicated a marked coolness towards wage and benefits policies which would unduly advantage industrial labor.[32]

In asserting the need for the state both to recognize and to reconcile divergent interests (embodied in Mao's 1957 concept of "the correct handling of contradictions among the people"), Mao in effect again affirmed his multiclass (multiinterest) mass line approach, in which the role of the five hundred million peasants loomed particularly large.[33] Through the vehicle of the people's communes and the range of new rural-oriented policies and revised priorities (Mao's 1957-1958 doctrine of "simultaneous development" of heavy and light industry and agriculture), a broadly dispersed and decentralized socialist economic base could be rooted in the countryside as a countervailing force to the increasingly powerful state urban industrial sector. Thus in the strongl revived propagation of Mao thought in 1958, in line with the Great Leap Forward policies of that year, the earlier standard definition of his thought moved towards a new characterization which would include not only "the concrete practice" of the already past era of revolution, but also of the ongoing process of socialist construction.[34]

The Tenth Plenum of the Eighth Central Committee, held in September 1962, marked a key Maoist response to the Liu Shao-ch'i-sponsored "readjustment" policies of the 1959-1961 post-Great Leap Forward period, a response leading to a "struggle between the two lines" which culminated in the Mao-led Cultural Revolution in 1966.[35] A major resolution of the Tenth Plenum, on the economy of the people's communes,[36] underlined the central role envisaged for the rural communes by describing their economy as "the nation's socialist agricultural industry"[37]--in effect placing the collective rural economy on a par with the urban state industrial sector. "The Central Committee believes," the resolution stated, "that investment in agriculture, including investments in industry, transportation, and scientific research which directly serves agriculture, should be systematically raised in proportion to the gross investment for economic construction. Within a given period of time, investment in this sector should occupy a more important position than that in other sectors. "[38]

The above resolution emphasized the need for the working class to "establish a deep and comradely friendship with the peasants and work in mutual assistance and understanding," and stressed (as had Mao in his 1956 report) the importance of correct pricing policies to achieve the equitable exchange of products between the rural and urban areas. "The more agricultural products a region sells to the state, the more industrial products it should receive," the resolution noted. "This is not only an economic problem, but also a problem of great political significance," it added. [39]

At an enlarged work conference of the Central Committee in 1962, which preceded and prepared for the Tenth Plenum, Mao emphasized the new linkup of his revolutionary era practice and principles with postliberation construction, while at the same time acknowledging that the latter would also have to unfold over time and through much experience. The "laws" of the Chinese revolution had been mastered in accordance with "the objective world of China," largely unperceived by the Comintern at that time, Mao stated. He then added: "In recalling the period of history during the era of democratic revolution, when our Chinese Communist Party with difficulty but successfully recognized the laws governing the Chinese revolution, I intend to guide our comrades to realize one thing: in order to recognize the laws governing socialist construction, it is necessary to have a process, to start from practice, to become experienced from being inexperienced, and to graduate from little to more experience. "[40] Mao significantly noted, "We did better before in our investigation and study of things. Since we entered the urban areas, however, we have not been as conscientious in this respect as we were before. "[41] And in the wake of the Cultural Revolution, the Maoist principles of a China-centered, populist-proletarian socialist construction model were strongly reaffirmed. "We study good foreign experience, not to imitate it, but to pioneer new things, to rely on our own efforts," an October 1969 ideological pronouncement declared. [42] "The path to industrialization indicated by Chairman Mao means in essence that, under the leadership of the working class, the enthusiasm of the broad masses of the Chinese peasants in building socialism should be brought into full play so as to vigorously support socialist industrialization. "[43]

The CCP concept since 1949 of a multiclass dictatorship including the national bourgeoisie (the people's democratic dictatorship) came in for specific Russian attack during the years of open Sino-Soviet polemics after 1960. Though politically motivated and generally overstated, such criticisms often clearly linked this multiclass formula to the CCP's rural orientation and to the altered and unorthodox role of the urban proletarian sector in Chinese Communism. In a 1964 speech to a Soviet party plenum, Otto Kuusinen, the late Soviet functionary and Comintern-era theoretician, spoke of the "petty bourgeois" populist "odor" of the Maoist notion of a "dictatorship of the people," and in particular attacked Mao's "opportunist idea" that "after winning power the working class cannot exercise dictatorship alone but must share it with the national bourgeoisie." He significantly stated that if the CCP leaders had wished to define their state system in Leninist terms, "they could have spoken, for example, of a revolutionary-democratic dictatorship of the working class and the peasantry developing under the leadership of the proletariat."[44] Here, obviously, was the orthodox formula of the entire soviet period of Chinese Communism. Kuusinen added that "It is difficult to rid oneself of the impression that the leaders of the Chinese Communist Party somehow fear an increase in the influence of the working class. . . . The Chinese leaders see their chief support and all of their political hopes in the peasantry and not in the working class. This wrong, in fact negligent, approach of the C.P.C. leadership to the development of the workers' movement in their country is not something new," he maintained. "In its time it provoked the justified criticism by the Communist International."[45] And Wang Ming, in a 1969 attack on Mao written from Moscow (where he died in March 1974 at the age of seventy), listed among the "ten major crimes committed by Mao Tsetung in China" Mao's attack on the working class, its organizations and economic interests, and his policy of doing "everything to protect the national bourgeoisie."[46] The Maoist proletarian dictatorship, as I shall briefly elaborate in a concluding section, had clearly taken on its own special character.

Postliberation Assessments of Canton

Postliberation Chinese treatment of the Canton Commune--the single outstanding urban-proletarian revolutionary achievement in Chinese Communist history--appears in essential respects to have followed the course of the post-1949 ideological and policy developments briefly sketched above. While in Mao's published works the Commune is in

substance ignored, there was some evidence in the early 1950s even
of the pre-1935 CI-CCP assessment of that event, and also a tendency
in historical commentaries on the Chinese revolution published in those
years to view Canton entirely positively. Interestingly, in the 1957-
1958 period of a strongly reasserted Maoist line, the Canton uprising
received greater recognition in the Chinese media, but now in order
ultimately to make the point of its "negative example" in illustrating
the pitfalls of an urban-focused outlook. In the aftermath of the Cultural Revolution, Canton seems to vanish from party historiography
at a time when the Mao-linked Autumn Harvest uprising was being
increasingly sanctified. In contrast, Soviet historians in 1967 published an important collection of essays and documents on the Canton
Commune, essentially oriented towards the Comintern position of 1928
and emphasizing particularly the pivotal revolutionary vanguard role
of the Chinese working class. It had been the CI-CCP intent from
1928 to the end of the soviet period in 1935 to place the primarily
rural soviet phase of the revolution within the political parameters
laid out by the Commune experience itself and by the larger significance subsequently attached to that event. It has been precisely these
political implications of the Commune from which the Mao-led CCP has
dissociated itself.

Mao's four-volume Selected Works, published during the 1950s,
contain a few narrative references to the Canton uprising, none of them
of any political substance or significance. It is of some interest, however, that in the original text of his November 1928 report to the party's
Central Committee on his operations in the Hunan-Kiangsi border area
and on the establishment of Communist political power there under his
leadership, Mao appeared careful to attribute the political forms set
up there, including soviets, at least partially to the example of the
Commune. As Stuart Schram notes, Mao ascribed these political forms
not only to his own "clumsy inventions," but also credited them to
'the practices and terminology of the 'Canton Commune,' about which
Mao and his comrades had read in the newspapers."[47] In citing this
detail from the earlier edition of Mao's works,[48] Schram points out
that in the post-1949 official version "all mention of the influence of
the Canton Commune, and even the term 'people's committees' copied
from it, has been eliminated."[49]

However, in a brief history of the Chinese labor movement seri-
alized in a major Shanghai newspaper in 1950-1951,[50] the Canton revolt
reemerged basically in the pre-1935 political formulation. Significantly,

this was now in Shanghai in the context of the "return to the cities" orientation of the early 1950s and of the reactivation of an urban labor constituency. As I have noted, there were efforts within the party in this period to "proletarianize" the CCP in a more orthodox sense and to enhance the revolutionary role and image of the working class.[51] The brief Shanghai history was clearly designed to further this latter aim; it thus declared that "from the production front to the national defense front, the Chinese working class has from start to finish been the vanguard of the revolution of the Chinese people."[52] The Canton uprising, this account stated, "showed once again the resolution and courage of the Chinese working class in the revolutionary stage . . . [and] it has left a splendid page in the history of the revolutionary struggle of the Chinese people. This uprising ended the Great Revolution of China and at the same time unfolded a new banner in the Chinese revolution--the Chinese Soviet Movement."[53]

A standard Communist history of the revolution, published in various editions in the 1950-1953 period,[54] also dealt approvingly with the Canton uprising, though not in the politically anachronistic terms of the labor history cited above. In the course of its brief account it noted the activist role of the Canton laboring masses in demanding an armed uprising, their "warm support" of the decision to revolt, and the resolute and heroic participation of the working class in the battle. Despite the courageous resistance of the workers, the poor people and the revolutionary soldiers, this account stated, the new political power was toppled by the overwhelming forces of the enemy. Though the Canton uprising failed, the author concluded, it had "glorious historical significance" in the history of "the new democratic revolution."[55] Though sparing in its account, and rather cryptic and ambiguous in its concluding assessment, the perspective on Canton was clearly most positive.

By the late 1950s such historical accounts of Canton as that by Hu Hua cited above had undergone some modification. Thus an essentially similar version in a 1959 volume edited by the same author[56] omitted the concluding evaluation of Canton found in the earlier history. It also pointed to the isolation of the Canton revolutionaries by the surrounding enemy forces, and noted that only a small number of the rebels were able to break through to the East River (Hai-lu-feng) region.[57] And Ho Kan-chih's well-known History of the Modern Chinese Revolution, published in an English edition in 1959, took note of the "overwhelming odds" faced by the revolutionaries in mounting an up-

rising in a big city, pointed to the failure to coordinate with the
Hai-lu-feng peasant risings, and concluded that the rapid and bloody
suppression of the revolt "went to prove that it was impossible to
occupy big cities like Canton for long when the revolution was at a
low ebb and the revolutionary forces were greatly outnumbered. "[58]
Yet while such accounts reflected to a limited degree the new CCP
outlook of the late 1950s, they still avoided a more searching "Maoist"
political critique of the basic weakness of the urban-proletarian-cen-
tered revolutionary line exemplified by Canton.[59] It is noteworthy in
this regard that although Ho Kan-chih's history, for example, was
written from the overall standpoint of the Mao-led CCP, in key respects it appeared to represent the "Marxist-Leninist" tendencies in
the party which later came to be associated with the Liu Shao-ch'i
forces.[60] It was in the party press, however, in 1957 and 1958, that
Canton took on fresh political meaning in support of the new Maoist
criticisms of the urban-centered developmental policies of the previous
half decade.

The thirtieth anniversary of the Canton Commune in December
1957 provided the occasion to spell out some of the new lessons of the
1927 revolt. A leading article in the central party organ, People's
Daily, began by hailing the uprising as an inspirational example of
self-sacrificing spirit and resolute commitment to armed revolutionary
struggle under the most adverse circumstances, with Canton's spirit
of revolutionary daring linked to the subsequent Maoist armed struggle
approach.[61] However, the article went on to elaborate, Canton's revolutionary élan proved futile in the absence of a correct revolutionary
orientation and strategy--one based on the unswerving consolidation of
"the worker-peasant alliance." In observing that Canton had proven
the impossibility of sustaining revolutionary power over a protracted
period through the big cities, it added that the revolt's sole dependence
on the urban workers, and its failure to cooperate and coordinate with
the vast peasantry, were critical factors in its inability to preserve its
forces, shift to the countryside and establish revolutionary bases there.
Thus despite its initial revolutionary impetus, Canton inevitably headed
for failure.

The main orientation for the revival of the revolution in 1927,
the article continued, was at that time "not clear to us." According
to "Western" (i. e. , Soviet) revolutionary experience, armed uprisings
must rely mainly on big cities as the center (emphasis added). If
these cities could not be occupied and the revolution soon expanded to

nationwide victory, failure unavoidably ensued. The CCP, the article noted, had organized three major uprisings in the latter part of 1927, two of which (Nanchang and Canton) had relied on big cities as the center. Only Autumn Harvest had depended on the countryside. Nanchang and Canton had thus failed, while the rural uprisings (ambiguously linked to Autumn Harvest), despite "a tortuous path," had been able to wage protracted struggle and build the foundation for the entire Chinese revolution. Canton, a typical city uprising, had thus provided the party with invaluable experience and historic lessons; namely, that the orientation of the Chinese revolution must be to rely on the countryside, and in the countryside to rely on the leadership of the working class (i.e., the CCP) to mobilize and organize the peasantry and build a solid worker-peasant alliance (the mass line), launch armed struggle and step by step achieve final victory.

In the course of the current construction of socialism in China, just as in the previous revolutionary period, the article concluded, there must also be reliance on a consolidated worker-peasant alliance. This was the great historic lesson and significance of Canton; on the basis of absorbing this lesson, an even better socialist society would be constructed. [62]

The relevance of the above evaluation of Canton to 1957-1958 policy issues in China was evident. Canton thus now illustrated the importance of moving away from an excessively urban-centered outlook towards a revitalization of a mass line "worker-peasant alliance," in which urban resources and leadership could be brought to bear on the mobilization and development of the rural sector.

The desire to dissociate Canton from its earlier role as symbol of the central role of the urban proletariat was manifested in the apparent failure to commemorate or mention this thirtieth anniversary during the eighth congress sessions of the All-China Federation of Trade Unions (ACFTU) in Peking from December 2-12, 1957, dates which included the Commune's December 11 anniversary. [63] Yet at the same time, reflecting the transitional nature of this phase in Chinese policy, a local commemoration of the event in Canton demonstrated both its traditional "internationalist" connotations as well as some of the newly asserted Maoist themes.

The observance in Canton appeared to serve essentially as testimonial to continued Sino-Soviet friendship. The Kwangtung governor,

Ch'en Yü, who had himself played an important role as Commissar of Justice in the Canton Soviet, paid tribute to the Soviet Russian martyrs of the revolt and also "drew attention to the fact that it was the Soviet people that had rendered sincere and selfless help to the Chinese peo- ple during this Canton Uprising as well as in their protracted revolu- tionary struggle."[64] And underscoring the "proletarian-internationalist" symbolism of the Commune, the Soviet consul in Canton, in a speech to the rally, expressed gratitude for the erection of a Sino-Soviet Friendship Pavilion in memory of the Soviet consular staff members executed in the suppression of the revolt, and presented to the meeting a red banner inscribed "To the glorious working class of Canton."[65]

T'ao Chu, the Kwangtung party leader at that time,[66] who was also apparently a participant in the Canton revolt, likewise spoke at the commemoration rally, with the text carried in the Canton party press the following day.[67] Also stressing the inspirational themes of heroism and martyrdom to the revolutionary cause, T'ao referred briefly in his concluding sentences to policies of the Commune that had now been fulfilled in China, such as the expropriation of the "big capitalists," the eight-hour day, land redistribution and the suppression of the landlords, national independence, and unity with the Soviet Union. On the last point he hailed "the one big socialist family" of the Soviet- led bloc. But in no sense did he portray the Commune as symbol or evidence of the pivotal revolutionary role of the working class. T'ao on the contrary expressed the newly surfacing Maoist theme on the uprising: the inevitable failure of the Commune against insurmountable odds had taught a vital lesson; i.e., that the revolutionary thrust should be directed instead at the rural villages, where strength could be built up in rural bases through armed struggle, encircling and ultimately capturing the cities. This, he added, was Mao's strategy and the path taken by the Chinese revolution which transformed failure into victory.[68]

These latter themes emerged even more sharply in a major article on the Canton uprising in People's Daily in mid-1958,[69] a high point in the rural-focused Great Leap Forward policies. The article carried particular weight, since it was written by Marshal Yeh Chien-ying, a leading CCP military figure who had been the deputy commander of the Communist military forces during the revolt. Yeh's article was an informative and sympathetic account of the role in the revolt of the cadet training regiment he commanded at that time, and of the circum- stances and conditions in Canton which were conducive to revolutionary action. He too now stressed the importance of the concept of CCP-led armed struggle which became the common thread linking all the uprisings following the break with the KMT in mid-1927. Yeh specifically rejected the earlier orthodox description of the Canton revolt as a "rear-guard battle" (t'ui-ping chih i-chan), but instead viewed it as a "positive" heroic counterattack in an ongoing struggle against the counterrevolutionary forces. As with the orthodox political formulas of the past, the significance of Canton's link to the subsequent armed rural revolutionary phase was given a Maoist content: it was now not the proletarian leadership symbolized by Canton that became the "banner" of the rural revolution, but rather its spirit of armed struggle.

The uprising, Yeh summed up, had taught certain lessons: under the conditions of an ebbing revolutionary tide, the most pressing task was not the impossible one of immediately seizing cities but rather of preserving the revolutionary forces and turning them towards the villages, there to organize and mobilize the vast peasantry in guerrilla war, build up rural bases, use the villages to encircle the cities and ultimately to seize them. It was this concept of a worker-peasant alliance and of the positive participation of the peasantry that made final victory possible.

Yeh noted that these lessons of Canton had not been recognized by "some of the party's leading comrades" for a fairly long period after the Commune's failure. At that time, "our minds were still full of bourgeois old-democratic revolutionary thought"--reliance on the city as the fundamental base (ken chu-ti) and an incorrect understanding of the strength of the peasantry. Only Chairman Mao creatively solved this problem which was crucial to the success or failure of the Chinese revolution. Had the Canton uprising not "hankered after the city" (liu-lien ch'eng-shih--a phrase apparently having pejorative self-indulgent connotations), but, instead, once the revolt started, had its forces moved consciously and quickly to the countryside to link up with the Hai-lu-feng peasant movement, then "the uprising would have achieved even greater victory."[70]

Thus the Canton revolt would have achieved real success if in fact it had not really been an urban-centered uprising at all, if its forces had instead left the city promptly and adopted a rural-base strategy. It is interesting to compare this idea with the Comintern-sponsored analyses of 1928, which cited the inability of Hai-lu-feng to send aid to Canton due to its distance away, and which noted that if the Canton revolutionaries had been able more effectively to activate and coordinate with peasant risings in the rural environs of Canton, such peasant forces could have helped cut off enemy reinforcements and thus helped the Canton defenders consolidate their position in the city.[71] Along similar lines, Lozovsky had written then that if there had been a general strike movement in coordination with the revolt, the Canton forces would have been able to wage their struggle for at least another week, allowing time perhaps for large-scale assistance from the countryside.[72] The concept of peasant coordination at that time was clearly viewed from the standpoint of reinforcing and assisting the urban revolutionary center.

The historical significance of the Canton Commune thus became one of "negative example": it underscored the need to shift to the rural-centered revolutionary strategy. The hegemony of the proletariat which had originally been proclaimed as the achievement of the Commune was transmuted into the Maoist "worker-peasant alliance," linked to the central role of the peasantry and the countryside, with urban resources harnessed to the rural struggle. The Canton Commune was thereby given a peculiarly aberrant role in the Chinese revolution as exemplifying the pitfalls of the urban standpoint. And most importantly, as already noted, these newly enunciated lessons of the Commune--with its "hankering after the city"--were clearly related to the increasing shift in the late 1950s to an "independent and self-reliant" socialist construction policy linked to the Maoist strategy and principles of the revolutionary period, while turning an increasingly critical eye towards the high priority status of the centralized, Soviet-patterned, urban-industrial sector in Chinese developmental policy.

At a relatively low-keyed thirty-fifth anniversary commemoration meeting in Canton in December 1962,[73] attended by Kwangtung governor Ch'en Yü and other local dignitaries (although not by party leader T'ao Chu), the memory of the uprising and its martyrs was invoked (as somewhat perfunctorily reported in the Canton press) in support of the then currently publicized party themes: fostering revolutionary spirit (reactionary classes will never voluntarily lay down their arms nor willingly withdraw from the stage of history); "never forget class struggle" in the course of socialist construction (Mao's emerging anti-revisionist line); and raise high "the three red banners"--the general line, the Great Leap Forward and the people's communes.[74] The "historical" Canton had receded even further from view, with its image invoked in this case, in what was (perhaps only formalistic) support of

Mao-identified ideological positions and policies within the party at that time.

During the Cultural Revolution of 1966-1969 (with its stronger affirmation of Maoist policies following the retreats of the early 1960s) and since, there has been an even more marked tendency to ignore completely any link of the Canton revolt to the Chinese labor movement, and indeed to remove that event entirely from its place in Chinese Communist history. The fortieth anniversary of the Commune in 1967, for example, appears to have passed unnoticed in the party media in both Peking and Canton. This policy of avoidance was also sharply illustrated in a September 1967 talk by Premier Chou En-lai to representatives of mass organizations in Canton. Referring to "the glorious tradition of the workers' movement" in Canton, Chou cited the major strikes in the Hong Kong-Canton area in the early and mid-1920s, adding that "Since then 42 years have passed. Workers of Canton have good traditions of struggle."[75] His failure to mention the Canton rising was the more striking, since he referred in the course of his speech to both the Nanchang and Autumn Harvest uprisings.[76]

This same pattern was evident in the CCP's most recent definitive ideological summation of its history, published on the occasion of the party's fiftieth anniversary in July 1971.[77] There is no reference to the Canton events in its recital of the revolutionary risings of the second half of 1927, the focus being on the origins of Mao's rural-based strategy, beginning with his leadership of the Autumn Harvest uprising.[78] The Nanchang uprising, though praised as an initial example of armed revolutionary struggle, is criticized for "taking the city as the centre and relying on aid from abroad" instead of "going to the countryside to arouse and arm the peasant masses and set up base areas."[79] Though much the same might presumably have been said of the Canton uprising, the latter's uniquely "old-proletarian" and internationalist connotations and earlier uses have evidently now ruled it out entirely. And Nanchang, after all, is historically linked to the founding of the Chinese Red Army, while Canton serves only as a negative example of excessive attachment to the city.

In sharp contrast to the vanishing role of Canton in CCP historiography, the 1967 fortieth anniversary was marked by the appearance in the Soviet Union of a major collection of articles, reminiscences, biographies and documents on the Canton uprising, with some additional materials on the related 1927 Kwangtung peasant movement.[80] Published under the auspices of the Institute of the Peoples of Asia of the prestigious Soviet Academy of Sciences, the volume commemorated the anniversary of the proclamation of the Canton Commune, and was dedicated to "the heroic events" of those days which had attempted "to establish the power of the Soviets" in Canton. [81]

In a very brief foreword, [82] the editor, L. P. Deliusin, noted that though this "dramatic episode" in the Chinese revolution had proved to be short-lived, "the uprising of the proletariat of south China left an indelible mark not only in the memory of eyewitnesses to the event, but also in the consciousness of future generations." Now viewing Canton from the vantage point of history, and presumably detached from the political infighting, sensitivities and conflicts which marked the 1928 Comintern debates and evaluation of Canton, Deliusin noted more forthrightly the key role of objective factors in predetermining the fate of Canton. He even cited here Chinese historian Ho Kan-chih's statement on the unfeasibility of attempting to occupy for long a big city like Canton in the face of greatly superior enemy numbers and an ebbing revolutionary tide. [83] Deliusin added (without mentioning the Comintern in this connection) that the CCP Central Committee, in adopting the decision to launch the uprising, had acted from "an incorrect evaluation of the forces of revolution and counterrevolution." However, Deliusin in no way indicated or implied that the urban-centered focus of the uprising went counter to the strategic perspectives of the Comintern's China policy at that time. Nor did he draw any larger implications impugning the basic notion of the proletarian revolutionary center exemplified by Canton.

It is interesting that Deliusin stressed the balance of forces concept, and the level of proletarian consciousness and organization as the crucial factors which should have been more carefully considered in opting for an armed uprising at that point. The Maoist commentaries of 1957-1958, on the contrary, had lauded Canton precisely for its spirit of taking up arms in the face of overwhelming counterrevolutionary force and revolutionary demoralization, though of course adding the crucial point that its revolutionary initiative had been misdirected to the city. One may speculate that the two positions reflected also the Sino-Soviet differences in the late 1950s and 1960s over the advisability of encouraging armed revolutionary struggles in various parts of the world. [84]

In any case, while the Chinese had underlined Canton's significance in pointing to the necessity for shifting to Mao's protracted, rural-centered strategy and policies, Deliusin focused instead on Canton's import as an example of proletarian revolutionary resolution and heroism. He sidestepped any ultimate judgment on Canton, observing that "The question of whether one should have taken up arms is more easily answered after the struggle has been won or lost." In paying "the tribute of sincere respect to the heroes of the Canton uprising," Deliusin declared that "the world proletariat valued their exploit highly." He concluded, in the words of the Comintern appeal of December 15, 1927, that "The unparalleled heroism of the Canton workers is an event of tremendous, truly worldwide [historical?] significance."[85]

In effect Deliusin, rather more frankly than the "rightist" elements in the Comintern in 1928, questioned the wisdom of launching the uprising under the unfavorable circumstances of that particular time; but, as was true of those critics at that time, he remained within the overall confines of the Comintern position and of its ultimate 1928 assessment of Canton. This is clearly reflected, both in the selection of source materials for the 1967 volume and in the orientation of the two new essays on Canton included in the book.[86] Most of the source materials are taken from the 1929 Comintern volume, Canton Commune,[87] and include the articles by Ch'ü Ch'iu-pai and Teng Chung-hsia from that collection--articles which clearly assert the role of Canton in affirming proletarian leadership of the Chinese revolution.[88] It also includes the definitive assessments of the Canton events from the resolutions of the February 1928 ECCI Ninth Plenum and the Sixth Congresses of the CCP and CI later that year.[89]

The opening essay in the Soviet collection, by A. G. Afanasiev, recounted in some detail the buildup of tensions and conflicts in Canton following the April 1927 KMT break with the left. The writer stressed the strong resistance of the unions under the Communist-led Council of Workers' Delegates to repressive measures, and depicted the rising tide of strikes, demonstrations, and revolutionary sentiment among the Canton workers, while citing also the growing incidence of peasant risings in Kwangtung during the latter part of 1927. He noted the steps taken by the Kwangtung party committee to establish and maintain contact with various peasant revolutionary areas in Kwangtung, including efforts to train peasant activists from the suburban areas around Canton. Overall, the writer portrayed the uprising as a genuine and virtually inevitable expression of the intensifying class struggle in Canton and of the determination of the left-led forces in that city to revolt (with some attempted coordination with the outlying peasant movement) against mounting counterrevolutionary repression.

Afanasiev delineated the organizational moves to set up the Canton Soviet and outlined its proclaimed program and policies. He cited the arrival in Canton during the uprising of some five hundred peasant activists, observing that "support from the peasantry encouraged the workers of Canton."[90] He underlined the heroic, last-ditch resistance of the worker Red Guards and of poorly trained and armed worker detachments in the fact of the overwhelming forces arrayed against them.

In summing up the causes of defeat, Afanasiev first listed a number of "objective factors": the ebbing revolutionary tide, the enemy ability to concentrate its forces on Canton, intervention of the foreign powers, internal divisions in the Canton labor movement, and the lack of military training and experience on the part of the rebelling workers. In concluding this recital, he wrote that "according to the plan of the organizers of the uprising, the workers, having seized power in Canton, were supposed to unite with the rebelling peasants and establish a revolutionary base in the south of China." But the peasant risings, he added, occurred unevenly and in regions distant from Canton, "and their participants could not, for a number of reasons, come to the aid of the Canton Commune."[91]

In enumerating "subjective factors" contributing to failure, Afanasiev again largely reiterated the criticisms in the 1928 CI-CCP documents and reports. (In fact, his entire essay is very closely based on those sources.) These factors included inadequate political mobilization (only some 27,000 took an active part, 20,000 of them workers), the absence of a general strike, incorrect tactics towards the workers in the "yellow" unions, weak political work among the enemy armed forces, insufficient attention to the antiimperialist struggle as a means of mobilizing the Canton masses, tactical military errors by the uprising's leaders, and failure to devise contingency plans for organized retreat in the event of defeat. He also cited the party's inadequate work among the peasants, as a result of which "it was impossible to surround Canton with a cordon of peasant actions which would have delivered a blow to the enemy's rear, in order to seal off the city from units which were coming to aid the counterrevolution, and in order to cut the path of retreat of the enemy's troops."[92] (This last point was clearly at variance with the 1957-

1958 CCP commentaries, which declared that the Canton revolutionaries should have immediately left the city and shifted their entire center of activity to the countryside.)

Afanasiev concluded: "Despite the errors committed by the leaders of the uprising, despite its defeat, the Canton Commune goes down in history as a model of the greatest heroism of the Chinese proletariat. The toilers of Canton undertook a selfless effort to continue the revolution and to raise it to a new level. And although the Canton uprising did not usher in a new period of revolutionary upsurge," he continued, "it was a valuable lesson for the Chinese and the international revolutionary movement. It once more pointed out the necessity for the closest union between the working class and its vanguard, the Communists, on the one hand, and the many millions of the peasantry on the other."[93]

The above was clearly the classic pre-Maoist concept of proletarian leadership of the Chinese revolution, in which the Communist vanguard, discretely linked to the urban working class, reaches out from this base and vantage point to unite with the peasant masses. The lesson of Canton thus emerged, not as a mistaken focus on the urban-proletarian revolutionary center, but instead as the failure effectively to consolidate that center by linking it to a coordinated and supportive peasant struggle.

The second essay on Canton, by T. N. Akatova, was focused on developments in the Canton labor movement in the months preceding the uprising, and on the role of the Communist-led labor forces in the preparations for the revolt. She detailed the pressures and difficulties faced by the left labor movement in Canton after April 1927--a combination of repression, reoganization, divisive tactics and political blandishments. She cited the cancellation of many of the political and economic gains won by labor during the revolutionary united front period, and of the growing strike movement in response to these cutbacks. She noted that from October 1927 "a wave of workers' actions grew in Canton, which reached their culmination during the December armed uprising."[94] Describing the steps taken by the CCP in militarily organizing and preparing the underground worker Red Guards, she stressed "the harsh blow" to the revolutionary forces caused by the forced dispersal from the city of virtually all of the twenty thousand Hong Kong strikers who, "strong in their organization, in their proletarian unity and consciousness, were the leading detachment of the working class."[95]

The absolute superiority of the forces of reaction in Kwangtung and throughout China determined the .defeat of the uprising, Akatova concluded, adding vaguely and ambiguously that the experience and lessons of the Commune had "tremendous historic significance" for the workers' movement in China and for the revolutionary struggle of the Chinese people.[96] It was evident, however, that the example of Canton was being utilized here to document and depict the historical revolutionary role and vitality of the Chinese working class.

Thus, as these recent Chinese and Soviet sources cited above illustrate, the differing historical treatment, lessons and symbolism of Canton appear also to reflect in many respects the currently applicable contrasting Chinese and Soviet standpoints on the substance and meaning of "proletarian" leadership.[97] A brief final examination of this issue, in the light of post-Cultural Revolution perspectives in China, will conclude this study.

FOOTNOTES

1. This dual standpoint was to some degree reflected in Mao's March 5, 1949, report to the Second Plenum of the Seventh Committee of the CCP, in which he declared that "The center of gravity of the Party's work has shifted from the village to the city. . . . Attention must be given to both city and village and it is necessary to link closely urban and rural work, workers and peasants, industry and agriculture. Under no circumstances should the village be ignored and only the city given attention; such thinking is entirely wrong. Nevertheless, the center of gravity of the work of the Party and the army must be in the cities; we must do our utmost to learn how to administer and build the cities." SW, IV, 363-364. With the new Maoist "return to the cities" through the mechanism of the Cultural Revolution, this report was republished and publicized in late 1968, refocusing attention on the key role of the "revolutionized" cities now increasingly integrated with and facing a developing countryside.

2. The Soviet Communist party, Mao wrote in 1949, "has built a great and splendid Socialist state," and "is our best teacher and we must learn from it." "On People's Democratic Dictatorship," p. 423.

3. For a discussion of these party recruitment patterns in the early 1950s, see Franz Schurmann, Ideology and Organization in Communist China (Berkeley, 1966), pp. 128-131.

4. See Charles Hoffman, Work Incentive Practices and Policies. People's Republic of China, 1953-1965 (Albany, 1967), pp. 79-90. These wage policies culminated in the wage reform of June 1956, which had been under preparation for some time previous to that date. Ibid., pp. 85-86. See also n. 32, below.

5. K. C. Yeh, "Soviet and Communist Chinese Industrialization Strategies," in Donald W. Treadgold, ed., Soviet and Chinese Communism, Similarities and Differences (Seattle, 1967), p. 339.

6. "Speech to Enlarged Work Conference of the CC, CCP," p. 52. See n. 42, below, for fuller citation of these Mao observations.

7. See The Agrarian Reform Law of the People's Republic of China. Together with Other Relevant Documents (Peking, 1950).

8. Thomas P. Bernstein, "Leadership and Mass Mobilization in the Soviet and Chinese Collectivisation Campaigns of 1929-30 and 1955-56: A Comparison," China Quarterly, no. 31 (July-September 1967), 36-47. While noting many abuses occurring during the Chinese cooperativization drive, Bernstein clearly points out the key differences in class strategies and policies between the 1955-1956 Chinese case and the 1929-1930 Soviet case. He points in particular to the much narrower rural base of support for the Soviet campaign, and their harsh treatment and confiscatory policies not only in relation to the kulaks but to the middle peasants as well. For Mao's more broadly based and "persuasive" rural class strategy, see "Selections from the Introductory Notes in The Socialist Upsurge in China's Countryside (September and December 1955)," in Selected Readings from the Works of Mao Tse-tung (Peking, 1967), pp. 345-347.

9. Bernstein, "Leadership and Mass Mobilization," p. 46, n. 138. According to this 1956 Chinese report cited by Bernstein, 60-70 percent of rich peasants were admitted as candidate members, 20-30 percent as probationary members, and 10 percent "were subjected to control."

    In September 1955, Mao stated that "we must offer the explanation [to the party and masses] that our division into the strata of upper-middle and lower-middle peasants is not a redrawing of class lines. . . . After a few years, all peasants will be admitted and there will be no distinction between strata." "Summing Up Speech at 6th Expanded Plenum of 7th CCP Central Committee" (September 1955), in Miscellany of Mao Tse-tung Thought (1949-1968), part I, JPRS 61269-1 (February 20, 1974), p. 23. This two-volume publication (JPRS 61269-1 and 61269-2) comprises translations from two confidential Chinese volumes, Mao Tse-tung Ssu-hsiang wan-sui [Long live Mao Tse-tung thought], published in 1967 and 1969 and made available through Taiwan sources. Hereafter cited as Mao Miscellany.

10. Mao Tse-tung, "On the Question of Agricultural Cooperation" (July 31, 1955), in Selected Readings, p. 335.

11. See "Selections from the Introductory Notes in The Socialist Upsurge," pp. 342-344, for an expression of this Maoist faith.

12. Bernstein, "Leadership and Mass Mobilization," pp. 20-21. In China, "Not only before the upsurge, but also during the drive itself," Bernstein writes, "vast efforts were made to recruit and train peasants for leadership roles." In each province, the number of such peasant "core elements" trained during the 1955-1956 upsurge ran into the hundreds of thousands. Ibid., p. 17.

13. "In China," Bernstein notes, "'Party building' and cooperative building were carried on simultaneously during the upsurge" (ibid., p. 21). See also, "Rely on Rural Party Branches for Running Agricultural Producer Cooperatives Successfully," People's Daily, November 2, 1955, in Survey of China Mainland Press (SCMP) (Hong Kong), no. 1168, November 10, 1955, p. 11. By the end of 1955, party cells were reported organized in 90 percent of the hsiang (China's basic-level rural political unit) and in virtually all hsiang by early 1958. Chao Kuo-chün, Agrarian Policy, p. 236.

14. "Study 'On Contradiction,' Overcome Dogmatism and Party Jargon, Hsüeh-hsi (Study), IV (April 10, 1952), in Current Background (CB) (Hong Kong), no. 202, pp. 32-34.

15. Hu Sheng and Yu Kuang-yuan, "Our Self-Examination," Hsüeh-hsi, V (August 1, 1952), in SCMP, no. 404, August 28, 1952, p. 24.

16. "Commemorate the 50th Anniversary of the Communist Party of China," by the editorial departments of People's Daily, Red Flag, and Liberation Army Daily; in Peking Review, XIV: 27 (July 2, 1971), 12.

17. Barry M. Richman, Industrial Society in Communist China (New York, 1969), p. 897. Richman observes that while the government "more than stuck to its end of the bargain with respect to interest payments to the capitalists," the initial valuation of their capital assets was "no doubt greatly understated in many cases" (ibid.). Chou En-lai, in a recently published 1971 interview, stated that payments to the former capitalists ended during the first year of the Cultural Revolution in 1966. William Hinton, "Chou En-lai: An Exclusive Interview," New China, I: 1 (Spring 1975), 12.

18. Richman, Industrial Society in Communist China, p. 898.

19. "Instructions at a Discussion Meeting Attended by Some of the Delegates to the Second Session of the First Committee of the All-China Federation of Industry and Commerce" (December 8, 1956), in Mao Miscellany, p. 38.

20. John Gardner, "The Wu-fan Campaign in Shanghai," in Chinese Communist Politics in Action, ed. A. Doak Barnett (Seattle, 1969), pp. 537-538.

21. "China and the Soviet Theory of 'People's Democracy,'" pp. 54-55.

22. Ibid., p. 57. Schwartz noted the differences in Chinese policy: the notion of carrying the national bourgeoisie all the way to socialism and the CCP's avoidance (up to that time) of the idea that the people's democratic dictatorship was a transitional stage to a proletarian dictatorship (pp. 58-59).

23. Malraux, Anti-Memoirs, p. 357.

24. "On the Historical Experience of the Dictatorship of the Proletariat" (April 5, 1956), in The Historical Experience of the Dictatorship of the Proletariat (Peking, 1959), p. 16.

25. As late as 1961 a CPSU fortieth anniversary message to the CCP stated: "The establishment of people's democracy in China furnishes proof of the new victory of the all-conquering doctrine of Marxism-Leninism. Ahead of the People's Republic of China, . . . lies an unprecedented brilliant prospect for building socialism." NCNA (Peking), July 1, 1961, in CB, no. 655, pp. 23-24.

26. Historical Experience of the Dictatorship of the Proletariat, p. 16.

27. Wang Shih, et al., A Brief History of the CCP.

28. Ibid., p. 109.

29. Ibid., pp. 302-303.

30. "On Ten Major Relationships" (April 1956), in "Collection of Statements by Mao Tse-tung (1956-1967)," CB, no. 892, October 21, 1969, pp. 21-34. In distributing this report for internal party guidance and study in December 1965, the Central Committee stated that "It plays a very important role in guiding present and future work" (p. 21). Mao had observed in 1958 that this 195 report "made a start in proposing our own line for construction." "Talks at the Chengtu Conference" (March 1958), in Mao Tse-tung Unrehearsed. Talks and Letters: 1956-71, ed. Stuart Schram (London, 1974), p. 101.

31. "On Ten Major Relationships," pp. 22-23, 26-27. "The basic reasons for the failure of some [socialist] countries in increasing production in agriculture," Mao observed, "are that the state policy towards the peasants is questionable, the tax levy on the peasants is very heavy, the price of farm produce is low while industrial products are expensive" (p. 23).

32. Ibid., p. 25. While acknowledging that it would be "improper to ignore" the pressures to readjust workers' wages in accord with increased labor productivity and greater daily output value, Mao added, "Since liberation, the workers' living standard has greatly improved. This is known to everybody. Jobs are now available to somebody in some families which basically were left unemployed in the past. Some families which were able to find a job for one member are now able to get jobs for two or three members. I came across such a family myself. . . . Generally speaking, our wages are not regarded as high, but because more people are employed, prices are low and stable, and they lead a settled life, the living standard of the workers basically cannot be matched by that of pre-liberation days" (ibid.). Mao's remarks here seemed to be obliquely critical of a major wage reform that was being adopted at that time in China, which provided for substantial increases for industrial workers based on skill and productivity. See n. 4, above.

Mao also noted that "In the exchange of industrial products and farm produce, we adopt here the policy of diminishing the labor gap, the policy of exchange of equal values or close to the exchange of equal values." "On Ten Major Relationships," p. 27.

33. A major People's Daily article in 1960 on Mao's concept of socialist construction stated that in "solving theoretically and

practically" the relationship between industry and agriculture,
Mao had charted "a road for further consolidating the worker-
peasant alliance and mobilizing the enthusiasm of the 500 million
peasants in building socialism." Su Hsing, "To Study Comrade
Mao Tse-tung's Thought on Building Socialism at High Speed,"
People's Daily, February 25, 1960, Union Research Service
(Hong Kong), XVIII: 20 (March 8, 1960), 302.

At the height of the Maoist Great Leap Forward in 1958, a CCP
anniversary editorial in People's Daily reviewed and reaffirmed
the central role of the peasantry to revolutionary victory before
1949, and added, "We consider the peasant question still the
fundamental one in the period of socialist construction," and
"any separation from China's more than 500 million peasants
would mean separation from the main base of support." "The
Peasant Question Still Remains the Fundamental One," July 1,
1958, in SCMP, no. 1815, July 21, 1958, pp. 10-11.

34. For example, Ch'en Po-ta, "Under the Banner of Mao Tse-tung"
(speech at Peking University meeting marking the 37th anniversary of the CCP), Hung Ch'i [Red flag] (Peking), no. 4 (July 16,
1958), in Extracts from China Mainland Magazines (Hong Kong),
no. 138 (August 11, 1958), pp. 5-17.

35. See Jürgen Domes, The Internal Politics of China, 1949-1972,
trans. Rüdiger Machetzki (New York, 1973), pp. 136-139. The
Tenth Plenum formally ratified the reversal of Chinese developmental priorities to the order of agriculture, light industry, and
heavy industry.

36. "Resolution on the Further Strengthening of the Collective Economy of the People's Communes and Expanding Agricultural Production" (September 27, 1962), in Rural People's Communes in
Lien-Chiang. Documents Concerning Communes in Lien-Chiang
County, Fukien Province, 1962-1963, ed. C. S. Chen, trans.
Charles Price Ridley (Stanford, 1968), pp. 81-89. This resolution was at that time classified by the CCP as a secret document.

37. Ibid., p. 81.

38. Ibid., p. 83.

39. Ibid., p. 84. In confidential notes on a Soviet text on political economy, Mao in this same period had called for developing industry in the countryside and transforming peasants into workers "on the spot." In furthering such a policy, he added, "rural living standards must not be lower than in the cities." "Reading Notes on the Soviet Union's 'Political Economics' [Economy]," (1961-1962), in Mao Miscellany, II, 313.

40. "Speech to an Enlarged Work Conference of the CC, CCP," pp. 48-49. Mao acknowledged at that time of continuing economic difficulties that "In socialist construction, we continue to grope our way, without clear vision." He noted, "We must be prepared to sustain defeats and setbacks because of our lack of vision, and thus gain experience to win the final victory" (p. 50).

41. Ibid., p. 51.

42. "Path for Industrialization," Ta Kung Pao (Hong Kong), October 23, 1969, p. 6 (excerpts from a Red Flag article, "China's Path for Socialist Industrialization," by the writing group of the Peking Municipal Revolutionary Committee). In 1962 Mao had characterized China's post-1949 economic construction policies through the First Five-Year Plan as follows: "Since we were inexperienced we had to imitate the Soviet Union in the field of building the economy, especially in heavy industry in which we imitated the Soviet Union in almost everything and had very few creations of our own. This was completely necessary at that time; but it was also a defeat, showing a lack of creativity and ability to maintain independence and keep the initiative in our own hands. . . . Starting in 1958, we adopted the guiding principle of self-reliance to be supplemented by seeking foreign aid." "Speech to an Enlarged Work Conference of the CC, CCP," p. 52.

43. "Path for Industrialization," p. 7.

44. "Extracts from Kuusinen's Speech," Carrère d'Encausse and Schram, Marxism and Asia, p. 331.

45. Ibid., p. 333. The Novosti press agency in Moscow posthumously published in 1974 what was declared to be the diary of the Tass correspondent in Yenan from 1942-1945, in which the author is cited as observing: "The Chinese proletariat does not even amount

to one percent of the population. It is completely submerged in the peasant-petty bourgeois element." Excerpts from Petr Vladimirov, China's Special District, 1942-1945, Der Spiegel (Hamburg), February 25, 1974, in Translations on People's Republic of China, JPRS 61534, no. 261 (March 21, 1974), p. 2. Vladimirov, who died in Moscow in 1953, had also functioned as Comintern liaison officer in Yenan.

46. "Cultural Revolution or Counterrevolutionary Coup?" Canadian Tribune (Toronto), March 19, 1969, pp. 14-23.

47. Schram, Mao Tse-tung, p. 119.

48. Hsüan-chi, Supplement, p. 55. This report appears in SW, I, entitled "The Struggle in the Chingkang Mountains" (November 25, 1928), 73-104.

49. Schram, Mao Tse-tung, p. 119n. Schram remarks on this deletion: "This flagrant example [the Commune] of the sacrifice of Chinese lives to Stalin's whim is something the Chinese Communists would rather forget." In my view this deletion is more likely to be related to the political implications associated with the Commune.

50. "Short History of the Chinese Labor Movement," originally published between November 1950 and February 1951 in Ta Kung Pao (Shanghai; not a CCP paper); reproduced in CB, no. 108 (August 20, 1951).

51. See, for example, a 1950 article in the party's theoretical journal: Yeh Huo-sheng, "Hsin-min-chu chu-i ko-ming yün-tung chung-ti ling-tao ch'üan wen-t'i" [The question of hegemony in the new democratic revolutionary movement], Hsüeh-hsi (Peking), II:7 (June 20, 1950), 15-16, for an affirmation of the leadership role of the working class. See also n. 3, above. These "proletarianization" trends were subsequently largely de-emphasized as more clearcut Maoist ideological and developmental policy lines reasserted themselves in the later 1950s.

52. "Short History of the Chinese Labor Movement," CB, no. 108, p. 43. The earlier sections of this history closely followed the

volume written by the CCP labor leader, Teng Chung-hsia, in
Moscow in 1928-1930, Chung-kuo chih-kung yün-tung chien-shih
[Short history of the Chinese labor movement], republished in
Peking in 1949. Teng's history covered only the 1919-1926
period.

53. "Short History of the Chinese Labor Movement," pp. 21-22.

54. Hu Hua, Chung-kuo hsin-min-chu chu-i ko-ming shih [History
of the Chinese new democratic revolution]; my citations are to
the 1953 Peking edition.

55. Ibid., pp. 115-116.

56. Hu Hua, ed., Chung-kuo ko-ming shih chiang-i [Lectures on the
history of the Chinese revolution] (Peking, 1959).

57. Ibid., pp. 216-217.

58. Ho Kan-chih, A History of the Modern Chinese Revolution (Peking,
1959), p. 185.

59. In this regard, Ho Kan-chih cited the clearly overstated figure
of "nearly 60,000 volunteers" as having joined in the uprising
in Canton, a figure used initially in the earlier Hu Hua history.

60. On the entire cheng-feng campaign of 1942-1944, for example,
which had represented the full Maoist ideological-political ascendancy within the CCP, Ho Kan-chih made no mention of the thought
of Mao, and described the movement as a "Marxist-Leninist educational campaign" (p. 383). He noted that the party "had learned
to solve the problems of the Chinese revolution in the light of
Marxism-Leninism" (p. 375)--a more equivocal statement than
the Mao thought formula of the integration of Marxism-Leninism
with the concrete practice of the Chinese revolution. Ho Kan-chih
also clearly sought to play down the concept of an overriding Mao
role in the party, referring consistently to "the leadership of the
Central Committee and Comrade Mao Tse-tung." This approach
was evident also in his treatment of Liu Shao-ch'i's major report
to the Seventh Party Congress in 1945 ("On the Party"), in which
Liu, then the party's leading Mao spokesman, projected the image
of Mao's brilliant leadership and genius and of the creative con-

tributions of his thought to Marxism-Leninism. Ho Kan-chih covered all this in a single brief sentence: "At this Congress, Comrade Liu Shao-ch'i made a report on the revision of the Party Constitution" (p. 423). Interestingly, as I shall note, it was Ho Kan-chih's assessment on Canton that was cited in a major 1967 Soviet volume on the Commune.

1. Yeh Hu-sheng, "Kuang-chou ch'i-i-ti wei-ta li-shih chiao-hsün" [The great historic lessons of the Canton uprising], People's Daily, December 11, 1957. This assessment was somewhat qualified by the observation that from "the objective point of view" the uprising had further alarmed the counterrevolutionaries and strengthened their attack on the revolution. But its subjective role in helping to revive the revolutionary spirit of the masses was more important.

2. Ibid.

3. The above observation is based on a perusal of the official news reports and documents of the congress. As I have noted elsewhere in this study, under the labor law of the Kiangsi Soviet Republic, the Canton anniversary date had been stipulated as one of labor's legal holidays.

4. NCNA, Canton, December 11, 1957, in SCMP, no. 1673, p. 39.

5. Ibid.

6. During the Cultural Revolution, T'ao Chu was subjected to virulent attack as a "double dealer" and "capitalist roader," and was ousted from power early in 1967. Ezra F. Vogel, Canton under Communism (Cambridge, 1969), pp. 328-329.

7. "T'ao Chu t'ung-chih-ti chiang-hua" [Comrade T'ao Chu's Speech], Nan-fang jih-pao [Southern daily] (Canton), December 12, 1957.

8. Ibid.

9. "The Failure of the Great Revolution and the Canton Uprising," People's Daily, July 30, 1958. See Chap. 2, n. 11, for Chinese title.

70. Ibid.

71. [Teng] Chung-hsia, "The Canton Uprising and the Tactics of the CCP," p. 57; Neuberg, Armed Insurrection, pp. 126-127.

72. Lozovsky, "Lessons of the Canton Uprising," p. 10.

73. "Sheng shih ko chieh chi-nien Kuang-chou ch'i-i 35 chou-nien" [Provincial and city circles commemorate the 35th anniversary of the Canton uprising], Nan-fang jih-pao, December 12, 1962. This brief report noted that some 200 people had attended the December 11 meeting, held in the Canton historical museum of the revolution. Perhaps significantly, only the vice-chairmen of the Kwangtung labor federation attended and spoke at the meeting.

74. Ibid. According to this press report, all the speakers "unanimously" expressed the themes cited above.

75. "Premier Chou's Speech to Representatives of the Mass Organizations of Canton Area" (September 27, 1967), SCMPS, no. 215, p. 4.

76. Chou complained in this speech of the "guild mentality" of the Canton trade unions, which he said had also been a problem to the CCP during the early revolutionary period. The unmentioned December 1927 Canton events were indeed a case in point.

77. "Commemorate the 50th Anniversary of the Communist Party of China" (by the editorial departments of People's Daily, Red Flag, and Liberation Army Daily), Peking Review, XIV: 27 (July 2, 1971) 5-21.

78. Roy Hofheinz has pointed out the exaggerations in the official CCP assessment of the Autumn Harvest uprisings as the "turning point" in the development of the Maoist strategy. Nevertheless, he concludes that "In conception, the Autumn Harvest Insurrection was a new type of tactic for the world Communist movement"--that of the countryside encircling the cities. Hofheinz noted that "although ultimately the decision about the insurrection rested with the Comintern, the actual form which it took was decided on by the Chinese comrades." Roy Hofheinz, Jr., "The Autumn

Harvest Insurrection," China Quarterly, no. 32 (October-December 1967), 86.

79. "Commemorate the 50th Anniversary of the Communist Party of China," p. 7.

80. Kantonskaia Kommuna. See Introduction, n. 2.

81. Kantonskaia Kommuna, title page note.

82. Ibid., pp. 3-4.

83. See nn. 58 and 60, above.

84. A 1974 Soviet Lenin anniversary article declared that the Peking leaders "incline [world] revolutionary forces toward adventurist actions, maintaining that the revolution may be accomplished without regard for objective conditions, on the basis of impulse alone." S. Aleksandrov and V. Yegorov, "Leninism and the World Revolutionary Process," Red Star (Moscow), April 21, 1974, in Daily Report, Supplement, Soviet Union, FBIS, May 8, 1974, p. 12.

85. Kantonskaia Kommuna, p. 4. See Introduction, n. 13, for citation of English text of this appeal, which gives a December 14 date, while Kantonskaia Kommuna gives December 15.

86. These essays are: A. G. Afanasiev, "The Heroic Uprising of the Proletariat of Canton, December 11-13, 1927" (pp. 5-31); T. N. Akatova, "The Working Class and the Canton Commune" (pp. 32-54).

87. See Chapter 2, n. 8, for citation of 1930 Chinese edition, which did not include some of the documentary materials in the Russian edition.

88. The Chinese edition of "The Canton Uprising and the Chinese Revolution" and of "The Canton Uprising and the Tactics of the CCP" have been cited frequently in my study.

89. Kantonskaia Kommuna, pp. 212-213.

174

90. Afanasiev, "The Heroic Uprising of the Proletariat of Canton," p. 21.

91. Ibid., p. 28.

92. Ibid., p. 29.

93. Ibid., p. 31.

94. Akatova, "The Working Class and the Canton Commune," p. 50.

95. Ibid., p. 52.

96. Ibid., p. 54.

97. These differences are illustrated also in the recent treatment of the Nanchang uprising. As I have already noted, the CCP's 1971 summation of its history criticized Nanchang for its urban-centered orientation. Akatova, by contrast, wrote that after having seized Nanchang with the aid of the local workers and peasants, "the revolutionary troops undertook a campaign to the south to liberate Canton and to reestablish a base for the revolution. The workers of Canton awaited with hope the arrival of the rebel detachments of Ho Lung and Yeh T'ing." She added that, on the approach of these forces to Swatow, "the workers of that city began a strike and then revolted and assisted in liberating the city," though after several days, by the beginning of October, these troops were "cruelly defeated," with the remnants breaking through to join P'eng Pai in the Hai-lu-feng region (p. 50). The difference in outlook is obvious.

CONCLUSION

The Canton Commune, both as revolutionary history and political symbol, has apparently run its full course in China to its present status as a virtual nonevent. During the Chinese soviet period the "banner" of the Commune affirmed a determination to keep the revolutionary movement ideologically on course by pointing out the classical proletarian-led Communist road to political power and socialism. The post-1937 Maoist new democratic phase of Chinese Communism eventually brought a clear departure from these earlier concepts and strategies and from the political formulas associated with them. However, as I have noted, the notion of the ultimately central role of the city continued to retain a strong hold within the CCP and was reaffirmed in major party pronouncements both on the eve of the defeat of Japan in 1945 and on the Communist entry into the major cities in 1949. The post-1949 urban-rural relationship in China has remained a complex and probably a still essentially unresolved issue. [1] But a more fully articulated Maoist line has now emerged which takes as its premise the idea that a communalized and gradually industrializing countryside can become a "proletarian socialist" base ("the great socialist countryside"), just as the rural areas had been made the new democratic revolutionary base before 1949. [2] At the same time, the urban (state industrial) sector retains an indispensable place, with its productive resources and human skills harnessed to the needs of a developing national (though more decentralized) socio-economic order which is still predominantly rural, peasant, and underdeveloped. Such urban-rural links seem to be in essence the current meaning of the "worker-peasant alliance" and of "proletarian consciousness." [3] The current accelerated pace in the massive movement of educated urban youth to the countryside is a significant aspect of this approach to the urban-rural relationship. [4] "The expansion of agriculture and transformation of the countryside," a People's Daily editorial declared in August 1973, "require that a great number of educated young people combine their political, cultural and scientific knowledge with the class struggle and socialist farming in the villages so as to contribute to building a new socialist countryside." [5] The countryside is "a university," it added, in which "young city-bred people" can be "reeducated" by the peasants, and thus "become integrated with the working people step by step and become workers with both socialist consciousness and culture." [6] Mao had observed in 1955 that "Chinese peasants are even better than British and American workers. Hence, they can achieve greater, better and faster results in reaching socialism.["7] No longer juxtaposed to each other, city and countryside are expected to develop an integrated, symbiotic relationship, in which the populist-proletarian concepts of Maoist Communism[8] become the key to the "proletarianization" of <u>both</u> city and countryside. "The thought, culture and customs which brought China to where we found her must disappear," Mao stated in 1965, "and the thought, customs, and culture of proletarian China, <u>which does not yet exist</u>, must appear" (emphasis added) These populist-proletarian virtues, whose values, methods and goals retain the strong influences of the party's rural, mass line experiences and ties, have in many respects continued to be epitomized by the PLA soldier--who remains very largely the "peasant transformed" and the contemporary adult version of the "little devil" of the Yenan period.[10]

A Canadian visitor to China in 1971 quoted a Chinese official as remarking: "We are attempting to urbanize the countryside and ruralize our cities. . . . . Why is it necessary to have massive urbanization and rapid industrialization all at once? Then you ignore the peasantry --look what happened in the Soviet Union when Stalin chose to industrialize at the expense of the countryside."[11] In its far-reaching impact on urban political organization, institutions and values, the Cultural Revolution may thus in effect have been a second and more fundamental move to "capture" the cities by the Maoist forces.[12]

And probably for the first time since the return to the cities in 1949, a strong Maoist foothold has been established in the "revolutionized" and restructured urban labor movement.[13] Wang Hung-wen, the young Shanghai "rebel" worker leader who rose to be a vice-chairman of the Central Committee at the 1973 Tenth CCP Congress, evidently symbolizes this new Maoist political base among the younger urban labor forces.[14] Reports on the convening of municipal and provincial trade union congresses throughout most of China in mid-1973, as part of the longer-term process of rebuilding a national labor federation,[15] were accompanied by a publicized focus on the key role of the workers which at the same time accentuated the proclaimed "new labor attitude" against special incentive rewards for increased labor productivity.[16] But that the notion of an economically favored position for the more productive urban industrial labor sector remains an important issue in China was manifested in the <u>People's Daily</u> editorial reporting on the 1973 Peking and Shanghai labor congresses. It noted that it was necessary to criticize such ideas as "economism" and "the negation of party leadership over the trade unions which had been put about by Liu Shao-ch'i and other political swindlers, " and that the now restructured party committees should "strengthen their leadership over the trade unions. "[17] It is clear that these issues (as well as the rustication campaign for urban youth) play a role in the current (1974-1975) "anti-Confucius, anti-Lin Piao" movement, with reports of struggle campaigns in factories against the "evil tendency" of using special material incentives to stimulate production. [18]

The continuing divergences over and the importance of these issues have been further reflected in key political documents and pronouncements early in 1975. With Mao himself (now eighty-one) possibly beginning to fade from the active political scene, [19] there appears also to be a more concerted effort by the Mao-oriented forces in the party leadership to build firmer (and more long-term) Marxist-Leninist ideological underpinnings for Maoist principles and goals. This has been evidenced in a flow of articles on "the dictatorship of the proletariat" which links this concept to orthodox Marxist-Leninist writings on the subject, while at the same time affirming its role in moving China continuously towards Mao-projected egalitarian and pop-ulist goals. This trend has been most importantly exemplified in a major article by Yao Wen-yuan, [20] the Maoist ideologue who emerged to political prominence in the course of the Cultural Revolution. Per-haps in response to certain inclusions in the new state constitution adopted in January 1975, [21] Yao took up the newly emerging Maoist issue of the continuation of "bourgeois right" in socialist societies, such as the commodity system and the "unequal" eight-grade wage system. He inveighed against those (linked now to the fallen Lin Piao) who used "bourgeois right" to oppose basic Maoist policies aimed at narrowing the "three major differences" (between industry and agriculture, city and country, and mental and manual labor). [22]

Yao specifically focused his attack on labor policies which stressed material incentives and rewards according to work done. Those who advocated this approach "wanted to widen without any limit the differ-ences in grade among the workers in order to foster and buy over a small section of the working class, " Yao declared, and "turn it into a privileged stratum which betrays the proletarian dictatorship and the interests of the proletariat, and split the unity of the working class. "[23] The creation of such a labor aristocracy imbued with "the idea of bourgeois right, " would thus presumably be a "revisionist" force opposing Maoist-style "proletarianism." Yao also inveighed against similar efforts to "incite" the peasants to greater personal accumulation and consumption at the expense of the socialist collective economy.

Thus, according to Yao, there continued to be factors and circumstances in China which could breed "new bourgeois elements" and potential capitalist restoration. "In order to gradually reduce such soil and conditions and finally eliminate them altogether," he added, "we must persevere in continuing the revolution under the dictatorship of the proletariat" (the classic formula of the Cultural Revolution).[24]

Yao thus clearly reasserted the key Maoist principles, sought to reinforce "revolutionized" labor attitudes in the face of continuing dangers of a privileged urban labor stratum and an intellectual-bureaucratic elite, and to uphold the rural socialist base. That conflicting interests and approaches remain over these issues is apparent from the 1975 state constitution which, while reiterating the basic Maoist themes and the leadership role of the Mao-led party over government and military affairs, seems also to give constitutional sanction to a number of the "bourgeois rights" under attack by Yao Wen-yuan.[25] Though the constitution presumably reflects current political and economic realities in China, while Yao was charting the path to future Maoist Communism, the two documents nevertheless appear to have differing emphases.

The question remains whether in fact Maoist policy lines and approaches can be consistently and effectively applied to divergent interest groupings over a lengthy period of time (Mao cautiously estimated in 1962 that it would take China at least one hundred years to build "a strong socialist economy").[26] As for the ultimate prospect of eliminating the rural-urban dichotomy and uplifting the vast rural sector of Chinese life in line with Maoist values while at the same time promoting reasonably efficient economic growth--these are issues beyond the scope of this study. But it is evident that the strongly urban-industrial, proletarian bias of western Marxism and Leninism, on the basis of which the contemporary urban elite of Soviet society was built,[27] has undergone a transmutation in China as a result largely of what the Comintern in its time acknowledged to be "the profound national peculiarities" of China. The current urban-elitist Soviet attitude towards the "peculiarities" of China was strikingly illustrated in an authoritative 1968 political critique of "Maoism" by a Pravda editor, which stated: "[In China] as in the past, the peasant population predominates. To a considerable extent, the urban population also consists of petty bourgeois strata. The working class constitutes a small percentage of the urban population and, what is more, is principally made up of workers with a low skill level and recent arrivals from the villages. The creation of an army of the industrial proletariat remains a matter of the future. This will apply all the more so to the scientific and engineering intelligentsia."[28] This view is further documented in a recent article on contemporary China scholarship in the Soviet Union.[29] The author notes that Soviet analysts see Maoist developmental policies since the late 1950s as a deviation from the proper proletarian socialist path--a path which these writers view as essentially entailing "the cultivation of an urbanized and relatively educated core of workers, scientific and technical personnel and intellectuals, who act as intermediaries in enabling the masses to master modern science."[30] Mao, on the other hand, had observed in a confidential 1958 speech that "Stalin only stressed technology and technical cadres. He only stressed cadres but ignored politics and the masses."[31]

It is China's peculiarities which have shaped the "concrete practice" of Maoist revolution and construction and the current Chinese Communist concept of proletarian leadership as well. "Working class leadership means leadership by Mao Tse-tung Thought," a workers' PLA propaganda team wrote in 1970,[32] while a further article stated: "Whether a person can represent the working class or not depends, . . . first and foremost on his ideology, that is to say, we should see whether he makes conscious efforts to study and apply Mao Tse-tung Thought in a living way and uses it to guide all his actions. This is decisive and fundamental. Class origin is of course important, but not decisive. The decisive factor is whether he has the revolutionary ideology of the proletariat."[33] Proletarian ideology-- the decisive key to proletarian leadership--is the theory and practice of Mao's thought, mass line proletarianism.

Ch'ü Ch'iu-pai had declared to the Sixth Congress of the Comintern in 1928, in reference to the Canton uprising, that a Chinese "peasant war" should serve to support the proletarian revolution in China.[34] This perspective has in effect been reversed in the Mao-led phase of Chinese Communism. The strategies and political-economic imperatives of the protracted peasant war became in time its own rationale and interest, transforming the meaning and content of the "proletarian revolution" in China. And similarly, the current leadership role of a "revolutionized" working class and the interests of the urban sector have been redefined to encompass and serve the populist needs of the Maoist "worker-peasant alliance." The concept of proletarian hegemony symbolized by the Canton Commune and the latter's originally proclaimed significance in transcending the peculiarities of a semicolonial peasant society are clearly as inappropriate to the current phase of socialist construction in China as they were to the evolving revolutionary strategies and policies of the rural base areas in the decade following the Long March.

FOOTNOTES

1. John Wilson Lewis, ed., The City in Communist China (Stanford, 1971), contains informative essays on various aspects of CCP urban policy since 1949. See in particular Lewis' introductory chapter, "Order and Modernization in the Chinese City," pp. 1-26, for an overall analytical view of urban policy patterns, issues and problems, and the significant changes brought about by the Cultural Revolution.

2. See Chapter 6, n. 39.

3. Joseph Lelyveld, the New York Times's Hong Kong correspondent, cites the publicized case of a former Red Guard urban youth who had declared his determination to settle permanently in the countryside: "Young Chai says, 'continuing the revolution under the dictatorship of the proletariat' means going to the countryside" ("The Great Leap Farmward," New York Times Magazine, July 28, 1974, p. 6).

4. At least eight million (and possibly up to fifteen million) urban youths have been involved in this movement since the end of 1968. See ibid., pp. 6, 56-62. In the decade from the mid-1950s to the mid-1960s, some forty million young people had been sent to the countryside. John Gardner, "Educated Youth and Urban-Rural Inequalities, 1958-1966," in Lewis, City in Communist China, p. 268.

5. Text of August 7, 1973, editorial, Peking radio, NCNA, August 7, 1973, Daily Report, People's Republic of China, FBIS, August 8, 1973, p. B 1.

6. Ibid.

7. "Talk Opposing Right-Deviation and Conservatism" (December 6, 1955), in Mao Miscellany, I, 27.

8. Chairman Mao "sets forth the theory of dictatorship exercised by the masses under the leadership of the proletarian political party. This has greatly enriched and developed the Marxist-Leninist theory of the state." "The Dictatorship of the Prole-

tariat Is Dictatorship of the Masses," Proletarian Revolutionaries of the Political Academy of the PLA, Peking Review, XI: 44 (November 1, 1968), 15.

9. Malraux, Anti-Memoirs, p. 373.

10. It is significant that in the renewed stress on working class leadership during the final stages of the Cultural Revolution in mid-1968, such leadership was directly linked to and usually paired with that of the People's Liberation Army (PLA). See, for example, "Anniversary of Entry of Working Class into Realm of Superstructure -- Hailing the tremendous achievements of China's first workers' and P.L.A. men's Mao Tsetung Thought propaganda team in Tsinghua University during the past year," Peking Review, XII: 31 (August 1, 1969), 3-8.

11. B. Michael Frolic, "What the Cultural Revolution Was All About," New York Times Magazine, October 24, 1971, p. 122. A December 1970 article in the Chinese press stated that "a basic viewpoint of Mao Tsetung Thought" is that "with regard to the peasants, only exchange [of equal or approximately equal values] and not expropriation can be used." "Orientation of China's Socialist Commerce," Revolutionary Mass Criticism Writing Group of the Ministry of Commerce, Peking Review, XIII: 50 (December 11, 1970), 4-5.

In a sympathetic account of Maoist economic policies, based on a 1972 China visit, British economist Joan Robinson writes that "Prices of fertiliser and agricultural machinery are kept low as a matter of policy. Over the years since 1962, the terms of trade have shifted in favor of agriculture, as the prices of the main crops have been slightly raised and the prices of many manufacturers appreciably cut." Economic Management China 1972 (London, 1973), p. 13.

12. See Janet Weitzner Salaff, "Urban Residential Communities in the Wake of the Cultural Revolution," in Lewis, City in Communist China, pp. 289-323, for a discussion of the decentralized, grass roots reorganization of urban government through revolutionary committees at the street and district levels. It is interesting to compare these developments with Liu Shao-ch'i's sharp criticisms of CCP cadres in Tientsin in 1949 for applying such

"village formulas" of administration to the cities. "Talk to Tientsin Cadres' Meeting" (May 19, 1949), in Liu Shao-ch'i Wu-ko Ts'ai-liao [Five statements by Liu Shao-ch'i], p. 30. Reproduced from Red Guard sources by East Asian Institute, Columbia University.

13. Regarding the weak Maoist influence in the former All-China Federation of Trade Unions (ACFTU), Paul F. Harper states: "Generally speaking, the Maoists' revolutionary visions and ideology have been rejected by the workers, but ties to the objects of the Maoist attacks, the party and the industrial bureaucracy, remained firm. Much of the credit for consolidating the proletariat's loyalty to the [non-Maoist] CCP must go to the unions." Trade Union Cultivation of Workers for Leadership," City in Communist China, p. 152.

Joyce Kallgren has noted the key role played by union-administered welfare programs after 1949 in placing the industrial workers and the CCP trade union bureaucracy in a specially favored and separate position, with a correspondingly "conservative" stake in the state socialist industrial sector whose high priority status came under increasing Maoist attack. "Social Welfare and China's Industrial Workers," in Barnett, Chinese Communist Politics in Action, pp. 540-573. For a key Cultural Revolution attack on "welfare trade unions," see "The Struggle Between the Two Lines in China's Trade Union Movement," Proletarian Revolutionaries in the ACFTU, Peking Review, XI: 26 (June 28, 1968), 17-21.

An analysis of the Ninth Central Committee of the CCP, elected in 1969, concludes that it was "basically inward-oriented, more rural than urban and, as a group, lacks what might be considered a high standard of education." Jürgen Domes, "The Ninth CCP Central Committee in Statistical Perspective," Current Scene (Hong Kong), IX: 2 (February 7, 1971), 13. There is no reason to believe that these patterns have been substantially altered in the Tenth Central Committee, elected at the August 1973 Tenth Congress. While the exceptionally powerful role of the military in the Ninth Central Committee (43 percent of the membership) has been cut back (reflecting Lin Piao's downfall) to a still significant 32 percent in the Tenth Central Committee, the percentage of grass-roots worker-peasant members has risen to almost

30 percent of the total. Byung-joon Ahn, "The Cultural Revolution and China's Search for Political Order," China Quarterly, no. 58 (April-June 1974), 281.

14. In regard to the revived struggle against economist tendencies, a March 1974 NCNA report described advances in production that had been made in the Shanghai cotton mill where Wang Hungwen had been a former cadre, as a result of the reliance in that factory on ideological struggle rather than material incentives. Lelyveld, Hong Kong dispatch, New York Times, March 6, 1974.

15. China Quarterly, no. 55 (July-September 1973), 604. Apparently as a forerunner of the 1973 trade union congresses, a "Conference of Representatives of Shanghai Revolutionary Workers" was reported to be functioning in May 1972. Peking Review, XV: 21 (May 26, 1972), 4, 19.

16. See, for example, "The Workers Are the Masters," Parts 1, 2, 3, Peking Review, XVI: 26 (June 29, 1973); XVI: 27 (July 6, 1973), XVI: 28 (July 13, 1973). For a description of national wage scales and grades, as of 1972, see Robinson, Economic Management China 1972, pp. 2-3. Continuing problems and complications in working out a "rational" wage and incentive policy in China are discussed in Christopher Howe, "Labour Organization and Incentives in Industry Before and After the Cultural Revolution," in Stuart R. Schram, ed., Authority Participation and Cultural Change in China (Cambridge, 1973), pp. 233-256. Wage adjustments made in August 1971 apparently favored the workers in the lower grades, who received a promotion in grade. Robinson, Economic Management China 1972, p. 3.

17. China Quarterly, no. 55 (July-September 1973), 604.

18. Lelyveld, Hong Kong dispatch, New York Times, March 6, 1974.

19. Mao failed to attend the January 1975 First Session of the Fourth National People's Congress in Peking.

20. "On the Social Basis of the Lin Piao Anti-Party Clique," Peking Review, XVIII: 10 (March 7, 1975), 5-10 (translation of an article in Red Flag, No. 3 [1975]).

21. Constitution of the People's Republic of China, adopted by the Fourth National People's Congress, January 17, 1975. Text in Peking Review, XVIII: 4 (January 24, 1975), 12-17.

22. "On the Social Basis of the Lin Piao Anti-Party Clique," p. 7.

23. Ibid.

24. Ibid., p. 8.

25. While Yao criticized those who advanced "the principle of to each according to his work and of material benefit" (ibid., p. 7), Article 9 of the constitution affirms the "socialist principle" of "'from each according to his ability, to each according to his work.'" Constitution of the People's Republic of China, p. 14. Article 7 also sanctions small private plots and "limited household sideline production" for commune members (ibid.).

26. "Speech to an Enlarged Work Conference of the CC, CCP," p. 49.

27. In an analysis of the changing composition of the Soviet Communist party, Merle Fainsod has noted that by 1940, "Although the party remained predominantly urban in composition, the newly favored categories both in town and country were the administrators, engineers, technicians, and the so-called leading workers, the shop chiefs, foremen, brigadiers, and Stakhanovites who represented the aristocracy of labor." "Transformations in the Communist Party of the Soviet Union," in Treadgold, Soviet and Chinese Communism, pp. 54-55.

Though the mass of the industrial workers were themselves ultimately subordinated to this new elite strata, the latter were linked to and sustained and nourished by the expanding and favored state urban industrial sector. Fainsod observed, in turning to the party recruitment patterns of the 1956-1961 period, that "the party still emphasized the recruitment of 'leading' rather than rank-and-file workers and collective farmers." (Of those newly admitted to membership in the Soviet party between 1956 and 1961, workers constituted 40.7 percent, collective farmers 22.7 percent, employees 35.3 percent, and students 1 percent.) Fainsod noted that, as of 1961 (in line with the needs of rapid industrialization), "The

administrative, managerial, and technical intelligentsia continued
to represent the preponderant element in the party, and their
predominance was particularly marked in leading posts" (p. 57).

A recent article reinforces Fainsod's conclusions in noting that
Stalin's policy during the 1930s of spawning a new group of
politically loyal technical specialists led to the. latter's assertion
of party leadership in the post-Stalin era. Kendall E. Bailes,
"The Politics of Technology: Stalin and Technocratic Thinking
Among Soviet Engineers, " American Historical Review, 79: 2
(April 1974), 445-469. The writer also cites Stalin's concomi-
tant policy of accentuating wage differentials (p. 468).

28. Fedor Burlatsky, "Maoism--The Threat to Socialism in China, "
from the book published in Moscow, 1968, translated in JPRS
47958 (May 6, 1969), p. 66. The new CCP policy line of
putting agricultural development first "runs completely counter
to Marxism-Leninism, " a 1964 Soviet Novosti Press commentary
declared. Certain Aspects of the Inner Life of the CCP (Moscow,
1964), pp. 19-20.

29. Gilbert Rozman, "Soviet Reinterpretations of Chinese Social
History: The Search for the Origins of Maoism, " Journal of
Asian Studies, XXXIV: 1 (November 1974), 49-72.

30. Ibid., p. 51. From the viewpoint of these Soviet sources,
Rozman writes that "socialism must be realized by increasing
the percentage of the population in the working class, raising
their mastery of specialized techniques and providing them with
advanced means of production" (ibid.).

31. "Speech on the Book, 'Economic Problems of Socialism'"
(November 1958), in Mao· Miscellany, I, 129.

32. "Strive to Build a Socialist University of Science and Engineering,'"
Workers' and PLA Men's Mao Tse-tung Thought Propaganda Team
in Tsinghua University, Peking Review, XIII: 31 (July 31, 1970),
5.

33. Wang Shu-chen, "Study Materialist Dialectics and Be a Vanguard
Fighter in Consciously Making Revolution, " Peking Review, XIII:
49 (December 4, 1970), 15.

34. <u>Inprecorr</u>, VIII: 78 (November 8, 1928), 1476. These observations were reinterated by Ch'ü in his article on Canton included in the 1967 Soviet collection, <u>Kantonskaia Kommuna</u>,
pp. 81-93.

MICHIGAN PAPERS IN CHINESE STUDIES

No. 1. The Chinese Economy, 1912-1949, by Albert Feuerwerker.

No. 2. The Cultural Revolution: 1967 in Review, four essays by Michel Oksenberg, Carl Riskin, Robert Scalapino, and Ezra Vogel.

No. 3. Two Studies in Chinese Literature: "One Aspect of Form in the Arias of Yüan Opera" by Dale Johnson; and "Hsü K'o's Huang Shan Travel Diaries" translated by Li Chi, with an introduction, commentary, notes, and bibliography by Chun-shu Chang.

No. 4. Early Communist China: Two Studies: "The Fu-t'ien Incident" by Ronald Suleski; and "Agrarian Reform in Kwangtung, 1950-1953" by Daniel Bays.

No. 5. The Chinese Economy, ca. 1870-1911, by Albert Feuerwerker.

No. 6. Chinese Paintings in Chinese Publications, 1956-1968: An Annotated Bibliography and An Index to the Paintings, by E. J. Laing.

No. 7. The Treaty Ports and China's Modernization: What Went Wrong? by Rhoads Murphey.

No. 8. Two Twelfth Century Texts on Chinese Painting, "Shan-shui ch'un-ch'üan chi" by Han Cho, and chapters nine and ten of "Hua-chi" by Teng Ch'un, translated by Robert J. Maeda.

No. 9. The Economy of Communist China, 1949-1969, by Chu-yuan Cheng.

No. 10. Educated Youth and the Cultural Revolution in China by Martin Singer.

No. 11. Premodern China: A Bibliographical Introduction, by Chun-shu Chang.

No. 12. Two Studies on Ming History, by Charles O. Hucker.

No. 13. Nineteenth Century China: Five Imperialist Perspectives, selected by Dilip Basu, edited with an introduction by Rhoads Murphey.

No. 14. Modern China, 1840-1972: An Introduction to Sources and Research Aids, by Andrew J. Nathan.

No. 15. Women in China: Studies in Social Change and Feminism, edited with an introduction by Marilyn B. Young.

No. 16. An Annotated Bibliography of Chinese Painting Catalogues and Related Texts, by Hin-cheung Lovell.

No. 17. China's Allocation of Fixed Capital Investment, 1952-57, by Chu-yuan Cheng.

No. 18. Health, Conflict, and the Chinese Political System, by David M. Lampton.

No. 19. Chinese and Japanese Music-Dramas, edited by J. I. Crump and William P. Malm.

No. 20. Hsin-lun (New Treatise) and Other Writings by Huan T'an (43 B.C.-28 A.D.), translated by Timoteus Pokora.

No. 21. Rebellion in Nineteenth-Century China, by Albert Feuerwerker.

No. 22. Between Two Plenums: China's Intraleadership Conflict, 1959-1962, by Ellis Joffe.

No. 23. "Proletarian Hegemony" in the Chinese Revolution and the Canton Commune of 1927, by S. Bernard Thomas.

Price: $3.00 (US) each
except $4.00 for special issues #6, #15, and #19
and $5.00 for #20

Prepaid Orders Only

MICHIGAN ABSTRACTS OF CHINESE AND JAPANESE WORKS ON CHINESE HISTORY

No. 1. The Ming Tribute Grain System by Hoshi Ayao, translated by Mark Elvin.

No. 2. Commerce and Society in Sung China by Shiba Yoshinobu, translated by Mark Elvin.

No. 3. Transport in Transition: The Evolution of Traditional Shipping in China, translations by Andrew Watson.

No. 4. Japanese Perspectives on China's Early Modernization: The Self-Strengthening Movement, 1860-1895 by K. H. Kim.

Price: $4.00 (US) each

Prepaid Orders Only

NON SERIES PUBLICATION

Index to the "Chan-Kuo Ts'e", by Sharon Fidler and J. I. Crump. A companion volume to the Chan-Kuo Ts'e translated by J. I. Crump. (Oxford: Clarendon Press, 1970). $3.00

Michigan Papers and Abstracts available from:
Center for Chinese Studies
University of Michigan
Lane Hall
Ann Arbor, Michigan 48104
USA

Printed and bound by CPI Group (UK) Ltd, Croydon, CR0 4YY

13/04/2025